Bundist Counterculture in Interwar Poland

Modern Jewish History
Henry L. Feingold, *Series Editor*

Other books in Modern Jewish History

Bearing Witness: How America and Its Jews Responded to the Holocaust
    Henry L. Feingold

Bondage to the Dead: Poland and the Memory of the Holocaust
    Michael C. Steinlauf

The Golden Tradition: Jewish Life and Thought in Eastern Europe
    Lucy S. Dawidowicz

Immigrants in Turmoil: Mass Immigration to Israel and Its Repercussions in the 1950s and After
    Dvora Hacohen

Jews, Turks, Ottomans: A Shared History, Fifteenth to Twentieth Centuries
    Avigdor Levy, ed.

Lest Memory Cease: Finding Meaning in the American Jewish Past
    Henry L. Feingold

New York Jews and the Decline of Urban Ethnicity, 1950–1970
    Eli Lederhendler

New York Jews and the Great Depression: Uncertain Promise
    Beth S. Wenger

Torah and Constitution: Essays in American Jewish Thought
    Milton R. Konvitz

An Uneasy Relationship: American Jewish Leadership and Israel, 1948–1957
    Zvi Ganin

Will to Freedom: A Perilous Journey Through Fascism and Communism
    Egon Balas

BUNDIST
Counterculture in Interwar Poland

■ ■ ■

Jack Jacobs

Syracuse University Press

Published in cooperation with
The YIVO Institute for Jewish Research

Copyright © 2009 by Syracuse University Press
Syracuse, New York 13244-5290

All Rights Reserved

First Paperback Edition 2021

21 22 23 24 25 26   6 5 4 3 2 1

Published in cooperation with The YIVO Institute for Jewish Research

∞ The paper used in this publication meets the minimum requirements of the American National Standard for Information Sciences—Permanence of Paper for Printed Library Materials, ANSI Z39.48-1992.

For a listing of books published and distributed by Syracuse University Press, visit https://press.syr.edu.

ISBN: 978-0-8156-3226-9 (hardcover)
      978-0-8156-2739-5 (paperback)
      978-0-8156-5143-7 (e-book)

Library of Congress has cataloged the hardcover edition as follows:

Jacobs, Jack Lester, 1953–
Bundist counterculture in interwar Poland / Jack Jacobs. — 1st ed.
p. cm. — (Modern Jewish History)
Includes bibliographical references and index.
ISBN 978-0-8156-3226-9 (hardcover : alk. paper)
1. Jews—Poland—Social conditions—20th century. 2. Jewish youth—Poland—Societies and clubs—History—20th century. 3. Jewish socialists—Poland—History—20th century. 4. Poland—Ethnic relations. 5. Ogólny Zydowski Zwiazek Robotniczy "Bund" w Polsce—History. I. Title.
DS134.55.J33 2009
305.892'4043809042—dc22
                                            2008051730

Manufactured in the United States of America

To my mother, Hinda Jacobs

Jack Jacobs is acting associate provost and dean for academic affairs at the Graduate Center, City University of New York, a member of the doctoral faculty of the Graduate Center's Program in Political Science, and professor of government at CUNY's John Jay College. He is the author of *On Socialists and "the Jewish Question" after Marx* (1992) and the editor of *Jewish Politics in Eastern Europe: The Bund at 100* (2001).

Contents

Illustrations   *ix*

Acknowledgments   *xi*

Introduction   *1*

1. The Youth Bund Tsukunft   *8*

2. SKIF: *The Bundist Children's Movement*   *29*

3. Morgnshtern
    A Bundist Movement for Physical Education   *48*

4. The Medem Sanatorium   *62*

5. The Bundist Women's Organization   *82*

   Conclusion   *98*

   Notes   *105*

   Glossary   *153*

   Selected Bibliography   *155*

   Index   *171*

Illustrations

1. An issue of *Yugnt-veker* published on May Day, 1926   14
2. Poster, created by H. Cyna in 1936, reading "Into the 'Tsukunft'"   16
3. Presidium of the first countrywide SKIF conference, Warsaw, October, 1936   43
4. Anna Heller Rozental, a leading member of the Bund, addressing children and youth at a SKIF-sponsored summer camp, 1937   45
5. Morgnshtern membership booklet of Eljasz Kulkes, Vilna, 1927   50
6. The managing committee of the Warsaw Morgnshtern, 1937   55
7. Gymnasts of the Warsaw Morgnshtern   57
8. Costume ball and carnival in the Medem Sanatorium   73
9. Naptime at the A. Litvak Day Care Center, which was run by YAF, Vilna, 1934   92

Acknowledgments

MY THANKS TO Prof. Henry Feingold, whose encouragement greatly facilitated publication of this book. My thanks as well to the late Abraham Brumberg, the late Victor Erlich, Solomon Krystal, Yitskhok Luden, and the late David Rogoff, all of whom lived in interwar Poland and commented on various portions of my work.

Motl Zelmanowicz, who also lived in interwar Poland, and who grew up in the Bundist counterculture, provided me with much-appreciated material and moral support over an extended period of time. I also received material support for this project in 2003–4 as the recipient of a PSC-CUNY Research Award and as the Workmen's Circle/Dr. Emanuel Patt Visiting Professor at the YIVO Institute for Jewish Research, and am delighted to be able to acknowledge my thanks in print.

Dr. Diethelm Blecking of Freiburg, and Professors Roni Gechtman (Mount Saint Vincent University, Halifax, Nova Scotia), Samuel Kassow (Trinity College, Hartford, Connecticut), Ellen Kellman (Brandeis University), and Gertrud Pickhan (Freie Universität, Berlin) generously shared materials and unpublished papers with me. The trust and collaboration of these scholars means a great deal to me.

I did the bulk of the research for this book at the YIVO Institute and am grateful to all of those affiliated with the institute. I am also honored by YIVO's decision to issue this work in conjunction with Syracuse University Press. Dr. Carl J. Rheins, the YIVO's executive director, deserves special mention, as do Jesse Aaron Cohen, Krystyna (Krysia) Fisher, Leo Greenbaum, Chana Mlotek, Fruma Mohrer, and Marek Web, all of whom are on the staff of the YIVO Archives, as well as Yeshaja Metal, its public service librarian. My friend Nava Schreiber of Tel Aviv helped me to locate suitable illustrations from the YIVO's collections. I have also benefitted from the expertise and cordiality of staff members at other institutions, including Dr. Gail Malmgreen, Associate Head for Archival Collections of the Robert F. Wagner Labor Archives at New York University, Eleanor Yadin of the New York Public Library, Rena Fuks-Mansfeld of the International Institute of Social History, and Misha Mitsel at the American Jewish Joint Distribution Committee Archives.

I delivered papers on themes discussed in this book, at various points in time, in Australia, France, Germany, Israel, Lithuania, Poland, and in the United States and learned a great deal from the reactions of audiences. I am sincerely grateful to my hosts for inviting me to present my ideas. From among many, I single out Bobbi and Michael Zylberman of Melbourne, the staff of the Centre for Studies of the Culture and History of East European Jews in Vilnius, Claudie Weill of the École des Hautes Études en Sciences Sociales in Paris, Prof. Dan Diner of the Simon-Dubnow-Institut für jüdische Geschichte und Kultur, Leipzig, Prof. Feliks Tych of the Jewish Historical Institute, Warsaw, Prof. Michael Brenner of the Institute of Jewish History and Culture at the University of Munich, Prof. Jack Kugelmass, currently at the University of Florida, Gainesville, and Dr. Rachel Rojanski of the University of Haifa.

Jeffrey Broxmeyer of the Ph.D. program in political science at the CUNY Graduate Center helped to format the typescript and provided additional support services. I thank him for his careful work and genuinely appreciate the help provided by all those who aided me in preparing this study. Susan Milamed has been an anchor in times of despair. I would not have been able to complete this book without her.

Bundist Counterculture in Interwar Poland

Introduction

IN THE YEARS BETWEEN the two world wars, the Jewish community of Poland was larger than any other Jewish community in Europe. The General Jewish Workers' Bund, a political party that had been founded in Czarist Russia in 1897, exerted a growing influence among Polish Jews in the 1930s.[1] Indeed, some argue that the Bund was the most powerful political party within Polish Jewry on the eve of the Second World War.[2] Both the extent of Bundist power, however, and the degree to which it could be fairly claimed that the Bund emerged as the strongest Jewish party in Poland in the late 1930s have been hotly contested.[3] A great deal of light can be shed on such matters by close examination of the constellation of organizations that revolved around the Polish Bund, including the Bundist youth movement, the Bundist children's movement, the Bundist movement for physical education, the Bund's women's organization, and the Medem Sanatorium (an institution for children at risk of contracting tuberculosis). It is the intent of my book to substantiate this claim.

■ ■ ■

Scholarly disputes as to the power of the Polish Bund have often hinged on analysis of electoral results. There were no Bundists elected to the Sejm, Poland's national parliament, at any point in the interwar era. Other Jewish movements—including both the Zionist movement and a political movement committed to representing the interests of Orthodox Jewry—were far more successful in this arena.[4] In 1919, the poor results obtained by Bundist candidates could be attributed, in part, to sharp divisions within the Bund itself. The Bund's single largest local organization in Poland, the Warsaw Bund, ultimately chose to boycott the 1919 election (against the will of the Bund's Central Committee), as did its organizations in Lublin and in Chelm.[5] Moreover, the Bund's daily newspaper, *Lebens-fragen,* was closed by the Polish government in the two weeks leading up to the election. Thus, the fact that the Bund did not elect any of its candidates to the Sejm in 1919 was not surprising.

But the Bund also failed to obtain any mandates in 1922. It ran a vigorous campaign in that year's Sejm elections, and the party's most prominent leaders headed its list. Bundist candidates obtained over eighty thousand votes, including almost nineteen thousand in Warsaw, more than twelve thousand in Lodz, and fifty-five hundred in Bialystok. However, because the mandates were won by candidates with the highest vote tallies in each of the sixty-four voting districts into which Poland was divided at that time, and because none of the Bundist candidates obtained the highest number of votes in the districts in which they ran for office, none of the candidates elected to the Sejm in 1922 were Bundists.[6]

The total vote obtained by Bundist candidates went up, to approximately one hundred thousand, in the Sejm election of 1928. Nevertheless, the end result, from the Bund's perspective, remained the same. Not one Bundist candidate was victorious.[7] Moreover, the number of votes received by Bundist candidates, running on a joint list with the Independent Socialist Party and the Right Poalei Zion, went back down in the Sejm elections of 1930, the last nationwide election in interwar Poland in which the Bund participated.[8] The results obtained by Bundists in Poland's parliamentary elections, in sum were, from the Bund's point of view throughout the interwar years, consistently disappointing.

However, the Bund performed very impressively in many of the Jewish communal and municipal elections held in Poland's largest cities and towns in the latter half of the 1930s. The first significant victories of this kind took place during elections to the boards of the *kehiles* (organized Jewish religious communities) in 1936. In Warsaw, which was home to some 350,000 Jews in the late 1930s—a far larger number of Jews than lived in any other city in Poland—the Bund received a plurality of the votes cast in the *kehile* election and thereby won considerably more seats on the governing body of the Warsaw *kehile* than any other party.[9] Whereas the Bundist list attracted 10,767 votes in an election characterized by relatively heavy voter turnout, its closest competitor, the National Bloc (a Zionist electoral list), obtained 6,982 votes, and Agudes Yisroel (a non-Zionist party committed to Orthodox Judaism), only 5,256.

Bundist lists obtained an even higher proportion of the vote than they had in Warsaw in the *kehile* elections that took place in 1936 in Grodno, Lublin, and Piotrków.[10] Examination of *kehile* election results in ninety-seven cities and towns in central Poland outside of Warsaw demonstrates that the Bund did not do as well overall in this region as either Agudes Yisroel or the General Zionists.[11] Nevertheless, the Bund's success in Warsaw and in other specific, important cities, was a stunning one, widely commented on in the Jewish press.[12]

The victory of the Bund in the Warsaw *kehile* election was followed by a major victory in the elections to the Lodz City Council. There were two hundred thousand Jews in Lodz during this period, making the Jewish community of that city the second largest in Poland. As in the Warsaw *kehile* election, turnout was high in Lodz.[13] The proportion of votes for Jewish lists won by the Bund-led slate in the municipal elections in Lodz was even larger than the proportion obtained by the Bundists weeks earlier in the Warsaw *kehile* election. The total number of votes cast in Lodz in 1936 for the Bund-dominated list (which also contained representatives of the Left Poalei Zion, the Council of Trade Unions, and other smaller entities) was 23,685. While the United Jewish Electoral Bloc (in which Agudes Yisroel played a key role) won three seats, and the United Zionist Bloc won two seats, the list headed by Bundists won six.[14]

The *kehile* election in Bialystok, held at the end of December 1937, had similar results. The Bundist slate won eight seats while Agudes Yisroel and the Labor Zionists each won three seats; the General Zionist slate won only two.[15]

The best-known examples of Bundist electoral victories date from the years 1938–39, at which point elections to city councils were held in major cities throughout Poland. In Warsaw, the Bundist-dominated slate, which attracted 61.7 percent of votes cast for Jewish lists, won seventeen seats on the city council in the elections conducted in 1938.[16] The lists run by other Jewish parties in Warsaw, in contrast, won a total of only three seats. In Lodz, seventeen Jewish city council members were elected from explicitly Jewish slates in the balloting that took place on December 18, 1938. Eleven of these were elected on a list that contained members of the Bund, of Jewish trade unions, and of the Left Poalei Zion. At least seven of the eleven were Bundists.[17] Bundist candidates also scored significant victories in city council elections in Vilna, Bialystok, and Lublin—which is to say that the Bund obtained more votes than any other Jewish party in five of the seven largest Polish Jewish communities. In addition, the Bundist lists did well in certain somewhat smaller but still significant Jewish communities such as Grodno, Radom, and Zamość. Representatives of the Bund were elected in 102 different cities and towns.[18] In Galicia, an area with different political traditions than Congress Poland, and one in which the Bund had never succeeded in picking up much traction, Zionist candidates outperformed Bundists in Cracow and in Lwów (in the latter of which the Bund's list was simply crossed out by the authorities) in the last set of pre–World War II elections.[19] Nevertheless, even in Galicia, the Bund made some inroads in the late 1930s.[20]

■ ■ ■

Scholars of Polish Jewry universally acknowledge that Bundist candidates won specific local elections. Both the reasons for these electoral victories, however, and the significance of these results have been subject to debate. Bernard K. Johnpoll, author of the first serious academic study of the Bund in Poland, suggests that the Bund benefitted indirectly from foreign affairs as well as from events within Poland: "Three major events, one in neighboring Germany" (that is, the rise of Hitler), "the second in neighboring Russia" (the Moscow trials, which purportedly led the Bund to reexamine its attitude toward the Soviet Union), "and the third within Poland itself" (a reference to an increase in anti-Semitism), argues Johnpoll, handed the Bund the leadership of Polish Jewry. "Because the Bund was an ecclesia militanta, it was able to defy the threats from within and without, and to lead the Jewish people during a period of despair."[21]

Joseph Marcus has also pointed to events outside the ranks of the Bund as helping to explain its electoral successes. To Marcus, however, the most significant of these events was apparently the disbanding of the Communist Party of Poland in 1938 by order of the Comintern. "When [that party] finally disintegrated," Marcus has written, "the ranks of Bund supporters swelled. In the last years before the outbreak of the 1939–45 war, the Bund emerged as the strongest Jewish party in Poland."[22]

Ezra Mendelsohn has sought the seeds of the Bund's electoral victories in its leading role in the struggle against anti-Semitism, in the perception that the Bund had allies in the non-Jewish world when other Jewish parties did not, and also in "the Jewish public's growing disgust with the failure of the General Zionists' political strategies and, above all . . . the collapse of the Zionist movement's program for Palestine after 1936." According to Mendelsohn, the British decision to prevent substantial immigration by Jews to Palestine "led to disillusionment with Zionism in general and a readiness to support [the Bund,] a party whose *doikeyt* [focus on Poland rather than on Palestine or some other potential land of emigration] was accompanied by excellent organization, ties with the Polish left, and the courage to demonstrate against Polish fascism."[23] As Mendelsohn put it in another, more recent, work, "The Bund owed much of its newfound popularity to the Zionist debacle."[24] Thus, from his perspective, the Bund's success was due not first and foremost to the conversion of massive numbers of Polish Jews to revolutionary socialism or to any other component of the Bundist orientation, but rather to the collapse of the Bund's ideological opponents.[25]

Daniel Blatman has taken a somewhat different tack. His study of the Bund in Poland in the latter half of the 1930s suggests that the Bund's electoral victories were the result of internal ideological alterations: "By the second half of 1933 . . . the Bund . . . came to the end of a process of crystallization, reorganization, and ideological change that had begun in the early 1930s. As a result of these changes the Bund was able to play a central role in the political struggle of that decade."[26] Blatman underscores the Bund's 1930 decision to join the Labour and Socialist International (LSI) as both indicating a new direction on the part of the Bund and as a reason why it began to attract new members during that decade. He points as well to the Bund's role, in March 1936, in organizing a general strike in response to a pogrom in Przytyk; its role in defending Jews against anti-Semitic attacks; its attempt to organize a Workers' Congress for the Struggle Against Anti-Semitism (which was to have convened in June 1936, but which was prevented from taking place by the Polish government); and its opposition to a ban on kosher slaughtering, among other matters, as indication of a reorientation on the part of the Bund, and as clarifying why it attracted more voters beginning in the mid-1930s than it had in the past: "There was . . . a clear connection between the Bund's new ideological direction and the continuous rise in the movement's strength at that time."[27]

Gertrud Pickhan, author of the single best study of the Bund in interwar Poland, puts particularly great stress not so much on the Bund's purported ideological alteration, but on changes in the socioeconomic composition of Polish Jewry in explaining the party's political rise. According to Pickhan, an increase in the number of wage laborers among Polish Jews led to an increase in the significance of the Jewish trade unions. Since these unions were tied to the Bund, the increase in the power of the unions ultimately led to an increase in the power of the party.[28]

Several prominent academics have cautioned against making too much of the Bund's late victories. Antony Polonsky, for example, in a piece published in 1988, argued that Jewish political opinion had some pendulumlike qualities in interwar Poland, and thus that the Bundist electoral gains in 1938–39 were not necessarily the result of major changes in Jewish life or indicative of long-term trends:

> Jewish political life in Poland, partly as a consequence of the perilous situation of the Jews, was subject to violent swings of mood. The Bundist upswing was partly the result of Jewish hopes that the Bund could intercede on their behalf with a victorious Polish Socialist Party. Had the socialists not been able to take power . . . or had they failed to fulfill the hopes the Jews placed in them, these attitudes could very quickly have changed.[29]

It is my contention that the electoral victories of the Bund in the late 1930s were not ephemeral but rather the result of deeper tendencies. The fact that such tendencies existed may best be demonstrated by focusing on the attempts made by Bundists in the 1920s and 1930s to create a Bundist counterculture.[30] The Bund in Poland was not simply an American-style political party concerned primarily with electing candidates to office or passing legislation that furthered the interests of its members. It was a nucleus eager to instill in the movements revolving around it a set of values and ideals sharply different than those dominating Polish society or traditional Jewish religious institutions. The total number of individuals involved in the constellation of Bundist movements was significantly larger than the number of Bund members per se. Most, though not all, of these peripheral movements grew dramatically in size over a period of years, beginning in the mid-1920s.

Neither the significance of the Bund, nor, for that matter, the movement's limitations can be properly assessed without study of the attempt to create a Bundist counterculture. However, the Bundist constellation of movements has never been systematically explored. My hope, in the chapters that follow, is that I will be able not merely to describe the functioning of some of the major movements and institutions that circled the Bund, but also to suggest ways in which the histories of these movements and institutions help to explain the electoral victories of Bundist candidates in the years immediately preceding the Second World War.

1

The Youth Bund Tsukunft

THE YUGNT-BUND TSUKUNFT (Youth Bund Tsukunft) occupies pride of place among the constellation of organizations associated with the Bund in interwar Poland.[1] By the late 1930s, the Tsukunft, as this movement was widely known, had more than twelve thousand members, and had undergone a growth spurt in the Polish capital and elsewhere. The Tsukunft, which provided a sense of power and a reason for optimism to the desperately poor and beleaguered Jewish youth of Poland, attracted them for many reasons. The fact that the movement discussed the sexual concerns of its constituency was among them.

Unlike the other major components of the system of Bund-affiliated movements, which came into being in independent Poland in the 1920s, the Tsukunft had its roots in the czarist era. Moreover, it differed from the Polish Bund's movements for women, for children, and for physical education in that it was not established as an explicitly Bundist organization or under Bundist auspices. One of the czarist-era organizations from which the Youth Bund Tsukunft was directly descended was an illegal youth group, founded in Warsaw and active in 1909–11, many of whose members were sympathetic to the Social Democratic Party of the Kingdom of Poland and Lithuania (SDKPiL)—a party with which the Bund was not always on the best of terms. This youth group, which had both Jewish and non-Jewish members, soon merged with an independently created grouping of Jewish working youth and students also based in Warsaw, also socialist in its orientation, and also operating illegally; however, the bulk of its members were closer to the Bund than to the SDKPiL. The new combined entity, which emerged in 1911, adopted the name Social Democratic Youth Organization Tsukunft—and in 1916, this Warsaw-centered organization adopted a resolution declaring that it considered itself to be an autonomous organization operating under the leadership of the Bund. The Tsukunft remained an organization closely tied to the Bund throughout its remaining years of existence.[2]

In the period following the First World War, the Warsaw Tsukunft took proactive efforts to help establish Tsukunft groups in other areas of the newly independent Polish state. However, the early 1920s were difficult years in the organization's history. During the Polish-Russian War of 1920–21, the Polish government hounded the Tsukunft, which opposed the war. The organization was unable to issue a regularly appearing periodical, a number of its activists were arrested, and certain of its local organizations stopped functioning altogether. The Tsukunft began to operate somewhat more normally when the war ended and had at least 112 local organizations at the time of its third countrywide conference in April 1922, but it was rocked once again by sharp divisions revolving around its relationship to the Communist Youth International.

From 1916 onward, the political line of the Tsukunft mirrored that of its parent party. This fact is made manifest precisely by examining the important issue of affiliation with the international organization of Communist youth.

In 1920, the Polish Bund resolved to join the Comintern (the Communist International). However, the conditions for membership subsequently set by the Comintern were, in 1921, rejected in part by the Polish Bund. A minority of members of the Bund in Poland broke from the party, created an entity known as the Kombund (the Jewish Communist Workers' Bund of Poland), and accepted all of the Comintern's membership conditions.[3] The Bund itself, in contrast, remained outside the Comintern and later affiliated instead with the International Information Bureau of Revolutionary Socialist Parties (the Pans Bureau), which occupied the sliver of political space between the worldwide association of the communist parties and the worldwide association of social democratic parties.[4] In 1930, having undergone something of a political evolution, the Polish Bund became a member of the Labour and Socialist International, a Comintern rival that contained both socialist and social democratic parties.[5]

A few weeks following the Bund's decision to seek membership in the Comintern, the Tsukunft resolved to apply to the Communist Youth

International, the political positions of which were comparable to those of the Comintern. However, the Communist Youth International, at its second congress, set membership conditions unacceptable to the Tsukunft. Late in 1921, a group of pro-Comintern members of the Tsukunft broke with the Bundist youth movement and created the Komtsukunft, which later that same year affiliated with the Communist Youth International.[6] In contrast, the Youth Bund Tsukunft proclaimed, at its fourth conference in 1925, that the Paris Bureau ought to create a bureau of youth movements.[7] In a report apparently dating from 1928, the movement noted that the Tsukunft "maintains brotherly relations with the socialist youth organizations which group themselves around the Paris Information Bureau."[8] Shortly thereafter, the Tsukunft began to move closer to the Socialist Youth International (SYI), which was itself allied with the LSI, and in 1936 the Tsukunft became an official member of the SYI.[9] The Tsukunft followed the Bund's lead on this issue, as it consistently did on all major issues.

The 1922 break between the Tsukunft—which that year changed its official name to the Yugnt-bund "tsukunft" in poyln (Youth Bund "Tsukunft" in Poland)—and the Komtsukunft resulted in a loss of members for the Bundist youth movement. Some of the Tsukunft's one-time members sided with the Komtsukunft and, when that organization folded itself into the Communist Youth Association, joined the latter. Other one-time members drifted away altogether from political involvement. In 1924, the Tsukunft had only seventy active local groups. However, it apparently had 171 local groups in 1928 and claimed 184 local affiliates at the time of its sixth (and final) pre–Second World War conference in 1936.[10]

Both the membership of the Youth Bund Tsukunft in interwar Poland and the movement's potential constituency were made up primarily of Jewish working youth, who were surveyed under the auspices of the Tsukunft in 1925–26. The results of the survey were analyzed by distinguished scholar Jacob Lestschinsky, by no means fully committed to the program of the Bund. They provide a snapshot of the demographic group that the Tsukunft hoped to bring into its ranks and suggest that the Tsukunft had a tough job ahead.[11] The survey—which contained questions dealing with age, literacy, living conditions, religious observance, working conditions, and other matters—was ultimately completed by 3,889 youths (a rather respectable number for a survey of this kind). Precisely because the survey was conducted under the auspices of the Tsukunft, the young men and women who submitted survey forms were almost certainly not typical of Polish Jewish working youth as a whole. There is reason to believe that respondents were disproportionately members of either the Youth Bund Tsukunft, the trade union movement, or both.[12] It should also be noted that, while the survey was conducted in twelve large cities and fifty-five smaller locations in Poland, the largest number of respondents lived in Youth Bund bastions. The single largest number of those who responded, for example, lived in Lodz; the second largest number lived in Warsaw; and the third largest lived in Bialystok. In fact, 38 percent of all those who replied were from these three major cities. This, too, will help to explain why the survey's results were likely quite troubling from the perspective of the Tsukunft's leadership.

A survey question regarding religious observance provides us with an indicator of the yawning gap that existed between the leadership—which was secular and anticlericalist—and the youth that it was striving to organize. More than 50 percent of the boys and young men who responded to the survey indicated that they prayed.[13] To be sure, many of those also claimed that they were not believers and prayed in order to avoid confrontations with their parents or with their community. Nevertheless, the survey suggested that the Jewish working youth of interwar Poland was far more tied to tradition than were the leaders of the Bund or of the Tsukunft. Given that those responding to the survey were likely to have been well aware of the Tsukunft's ideologically secularist orientation, it is altogether possible that any number of respondents who prayed may have declined to report that they were doing so. Thus the proportion of Jewish working youth in interwar Poland who were to some degree religiously observant may well have been even higher than the survey suggests. Similarly, the contention made by some of those who reported that they prayed that they did not do so on the basis of conviction should also be treated with caution. Certain teenage members of the Tsukunft replying to a survey conducted under the auspices of a movement with which they were affiliated and with which they strongly identified may have misrepresented their actual beliefs by providing "politically correct" answers—that is, by reporting that they were not believers when in fact they were.

Since both the Bund and the Tsukunft were generally strongest in Poland's largest cities, the Tsukunft's leaders may have hoped that a breakdown of respondents by geographic location would show that Jewish working youth in the cities were less likely to pray than were their counterparts in small towns. In point of fact, the survey found the opposite to be the case. The proportion of Jewish working youth in the large cities who reported that they prayed was marginally larger than that of Jewish working youth who prayed and who lived in small cities.[14]

But to the Youth Bund Tsukunft, the potential problems raised by the very high level of nominal religious observance among the youngest Jewish workers were only a small part of the challenge facing the group. In 1930, Pinkhes Shvarts, a Bundist journalist repeatedly elected to the Tsukunft's Central Committee, wrote a series of articles for the *Yugnt-veker*, the major organ of the Tsukunft, analyzing the results of the Tsukunft's survey, in which he explicitly noted that the phenomenon of having very young children in the workforce appeared to be growing, and that this did not bode well for the Youth Bund Tsukunft. "The younger the child is brought into the world of work," Shvarts writes, "the more dejected and morally neglected he becomes. It is harder to organize these children than the older ones. The street, with all of its peculiar means of attraction, 'organizes' them."[15]

Other elements of the Tsukunft's survey were equally sobering, from the Bundist point of view. The living conditions, the working conditions, and the cultural level of the Jewish working youth were all demonstrated by the survey to have been grim.[16] A few examples: More than 40 percent of the Jewish working youth reported that they were living five or more to a room. The average work day was close to ten hours (leaving little or no time for formal education). Moreover, the youths tended to have extremely small incomes (and thus little or no money available for purchasing periodicals or books, or for traveling to organizational meetings).[17] Though there is precious little in the way of comparative data available, a study of Polish working youth conducted during the same era as the Tsukunft's survey suggests that in certain respects Jewish working youth were worse off than their non-Jewish counterparts. The average working day of the non-Jewish working youth, for example, was apparently substantially shorter than that of the Jewish youth responding to the Tsukunft's survey (explicable, I would hypothesize, by the fact that the two groups did not necessarily work in the same fields).[18]

One last telling statistic: Seven percent of the Jewish working youth reported that they were unable to read or write in any language—and the proportion of Jewish boys or young men who could be described as completely illiterate was higher still. The demographic results of the survey suggested that the Tsukunft leadership had its work cut out for it.

It was, however, not merely the makeup of the Jewish working youth in Poland in the 1920s that suggested that it would be difficult for the Tsukunft to make much headway. The Communist youth movement was bitterly opposed to the Tsukunft, was actively engaged in attempting to organize the same constituency as was the Youth Bund, and was prepared to use hardball tactics in order to undercut the Tsukunft's activities. At various times, the *Yugnt-veker* printed reports on an attempt by Communist youth to break up a meeting of the Tsukunft,[19] on Communist attempts to infiltrate and to disrupt local branches of the Tsukunft,[20] and on the physical intimidation of an individual who attempted to leave the Communist youth organization in order to affiliate with the Tsukunft.

And yet, despite the fact that much of the Youth Bund Tsukunft's potential constituency was in bad shape economically, had little formal education, and seems to have been rather traditional by certain measures, the history of the Tsukunft in interwar Poland is marked by both growth and considerable success.

Limited information exists regarding countrywide membership trends in the Tsukunft as a whole. An internally generated, unpublished document notes that the Tsukunft had more than three thousand members in 1924.[21] The organization claimed to have five thousand members and two thousand supporters at the time of its fourth convention, which took place at the end of 1925.[22] Two years later, the Polish Ministry of the Interior estimated that there were around six thousand members in the Youth Bund Tsukunft.[23] The Tsukunft asserted in 1930 that it had almost ten thousand members,[24] and in April 1937 twelve thousand.[25] The last issue of the *Yugnt-veker* published before the beginning of the Second World War reported that the Tsukunft's membership had reached 12,300.[26]

There is no definitive statistical data available on the places or movements from which the Tsukunft drew its members in the 1930s. It is clear,

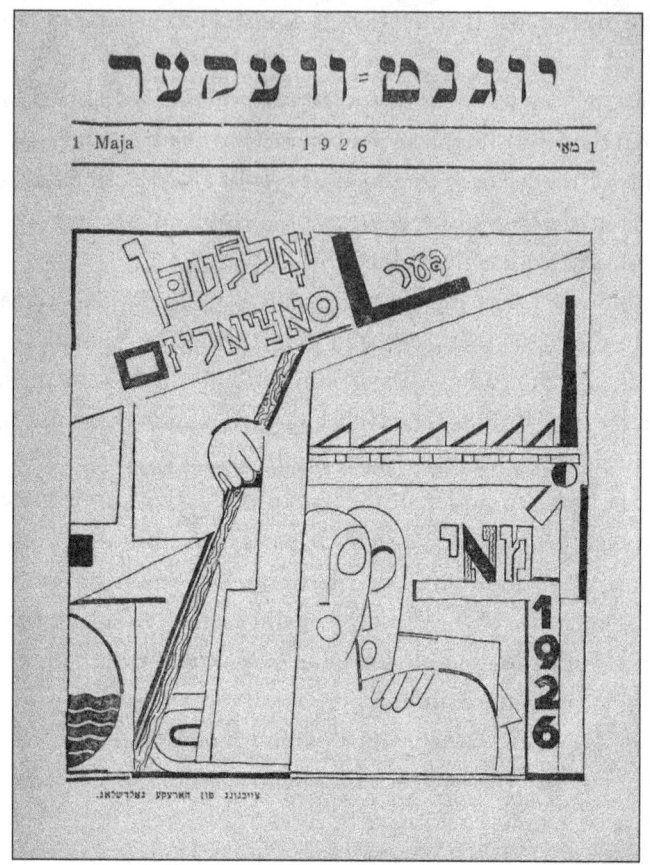

1. An issue of *Yugnt-veker* published on May Day, 1926. The cover reads, in part, "Long live socialism." *Yugnt-veker,* May 1, 1926.

however, that some became members after having been members of the Bundist children's movement, Sotsialistisher kinder-farband (SKIF). Others came from rival Jewish youth movements or from the illegal Communist youth movement.[27] A Bundist source notes that the very small Shtral youth movement (which had been affiliated with the Independent Socialist Party, and which entered the Frayland Lige, a territorialist organization, as an autonomous section in 1934) announced early in 1937 that the Shtral had decided to liquidate itself, and had encouraged its members to enter the Bund.[28]

In 1936, five young men and two young women who had all grown up in observant households and studied in yeshivas or in Beys Yankef schools (a system of girls' schools run under orthodox auspices), but had later broken from the orthodox world, became interested in forming a Bund-affiliated group made up of individuals with backgrounds similar to their own.[29] The Warsaw Committee of the Bund, sympathetic to this initiative, decided that this grouping ought to be guided by Bundists who had themselves been raised in observant homes, and delegated two local activists, Matvey Bernshtayn and Yankef Feldhendler, to take on the task. The Arkadi Group, as the new entity was known (in honor of Arkadi [Aleksandr] Kremer, one of the founders of the Bund), proved, to the great distress of Agudes Yisroel, to be somewhat attractive in the Polish capital city.[30] In the last years before World War II, several clusters of yeshiva students left the world of orthodox Jewry and became members of the group. "Many of them came directly from the great Yeshiva Hakhmei Lublin," stated Levi Mendelson.[31] The Arkadi Group, with nearly 250 members in Warsaw, may have sparked the creation of similar groups in other cities.[32] Emanuel Nowogrodzki, a leading Bundist, reports:

> It was necessary to teach the "Arkadniks" a trade, to arrange for work and apartments, to create special cooperatives and work collectives, since their parents had not prepared their children for anything in life except the Torah and biblical scholarship. But they brought chasidic exaltation from their homes and yeshivas and enriched the movement with new, prophetic/messianic overtones. In a very tangible way, the "Arkadniks" emphasized to Jewish society in Poland the Bund victory over the old Jewish religious world. They were the living witnesses and evidence of this victory.[33]

By 1938, a branch of the Tsukunft, made up of seventy-five young men and women and known as the Berkovitsh Circle, had been created within the Arkadi Group of Warsaw.[34] The sixteen-year-old founder of the circle, Tseshke Morgnshtern, was the youngest daughter of the Lukover Rebbe.[35]

At the same time, the Tsukunft also began to attract Jewish youth from more acculturated and linguistically assimilated environments than had earlier been the case. A report in the *Yugnt-veker* published in 1938, for example, notes that in Borislav, in East Galicia, the individuals who were at

2. Poster, created by H. Cyna in 1936, reading "Into the 'Tsukunft.'" Courtesy of the Archives of the YIVO Institute for Jewish Research, New York, RG 1400.

that time in the process of creating a Tsukunft branch in that city "stem in their greatest part from an assimilated environment. . . . a portion of them do not even know how to speak Yiddish."³⁶ This as well as the fact that this sector of the Jewish youth appeared, at least to some extent, to be open to the work of the Tsukunft, helps to explain why, in the years 1938–39, the Tsukunft began to issue a Polish-language organ, *Wolna Młodzież*, while continuing to publish the *Yugnt-veker*.³⁷ An article that appeared in *Yugnt-veker* in 1939 justified the publication of the Polish-language periodical in the following terms:

In recent years the process of broadening our influence among new strata of Jewish youth made great progress. We also managed to broaden our influence among linguistically assimilated Jewish youth. This phenomenon ripened the thought of creating a periodic Tsukunft newspaper in the Polish language.... From its first moment onwards, *Wolna Młodzież* earned for itself a mass readership. Many more copies appear today than of any other Jewish-Polish youth newspaper.[38]

To be sure, the movement of individuals among the youth organizations of interwar Polish Jewry did not occur in one direction only. It is certainly true that some young men and women who had been in the Tsukunft at one point or another forsook the Bundist group for other parties or youth movements.[39] Henakh Todres, for instance, who had not only been a member of the Tsukunft but who also had a job at the Bundist newspaper *Naye folkstsaytung,* became active in the Frayland Lige.[40] However, it seems that more youth moved into the Tsukunft than out of it in the late 1930s. It also appears that the Tsukunft was drawing on broader pools in the late 1930s than it had in earlier decades.

The Tsukunft's branch in Warsaw, which was, by a considerable margin, the largest and most important local group, underwent a particularly marked pattern of growth in the 1930s. In 1916, during the course of the First World War, the Warsaw Tsukunft had around three hundred members. In the period immediately following that war, in 1919, the Tsukunft claimed to have more than thirteen hundred members in the area. Membership in the Warsaw Tsukunft fluctuated during the 1920s and early 1930s, but it never dipped below eight hundred and never grew much beyond fifteen hundred during that period. In the late 1930s, in contrast, the group grew steadily and dramatically. It claimed to have 1,625 members in 1936, 1,973 members in 1937, 2,235 members in March 1939, and 2,400 members by May Day of that year.[41] The Tsukunft of Warsaw was twice as large on the eve of the Second World War as it had been in 1933, and it was larger in 1939 than it had ever been at any earlier point in its history. Membership trends in the Warsaw Tsukunft were not necessarily typical of those in Tsukunft locals elsewhere in Poland,[42] but the success of the Warsaw Tsukunft was a notable one.

A sense of the significance of the figures presented above may be gleaned by noting that the Bund itself had 1,899 members in Warsaw in March 1935 and 2,875 members in October 1936.⁴³ The total membership of the Poland-wide Bundist youth movement was comparable, at some points in its later history, to the countrywide membership of the Bund per se.

It must also be underscored that the Tsukunft was obliged to constantly replenish its ranks as members aged out. Bund members could remain in the party indefinitely, but Tsukunft members were in the movement for a limited period of time and were encouraged to graduate from the Tsukunft and to enter into the Bund after they turned eighteen years old (though there were apparently many cases in which somewhat older individuals were members of the Tsukunft). From January 1, 1937, through March 1, 1939, 245 members of the Warsaw Tsukunft were transferred from the ledgers of the Bund's youth movement to those of the parent party.⁴⁴ One source notes, "in the course of the twenty year existence of the [Poland-wide Tsukunft,] thousands who had already received their preparation in the Tsukunft entered the Bund."⁴⁵

Another way to reveal the significance of the Tsukunft's size may be by comparing the party with socialist youth movements active in other countries. In 1928, the socialist youth movement of Belgium had 14.29 members for every 10,000 inhabitants of that country. The counterpart movement in Germany had 9.43 members per 10,000 Germans, and the French movement had 0.76 members per 10,000 inhabitants of France.⁴⁶ There were 3,113,933 individuals of the "Mosaic faith" in Poland in December 1931, according to the census conducted at that time by the Polish government.⁴⁷ To say that the Tsukunft had something like 10,000 members in 1930 is to suggest that it had more than 31 members per 10,000 Polish Jews.⁴⁸ Its proportional strength compared very favorably with all but the strongest of the world's socialist youth movements.

Hashomer Hatsair, which had a leftist Zionist orientation, was the largest Jewish youth movement in interwar Poland.⁴⁹ However, Hashomer, which seems to have had a much larger percentage of middle class and bourgeois youth in its ranks than did the Tsukunft, was not thought of by the Tsukunft as a direct competitor precisely because it drew on such a different sector of the Jewish population.⁵⁰ The fact that Hashomer was significantly larger in size than was the Tsukunft even in the late 1930s was apparently not a matter of great importance to the Bundist youth. Far more important, from the perspective of the Tsukunft, was the size of the Bundist youth movement vis-à-vis other Jewish socialist movements that were made up of working-class youth. The Tsukunft's total membership in the late 1930s was impressive when compared to those movements. Yugnt, the youth movement of the Left Poalei Zion—and an obvious group with which to compare the Tsukunft—seems to have had precisely 5,492 members in Poland in 1919 and roughly 8,000 members in 1938.[51] Frayhayt, the youth movement associated with the political party formed by the merger of the Right Poalei Zion and the Zionist Socialist Party Zeire Zion, is said to have had some 3,000 members in 1926 and about 7,000 members in 1938.[52]

Given the fact that the Jewish working youth of Poland was at best a difficult constituency to organize, one must ask the following: How and why did the Tsukunft succeed? One answer may be connected to the organization's wide range of activities and services. The Tsukunft organized youth sections of trade unions in those fields in which large numbers of Jewish working youth were employed. It also organized demonstrations, meetings to discuss political events, study groups, hikes, choruses, libraries, dramatic circles, summer camps, winter camps, and athletic activities.[53] Tsukunftistn (members of the Tsukunft) were actively involved in attempts to elect Bundist candidates to various offices, participating, for example, in the dissemination of election materials and in house-to-house campaigning. In Warsaw, the Tsukunft maintained an emergency fund, beginning in late 1934, which provided grants to unemployed and sick members of the movement.[54]

From 1929 to 1939 the Bundist youth movement also fostered an armed, trained, paramilitary group, the Tsukunft-shturem (Tsukunft Storm), which consisted of some two- to three-hundred members in Warsaw. (The group also existed, on a smaller scale, elsewhere in Poland.) Tsukunft Storm, which was responsible for maintaining order at Tsukunft events, was chaired by Lucjan Blit, the onetime general secretary of the Tsukunft itself. Made up of a handpicked group of Tsukunftistn, it served primarily as a self-defense force. However, it also interceded on behalf of (non-Bundist) Jewish victims or potential victims of physical anti-Semitism—at various Polish universities in Warsaw, for example—and ultimately came to play a practical role in preventing actual incidents of physical violence as well as a symbolic or psychological function: "The uniforms, the marches, the visibility and the openness, were an expression of pride, security, and assertiveness—and it was here that the Tsukunft-shturem played an important role, not only for itself and the political movement it represented, but also for many other Jews. It provided a badly needed psychological lift."[55]

One of the Tsukunft's other particularly notable activities was the establishment of evening schools for Jewish working youth. Since a 1924 Polish law mandated that young people could not be employed if they were unable to provide documentation demonstrating that they had either attended school or were enrolled in a school, these evening schools increased the likelihood that Jewish working youth would be allowed to work without fear of the authorities.

But the Tsukunft was by no means the only organization to establish such schools (or the only Jewish youth movement to participate in political activities or to organize social events). Indeed, Moshe Kligsberg, a leading figure in the Tsukunft in the 1930s, has pointed to a wide variety of ways in which the various Jewish youth movements in interwar Poland were all remarkably similar. "Ideologically the youth organizations did indeed engage in a bitter struggle among themselves. . . . But as to the matter of their style of life: they were as similar to one another as drops of water, and together they presented a unified sector which was clearly conspicuous in Jewish life."[56] Thus, the roots of the Tsukunft's success (including its success vis-à-vis other Jewish youth movements) would appear to lie not in the activities or services it offered, or in its way of life, but rather in other factors.

Gertrud Pickhan has argued compellingly that the development of socioeconomic conditions in interwar Poland increased the social basis for the Bund and, thereby, the political chances open to it.[57] The same explanation ultimately helps to clarify the reasons for the success of the Youth Bund Tsukunft. The Youth Bund increased in size at the same time as its parent party and, to a significant degree, did so for the same reasons. In the 1930s, it was able to attract elements of the Jewish population that had earlier stood outside its ranks or sphere of influence.

There were, however, secondary factors that may have played a special role in the case of the Youth Bund. The Tsukunft, like its parent movement, was revolutionary socialist, Yiddishist, anti-Zionist, and secular. All of these aspects were important, but I suspect that it was the Tsukunft's commitment to socialism and the vision of so-called *naye mentshn* (new people) connected to it that best explains the Tsukunft's success.

The socialist Left in interwar Europe—including the Bund and the organizations connected to it—was committed not simply to an improvement of economic conditions for the working class but also to the creation of people of a new and different sort, people qualitatively better than those of the past. The vision offered by the socialist Left of what these people would and should be like was one that large numbers of adolescents, including large numbers of Polish Jewish adolescents, apparently found highly appealing.

The socialist vision of *naye mentshn* encompassed many qualities and attitudes, one of which concerned sexuality. By examining the Youth Bund Tsukunft's approach to sexuality in the late 1930s, and comparing this to its approach earlier in its history, I hope to provide a more nuanced understanding of how and why certain elements of Polish Jewish youth came to find the Tsukunft appealing.

The articles on sexual life appearing in the *Yugnt-veker* in the early 1930s were not particularly progressive. A 1932 piece by Dr. A. Goldshmid, for example, counseled abstinence "until the time of full development" and suggested that such development did not occur until one's mid-twenties.[58] Goldshmid advised that excess energy should be channeled into sports, organizational work, and hikes, and also cautioned that care should be taken to avoid sexual tension within the work of the organization. He suggested, for instance, that dancing be discouraged. While Goldshmid stressed that sexuality was natural and strongly supported maintaining coeducation rather than moving to single-sex schools or classes, most of his advice to the Tsukunftistn was very traditional: "Early marriages," Goldshmid wrote in the *Yugnt-veker* in 1932, "are the best state of affairs by which to solve the sexual problem in our conditions. . . . We maintain that so-called 'free love,' which is often translated as meaning that one lives with one person today and tomorrow with another, must in our circumstances always end to the detriment of the woman. Under bad conditions and low culture [free love] can even lead to prostitution."[59]

But in 1934–35, a number of articles with a different tone appeared in the *Yugnt-veker*. They were written by Sophia Dubnow-Erlich, a very well-known figure in Bundist circles who turned fifty in 1935. She was married to Henryk Erlich, one of the most prominent leaders of the Bund, was the daughter of world-famous historian Simon Dubnow, and was a respected author in her own right.

In the first of her articles in the *Yugnt-veker* touching on sexuality, entitled "To a New Way of Life," Dubnow-Erlich stressed the importance of sex education.⁶⁰ "The struggle for the new order," she noted, "can . . . not be conducted only on the economic-social front" but also on all others. She reported on work that had been done in Vienna, alluding to clinics that been organized by Wilhelm Reich in 1929 under the auspices of the Socialist Society of Sexual Advice and Sexual Research. These clinics—open to everyone, including youth and unmarried clients—had been established in several poor neighborhoods in the Austrian capital. They urged their working-class clients "to draw the political lessons which come from recognizing the social roots" of sexual and emotional issues.⁶¹ Dubnow-Erlich also commented positively on the work of a German radical and researcher on sexuality, Dr. Max Hodann, who had advocated "a revision of conventional sexual mores"⁶² and had given a series of talks on sexual themes in a school in a Berlin suburb.

During this period, Reich was deeply concerned with abortion, contraception, and with questions about adolescent sexuality. He believed that women ought to have the right to decide whether to terminate their own pregnancies, that adolescents should be taught about contraceptives and given access to them, and that advocacy of abstinence was unrealistic.⁶³ Hodann was likewise interested in sex education for youth and penned a "frank guide" entitled *Bub und Maedel*.⁶⁴

How familiar was Dubnow-Erlich with the ideas of Reich and Hodann? There is now no way of telling. Dubnow-Erlich did live in Berlin for a year in 1925–26, and also during the summer of 1932⁶⁵ (when Reich was also living there).⁶⁶ During these periods, she frequented Russian and Russian Jewish émigré circles. Dubnow-Erlich was well educated, intellectually curious, and politically engaged—and may well have had occasion to learn of the ideas and activities of Reich and Hodann while in the German capital or through contacts she made there. Whether or not she closely followed the work of Central European sex reformers, there can be no question that she ultimately echoed, knowingly or unknowingly, certain stances that they had taken.

In addition, and however familiar she may have been with the ideas of a Reich or a Hodann, Dubnow-Erlich was fully and completely aware of the ideas of those Polish intellectuals, who, in the period following her first extended trip to Berlin and her return to Warsaw from Germany, attempted to open

Polish society to progressive approaches to sexuality and sex education. Writing in her autobiography about this period of time, Dubnow-Erlich notes:

> I had before me the task of renewing my conversation with readers about what was new in literature and daily life. I realized that the newspaper I worked for was, for a very large number of readers, the only source of information on what was happening in the world: this created an obligation. Life suggested topics: one of these was the process of breakdown and restructuring of ways of life, family relations, and methods of education. In the milieu of the Polish progressive, though politically amorphous intelligentsia, a movement arose that had the aim of shaking up the stagnant, conservative way of life that had arisen over the course of centuries under the aegis of the Catholic clergy. Many talented writers, under the leadership of the apostle of secular Western literature Boy-Zalenski, tirelessly put on the agenda such demands as the liberalization of divorce, legalized abortion, and eliminating compulsory regulation of the relations between the sexes. To this the "Conscious Motherhood" society added the elimination of a system that made women into childbearing machines. The problems that troubled the minds of progressive writers . . . took on special significance for the young. . . . The changes taking place before our eyes urgently needed analysis, and I constantly returned to this topic.[67]

Dubnow-Erlich wrote on these themes for the *Naye folkstsaytung*, for *Nowe Pismo* (a Bundist organ published in Polish), and for the major periodical of the Tsukunft. Writing in *Yugnt-veker* in 1934, for example, and knowing full well that the bulk of her readers would be adolescents, Dubnow-Erlich explicitly noted that it was desirable that information be provided on the sexual act, on pregnancy, on birth, on menstruation, and on related issues.

In a piece entitled "The New Sexual Ethic," Dubnow-Erlich also declared that asceticism and suppression of the sexual instinct "rapes human nature," and pointed out that it was precisely when human passions do not find an outlet—that is, in churches or prisons—that they are most likely to flare up.[68] Citing Freud, Dubnow-Erlich advocated sublimation and argued that the movement ought to create the greatest possible number of opportunities for such, but she also underscored that the idea that a mature young person would find such sublimation sufficient was nonsensical.

Tsukunftistn, she clearly believed, could and should not be wholly stopped from expressing themselves sexually, but should be taught about sexuality and about healthy and unhealthy ways of relating to others. From Dubnow-Erlich's perspective, a healthy sexual relationship was one that was freely entered into by equal, physically mature, and sexually aware people. It was one which involved neither physical nor moral nor psychological force, and which was not based on economic dependency or lack of knowledge. Socialists, she suggested, should certainly caution youth against entering exploitative relationships—that is, from hiring prostitutes—but Dubnow-Erlich clearly implied that socialists should by no means work to prevent all expression of youthful sexuality.

Her pieces on sexuality for the *Yugnt-veker* touched on a range of specific themes. In one such piece, she indicates, in a manner reminiscent of Emma Goldman, that many marriages were entered into purely because they provided a lifeline to women who otherwise had no means of support. "The chasm," she wrote, "between a prostitute and this or another wife is by no means as enormously large as one might think. The chief difference lies in the fact that the prostitute sells herself because of need to many men. On the other hand many 'respectable' women sell themselves to one man in order to have a secure and quiet existence."[69]

To be sure, it would only be in a new and different order, under socialism, Dubnow-Erlich believed, that sexual relationships could be fully transformed—but, there were political, educational, and consciousness-raising steps that should be taken even under existing conditions. If, she argued, women received pay equal to that of men, they would be less likely to enter marriages solely to find a means of support. If young men and women received sex education, they would lead healthier and more satisfying lives.

Moreover, life in the Soviet Union provided hints, she asserted, both as to what a better world might look like and as to the mistakes socialists ought to avoid. On the one hand, she noted, the Soviet Union was the country in which the standard of equal rights for women had been most consistently implemented. "Women there have entrée to all fields of work and to all functions," Dubnow-Erlich writes. "Marriages have a secular character, and, if even one of the parties to the marriage so demands, can be annulled at any time. Women who want to end their pregnancies benefit from medical help.

The working mother benefits from a considerable help provided by the state in educating her child (places where they can breastfeed, day care centers, etc.). All of this is very important."[70] On the other hand, Dubnow-Erlich noted in another piece (also published in the *Yugnt-veker*) that there had been an oversimplification of sexual relations in the USSR, and mere physical intimacy too often had been allowed to replace deeper relationships.[71]

Dubnow-Erlich provided a view of sexual ethics that differed to a significant degree from the attitudes current in traditional Jewish society, from those accepted in contemporary Polish life, and, to a somewhat lesser degree, from those prevalent at that time in the USSR. Her view also differed notably from earlier views expressed in the *Yugnt-veker*, but nevertheless it was a view that was fully consistent with and a reflection of the larger socialist goal of creating *naye mentshn*.

To what extent did Jewish working youth in Poland pay attention to articles on sexuality in the *Yugnt-veker*? Dubnow-Erlich reports that her "articles on the problems of daily life found a response most of all among young readers," and that in the wake of the publication of certain of these articles she was invited to participate in a discussion held under the auspices of a Bundist youth organization.[72] This discussion, and her publications, apparently led to additional encounters: "My contact with the young people soon took the form of tête-à-tête talks: there were more and more frequent visits from girls needing advice or practical help."[73] In addition, Dubnow-Erlich explicitly reports that one of her pieces—a piece published in March 1935 that dealt with the extent to which the movement should involve itself in the personal lives of its members, and the extent to which there should be a limit on such involvement—"elicited a number of responses."[74] The Tsukunftistn, in other words, seem to have paid very close attention indeed to Dubnow-Erlich's pieces and to have sought her out for further suggestions and discussions.

There is documentary evidence that local branches of the Tsukunft discussed issues related to sexuality. A memoir written by a woman who, in her youth, had been active in Warsaw in a Tsukunft study group led by Leon Oler (vice chairman of the Poland-wide Tsukunft movement at the beginning of the Second World War) notes that her group, in which Dubnow-Erlich's older son, Alexander, was also active, frequently discussed current events and adds that

Oler . . . suggested that we discuss the question of sexuality. In the beginning, this ticklish subject evoked within us certain reservations. But when he himself brought in the tone of earnestness and sensibility and a whole series of concrete examples, we were no longer embarrassed. The majority of girls, who felt an inferiority complex because of the biological role of the woman and the possible impediments in their future activities, only now understood the importance of their role. The young men, on the other hand, received a lecture about decent, comradely attitudes, respect for emotions, and responsibility for their own behavior. Now their tongues came untied. They brought out thoughts that troubled them about relationships between men and women, as well as about various behaviors. We talked about our family life. It seemed to us that we were beginning to understand the concept of living together harmoniously. We arrived at the conviction that even in this aspect Oler was capable of being our trusted counselor.[75]

Another one-time member of this same Tsukunft group (who eventually became Dubnow-Erlich's daughter-in-law), when interviewed half a century after she had participated in the Bundist youth movement, responded to an open-ended question inquiring as to what members had done in her Tsukunft circle by noting, "We learned about Marxism. . . . We learned about sexual relations between man and woman."[76] Even when prompted by her interviewer, this respondent remembered these things above all others.

What of those members of the Tsukunft who did not have direct access to Dubnow-Erlich? Did they share her perspective? The youth autobiography contests conducted under the auspices of the YIVO provide rich material on the concerns, ideas, hopes, and dreams of Jewish youth in Poland in the 1930s—including those of certain young men and women who were in the Youth Bund Tsukunft.[77] An unpublished autobiography submitted to the YIVO by a seventeen-year-old male, who used the pseudonym S. Frejlich and who was active in the Tsukunft, for example, contains a passage referring to events in Warsaw in 1938 that reads: "Within our bunch there began to be a discussion about free love. All the girls . . . were against it. A portion of the boys were also opponents of free love. I was (and am) a strong supporter. . . . I have had strong discussions with the girls about this. . . . I do not think of getting married. I will never do this. I will live together with a girl in free love, without the petty-bourgeois religious ceremonies."⁷⁸ This was a declaration of principle on Frejlich's part, not a description of an actual choice. He never did find a female comrade with whom to put his plan into effect—or at least did not do so before submitting his autobiography to the YIVO in the summer of 1939. Moreover, Frejlich's text explicitly states that the Tsukunftistn in his circle were divided in their approach to the question at hand. It is by no means the case that all Tsukunftistn held views similar to or derived from those of Dubnow-Erlich.

The overwhelming bulk of the Tsukunft's attention was devoted to explicitly political issues and activities. The Tsukunftistn in the mid- and late 1930s devoted much of their time and energy to discussing current events, to exposing what they perceived as the fallacies of Zionism, to combating anti-Semitism, to organizing against war, and to working for Bundist slates in communal and municipal elections. The number of pieces in the *Yugnt-veker* and in other periodicals published by the Tsukunft that dealt with sexuality per se was small, and the organization was not concerned first and foremost with the issues raised by Dubnow-Erlich's articles. But there can be no question that the Tsukunftistn were interested in sexuality—and that the *Yugnt-veker* was one of the relatively few periodicals from which Jewish working youth in Poland could obtain practical advice, honest and open information, and guidance about sexual matters of enormous importance to them.

What the Tsukunft offered to the poor and poorly educated Jewish working youth of interwar Poland was not only a sense of power, not only a feeling that they were part of a worldwide socialist movement with many adherents among the largest nations of Europe, but also a sense that their own deepest needs and wants were natural, and that these desires could and would be addressed both by the contemporary Bundist youth movement and in the socialist future. To be sure, the dramatic growth in the membership of the Warsaw Tsukunft in the late 1930s cannot be attributed exclusively to a changed attitude on the part of the Youth Bund toward sexuality. There was also growth in the membership of the SKIF and of certain other Bund-affiliated movements during these same years—and no evidence that the increase had anything at all to do with sex. There were certainly deeper socioeconomic factors at work. Moreover, the Tsukunft was not necessarily the only game in town. It is quite likely that certain other Jewish youth movements—

for example, those affiliated with the labor Zionist movements—may also have broached the topic of sex education. And yet it is, I suspect, not merely coincidental that membership in the Warsaw Tsukunft was more or less stabile in much of the period during which the *Yugnt-veker* preached sexual abstinence, and that this membership multiplied in size after the Tsukunft's periodical began to proclaim the need for a new sexual ethic.

In the late 1930s, the members of Youth Bund Tsukunft, while not necessarily advocates of free love, were all eager to obtain accurate information about sex and responded positively to a movement that affirmed that their needs were natural and fully consistent with a progressive political ideology. The doubling in size of the membership of the Warsaw Tsukunft in the late 1930s had many causes. The feeling among Polish Jewish youth that the Bund was powerful and was able to respond to anti-Semitism in ways that other movements could not, was surely among them. But the adoption of a new attitude on the part of the Youth Bund's most significant periodical toward sex education and sexuality, an attitude that was part of the movement's larger goal of creating *naye mentshn,* may also have been among the hitherto unrecognized sources of the Tsukunft's popularity.

2

SKIF

The Bundist Children's Movement

IN THE FIRST FEW YEARS of the twentieth century, children living in the Czarist Empire created a new movement, one made up of youngsters attracted to the work and ideals of the General Jewish Workers' Bund.[1] A generation later, similarly, a Bundist-oriented children's movement was established in interwar Poland. These two movements, however, while comparable in their political orientations and in the age group to which they appealed, differed rather markedly from one another in their modes of development, in their social compositions, in their activities and size, and in their relations to the Bund itself.

I

The Bundist children's groups of the czarist era were not unified and never had a centralized leadership of any kind.[2] Because these groups were generally organized from below, they did not even operate under precisely the same name in all locations. The groups, however, most commonly referred to themselves as the Kleyner bund (Little Bund).

The Kleyner bund came into being more or less spontaneously in several different cities and towns in the beginning of the twentieth century and underwent a period of rapid growth in 1905. Members tended to be between the ages of ten and fifteen. The first such group—and the one about which there is the most data—reportedly emerged in Homel in 1901.[3] There were also relatively large groups in Lodz and Piotrków in the years immediately thereafter, and entities of various sizes in approximately forty other locations, including Bialystok, Bobruisk, Częstochowa, Dvinsk, Kovne, Lublin, Minsk, Odessa, Pinsk, Warsaw, and Vilna.

Members of groups from adjoining villages sometimes had sporadic relationships with one another.[4] There are also known to have been cases in which members from a large city would visit surrounding towns in order to spark activities or disseminate literature. The Bundist children's groups of the Russian Empire, however, never issued a periodical, and never held a countrywide conference or congress.[5]

The bulk of those attracted to the Kleyner bund were apprentices—that is, children who were already working in shops. A smaller percentage of the Kleyner bundistn (members of the Kleyner bund) were *kheyder-yinglekh* (boys who were students in traditional Jewish religious schools). During the period in question, there existed somewhat rarer cases of students in middle schools or *gymnasia* forming Bundist-oriented groups, or joining existing groups of the Kleyner bund in the cities or towns in which they were studying.

The overwhelming majority of participants in the Kleyner bund were boys. One authoritative source, writing in 1937, went so far as to indicate that there were no girls involved in the movement. Local reports, however, suggest that this was not in fact universally true. Frida Vayner, for example, who was raised in Kiever gubernye, is known to have been active in the Kleyner bund in her native *shtetl*.[6] Dina Pritkin, who became an activist in the Ukrainian and in the Bielorussian Bund in the years 1912–19, first identified herself with the Bundist movement in Homel, where she was involved in the Kleyner bund's activities.[7] Nevertheless, it does in fact appear to be the case that most participants in the Kleyner bund were male, and that some groups were made up exclusively of boys.

Significantly, the Kleyner bundistn often had an ambivalent relationship with the local branch of the Bund. Older Bundists in Czarist Russia worried—with good reason—that illegal political activities were too dangerous for children, and, at least initially, tended to discourage children from engaging in them. The Bund, after all, depended on the discipline of its members and relied on conspiratorial methods. Socialists who had been arrested by agents of the czar had, in specific instances, been sentenced to extensive terms in prison or to internal exile. Thus, in those areas in which children organized themselves despite the wishes of adult Bundists, the Bundists often attempted to dampen the fervor of the Kleyner bundistn by ignoring them. Kleyner bundistn were regularly prohibited from taking part in Bundist meetings and demonstrations, or simply laughed off.

These responses, naturally, annoyed and angered the children against whom they were directed. But significant numbers of children were nevertheless very attracted to the Bund, precisely because it was illegal and conspiratorial. They generally had a romanticized view of the activities and significance of the adult organization, particularly during the period of revolutionary optimism following Bloody Sunday in January 1905, when unarmed protesters were shot by the czar's imperial guard.[8] In those locales in which the children of the Kleyner bund were prevented from participating in Bundist events, they tended to create their own events echoing or mimicking the activities of their adult counterparts. A report on Bobruisk that was published in July 1905 in *Di letste pasirungen*, a Bundist organ, reads in part: "As in other cities, the Kleyner bund, as it calls itself, has formed among us. Boys from 12 to 14 join it. They organize meetings, at which their own speakers speak. They issue hand written leaflets and similar items. . . . They organized a demonstration during Passover [*khalemoyed peysakh*] at which a red flag was also not lacking. They shot revolvers and marched through *Shosay-gas* [Highway Street] with revolutionary proclamations."[9] The Bund Archives in New York contains the last known copies of a Kleyner bund flyer—written in a childish hand, orthographically incorrect, and hectographed. According to A. Litvak, Kleyner bundistn organized strikes of apprentices demanding better food and more humane treatment, strikes among Jewish students in Russian schools, and even strikes in *kheydorim* (Jewish religious schools) demanding that the length of the school day be cut.[10] In several cities, members of the Kleyner bund would gather daily in order to receive news and to make plans, mirroring the operations of adult Bundistn.

Attempts by parents or older Bundistn to prevent children from involving themselves in political activities repeatedly failed. In Piotrków the fathers of children active in the Kleyner bund agreed that on one specific *shabes* (Sabbath) during which their children had reportedly planned a demonstration, the fathers would wait until their families had eaten their Sabbath meal and then remove their children's shoes, clearly hoping thereby to keep their children close to home and out of trouble. The Kleyner bundistn of Piotrków, however, were not so easily dissuaded; they held their demonstration anyway, their lack of shoes notwithstanding, and the barefoot demonstration became a local symbol of the children's determination.

The Kleyner bundistn, not particularly well schooled in the finer parts of Marxist theory, relied heavily on direct action (though they did not use that phrase to describe their tactic). Bosses who mistreated workers or who refused to grant the demands of strikers would have their windows broken. A particular kind of sabotage was used, with problematic bosses involved in the production of food or baked goods. Members of the Kleyner bund would sneak into the shops of such bosses and mix noxious substances into their supplies. In Homel, the young toughs of the Kleyner bund used a distinctive weapon—a stick with an iron cap on a spring—against those perceived as enemies, and clearly relished beating their opponents. The Kleyner bundistn of Vilna went so far as to construct street barricades in October 1905. But, though some of the activities of the Kleyner bundistn are best described as playacting, all was not fun and games. There were a number of children killed in the demonstrations of 1905, including members of the Kleyner bund—that is, Avremele Himelshtayn of Minsk[11] and Yankl Moyshe Agranov of Homel.[12]

In some areas, including Lublin, older Bundists organized the children[13] or provided them with leaders after they had organized themselves. Khane Sore Gants, one of the pioneer members of the Bund in Lodz, served as a leader of the Kleyner bund in that city until she was killed by a Cossack while participating in a protest demonstration.[14] The Bund of Dvinsk took the children of the Kleyner bund in that city under its wing as the political situation grew more tense. The Kleyner bund in Dvinsk, according to Beynish Michalewicz, a prominent Bundist who had direct contact with Bundist-oriented children,

> was organized by a 13 year old baker's apprentice . . . in addition to workers and employees there were quite a few students in the Kleyner bund of Dvinsk. When the campaign to boycott Bulygin's Duma began, gymnasia students used to come to the semi-secret meetings and, speaking in Russian, used to ask for the floor in the name of the Kleyner bund. Since we did not recognize the Kleyner bund, we did not give them the floor. In October and November [of 1905], in the time of the two large Russia-wide strikes, we

needed to close the schools. Our organization handed the task over to the students of the Kleyner bund, and they carried it out. From that time on, the [Bundist] organization was in constant contact with them, and the Kleyner bund became the students' organization of the Bund in Dvinsk.[15]

In other areas as well—that is, in Homel—the Bund came over time to see that the Kleyner bundistn could be helpful to the party per se for specific tasks, such as distributing proclamations, and that it was also safer for the children to be under adult supervision than it was to leave them to their own devices. In Homel, the Kleyner bund was eventually provided with leaders drawn from the ranks of the Bundist intelligentsia, who organized the children into study groups devoted to the natural sciences, history, and political economy, among other subjects.

The Bund—though the strongest and largest of the Jewish socialist parties in the era of the Revolution of 1905—was by no means the only such party on the Jewish street during that era. Other Jewish parties competing with the Bund—notably the Zionist Socialist Workers' Party, most often known as the SS (the initials of its name in Russian)—also attracted children. By the end of 1905, the Kleyner SS (Little SS) was up and running in Warsaw, and it cosponsored a demonstration with the Kleyner bund of that city.[16] In Warsaw and elsewhere, there were, of course, also Jewish children sympathetic neither to the Bund nor to the SS but rather to mainstream Zionist or other groups. But not every Jewish party, or even every Jewish socialist party, attracted or attempted to organize children. There were groups for children with a General Zionist orientation. There were also children attracted to Labor Zionism. But there was, so far as I have been able to determine, no such thing as an organized children's movement of the Jewish Socialist Workers' Party.

The Warsaw demonstration cited above notwithstanding, relations between the Kleyner bund and children affiliated with other movements were apparently often very poor. Yankel Levin's memoir, *Fun yene yorn*, the single most detailed account of the workings of a local Bundist children's group in the years of the Czarist Empire, provides unusually interesting information as to the attitudes and activities of the Kleyner bundistn in Homel—Levin's native city. In Homel, Levin writes, "we used to get back at the rich children, many of whom were Zionists. On holidays, when they used to decorate their homes with Stars of David, we used to rip the decorations down. We used to disrupt their meetings. . . . We had the same hatred for the proletarian groups, like SS and the Labor Zionists. They consisted chiefly of well-to-do boys and girls."[17] Litvak notes that local groups of the Kleyner bund and of the Kleyner SS met not only for discussions but also for fights.[18] In fact, encounters between rival groups at points resembled the rumbles between street gangs depicted in the American film *West Side Story* and were characterized by a similar bravado. A fight between members of the Kleyner bund and of the Kleyner SS in Pinsk in which the children beat each other with sticks and other weapons was broken up by representatives of the adult parties who happened to be nearby, and led Moyshe Katz of the SS to formulate a plan to create study circles for children. These circles would have included members of both of the preexisting children's groups and would have transcended the distinctions between them. The plan, however, was never implemented.[19]

There is no way to accurately measure or even to estimate the total number of children who participated in the Kleyner bund as a whole. The Kleyner bund in Homel was founded by about fifteen children. One source indicates, however, that in the beginning of 1905, there were thirteen circles made up of Kleyner bundistn in Homel, and that the total number of members in that city at that time was 250.[20] At its height, later that same year, by which point the Homel group was devoting itself primarily to self-education, the Kleyner bund of Homel claimed three hundred adherents.[21] In the heyday of Minsk's Kleyner bund, similarly, it boasted two hundred members.[22] But Homel and Minsk were all but certainly among the movement's strongholds. The Kleyner Bund in Volkovishki, which was organized in the summer of 1905, claimed to have forty to fifty members.[23] Mariampol and Polotsk, each of which had groups of twenty-odd boys, are certainly more typical.[24] Thus, the numbers of children affiliated with the Kleyner bund may best be described as modest.

But there may well have been more children in the Kleyner bund than there were Polish or Russian children active in non-Jewish socialist children's organizations in the Russian Empire during that era. The appearance of children's groups in Eastern Europe specifically identified with left-wing political parties appears to have been primarily (though not exclusively) a Jewish phenomenon even during the era of the Revolution of 1905. There were anarchist children's groups in the Bialystok-Grodno region, scattered groups of Polish socialist students, and students known to have been sympathetic to the

SDKPiL. But there does not appear to have been during that era a Little Polish Socialist Party (PPS) movement among the Poles, or a Little Menshevik movement among Russian children, or at least no contact between any such movements and the Kleyner bund.

The absence of such non-Jewish contacts is indicative of the weak roots of the revolutionary groups at that time. These weak roots eventually undermined the viability of all socialist children's movements in the Czarist Empire. The crushing of the strikes of December 1905 and fear of pogroms, hunger, and fatigue all eventually contributed to a dissipation of the optimistic mood that had taken hold among the rank and file of the Jewish socialist movements in the year immediately preceding that event. During and after 1907, a marked decline in the size of the Bund (and of the other socialist movements that had been active in the empire) became evident.[25]

However sharp the decline of the Bund, the decline of the Kleyner bund was even sharper. "One distinctive dynamic of the process of demobilization," Tobias and Woodhouse have underscored in a study of adult Bundists in the post–Revolution of 1905 years, "is a tendency for the revolutionary organization, in the face of defeat, to fall back on or revert to types of activity and organizational resources which had existed earlier; and for individual members to choose their course of action by reference to the experience and resources they had acquired prior to entering the movement, or after entering it but prior to its defeat."[26] But the children of the Kleyner bund were too young to have had such experience or resources.

The Bund itself survived the years of reaction by such means as reducing its staff, devoting energy to unionization efforts, and by fostering economic, educational, and cultural work more than it had during the revolutionary period. The Kleyner bund, however, was insufficiently organized to be able to make use of such tactics. Demoralization, the lack of a central leadership and of an organ of its own, the difficulties of operating without material resources, the precipitous decline of the adult Bund, and the increasingly reactionary atmosphere in the country as a whole all contributed to the Kleyner bund's demise.

In Homel, the Kleyner bund dropped in size during the course of 1906 from three hundred members to sixty. At the beginning of 1907, those still active in Homel's Kleyner bund were absorbed into the Bund itself. Certain former Kleyner bundistn became members of the Committee of the Bund organization in Homel. Others became leaders in local trade unions. The children's organization, however, ceased to exist. In some towns or cities, the Kleyner bund probably lasted marginally later into that same year. It appears to have ground to a halt everywhere by 1908.

There are virtually no indications as to what became of most of its one-time members. Some of them remained in the Russian Empire and in the socialist movement. Yankel Levin, who played a prominent role in the Kleyner bund in Homel, worked for the Bund's Central Committee in various locations beginning in 1913 and wrote for Bundist publications.[27] He was elected to the Bund's Central Committee at its Eleventh Conference, held in Minsk in 1919,[28] and, with other members of the Bundist Left, later joined the Communist Party. Levin was involved with projects related to Jewish colonization of the Crimea, became secretary of the regional committee of the Communist Party of Birobidjan, and appears to have been executed by the Soviet state in 1941. Moyshe Goldshtayn, who was born in Ostropole, Voliner guberneye, and who was in the Kleyner bund when he was fourteen years old, later became a Bolshevik, adopted the name Volodarski, and was allegedly a popular leader of the workers in Petrograd. On June 20, 1918, however, he was shot and killed by a member of the Social Revolutionary Party.[29] Other former members of the Kleyner bund emigrated. I. Eberil, a leader of the Kleyner bund in Minsk, became a vice president of the Workmen's Circle after immigrating to the United States.[30] Frida Vayner, who immigrated to America in 1911, organized Workmen's Circle schools in Galevston, Texas, and was active in Jewish cultural organizations in the southern part of the United States for many decades.[31] Certain ex-Kleyner bundistn left political life—either immediately following the collapse of the Kleyner bund or at some point thereafter. Dina Pritkin, for one, was described as someone who still considered herself to be a Bundist in 1921, though she was no longer involved in "active [political] work."[32] The cases just mentioned, however, are not necessarily representative. The later lives of most members of the Kleyner bund simply cannot be traced.

But the Kleyner bund was not forgotten. It sparked several literary works, including Baruch Charney Vladeck's short story, "Tsvey yinglekh," and Dovid Kasel's *Meirke fun "kleynem bund."*[33] During the 1920s, moreover, Esther Frumkin, a prominent former Bundist who had become a leading figure in the *Evsektsiia* (the Jewish Section of the Communist Party of the Soviet Union), wrote a foreword to a memoir on the Kleyner bund in which she justified writing on the topic in the Soviet context, noting that the place of the Kleyner bund had been taken by the communist youth association, "which unites in its ranks . . . Jewish youth . . . and Russian youth." Furthermore, she insisted that the mistakes evidenced in the history of the Kleyner bund had been overcome since "the Jewish worker has found his true place in the iron ranks of the Communist Party."[34] The legacy of the Kleyner bundistn, finally, was also remembered and interpreted (though not emulated) by the leaders of the Bundist children's movement of interwar Poland.

II

There were no Bundist children's groups for a full generation following the collapse of the Kleyner Bund. In the fall of 1926, however, the Youth Bund Tsukunft sponsored a number of meetings in Warsaw to discuss organized work among the children of the Jewish working class.[35] The fact that these meetings took place late in 1926 was not accidental, for 1926 was the year in which Marshall Jósef Piłsudksi—who had, as a young man, been sympathetic to the Polish socialist movement—seized power in Poland. Though the Bund rapidly came to disagree quite strongly with Piłsudksi's antidemocratic policies, it initially supported his overthrow of the government that had governed Poland in the first half of the 1920s, and it benefited from the relative decrease in power of political anti-Semitism, which characterized the early years of the Piłsudksi regime. Piłsudksi's seizure of power in May 1926, which improved the atmosphere for Polish Jewry even if it did not further the socialist cause, thus helps to explain why not only the Polish Bund's children's movement, but also the Bundist movement for physical education and the Bundist women's movement all crystallized in that year.

The meetings sponsored by the Tsukunft in 1926 led those who participated in them to conclude that it would be advisable to establish a new, separate, Bundist-oriented children's organization rather than attempt to conduct work for children under the auspices of the Tsukunft itself. The new organization, known as the *Sotsialistisher kinder-farband* (SKIF), or the Socialist Children's Union, was created at a meeting held on the premises of the Bundist-oriented women's organization and began to operate in December

1926—originally, solely in Warsaw.³⁶ It eventually included children between the ages of ten and fifteen (although the precise ages for entering and leaving the organization were not precisely mandated).³⁷

A number of teachers and educators associated with the TSYSHO (the Central Jewish School Organization), which was secular and Yiddishist in orientation, and which attracted many students from Bundist homes, were initially opposed to the creation of a Bundist children's movement and argued that it could have a negative impact on the development and education of those children who became involved in it.³⁸ Those who opposed forming a Jewish socialist children's movement that would foster Bundist principles feared that such a movement would lead children to neglect their school work, that it would dampen children's natural playfulness and mischievousness by exposing them prematurely to serious political and social issues, and that it would impose undue psychological burdens upon them.³⁹ They also feared that SKIF leaders would undermine the authority of teachers by acting as their competitors.⁴⁰ But, these initial misgivings notwithstanding, the creation of the SKIF clearly touched a chord within the Polish Jewish working class. In the wake of a decision by the plenum of the Bund's Central Committee to encourage the establishment of children's groups, the creation of the SKIF in Warsaw was rapidly emulated in cities and towns throughout Poland.⁴¹ The successes of the SKIF soon brought around the most prominent of those who had originally doubted the wisdom of forming such a movement. Many of the teachers who had been among the SKIF's early opponents later devoted considerable time and energy to fostering its work.⁴²

The SKIF proved to be particularly attractive to children attending schools affiliated with the TSYSHO. These children were the SKIF's most obvious constituency because a sizeable portion of their parents were committed Bundists, and because a number of the teachers and administrators in these schools were also sympathetic to Bundist principles.⁴³ Emanuel Patt, the SKIF's second secretary, has claimed that in the months immediately following the formation of the SKIF, a great majority of the children in those TSYSHO schools under Bundist control became members of the new Bundist children's organization.⁴⁴ Available data suggests that Patt overstated the case.⁴⁵ SKIF, however, clearly had a strong presence among TSYSHO students.

But TSYSHO charged tuition, which made this school system inaccessible to some of the poorest sections of the Jewish community, including many families that would have preferred to have their children educated in Yiddish. Approximately 80 percent of the Jewish children in Poland who attended primary schools were enrolled in Polish-language public schools run by the government. Widespread poverty left many Jewish families "with no other way to meet the requirement of compulsory primary school attendance."[46] SKIF, therefore, reached beyond the TSYSHO, sought out children attending the state schools, and soon attracted significant numbers of them.[47]

It ought to be noted that some of the children who entered the SKIF were students in traditional Jewish religious schools or came from observant families. Vladka Meed reports that in the early 1930s, when a boy named Yulek Yunghayzer first came to a SKIF club, he was wearing a Chasidic hat and a black frock.[48]

Significantly, neither the children enrolled in state schools nor those in religious institutions were considered by the Bund's leaders to be peripheral. The Bund central leadership recognized as early as 1927 that it was necessary to reach such children because the schools attended by them were "implanting ... a hostile relationship to the Jewish socialist movement."[49] In fact, some pointed out, the children attending TSYSHO schools could actually be said to have needed SKIF less than those attending other types of schools.

Of course, many Jewish children in interwar Poland were not enrolled in any school, or left school at a very early age. SKIF also attempted to organize both children employed in workshops or factories and so-called street children, many of whom had never attended school (compulsory education laws notwithstanding) and who scratched out a living selling newspapers, beygls, or cosmetics on the streets for tiny sums.[50] Since most of these street vendors could not afford licenses to operate, the police regularly hounded them.[51] Though I know of no precise figures on the number of Jewish street children in interwar Poland, one SKIF activist indicated in 1936 that Poland had a total of one million street children at that time, only some of whom, presumably, were Jewish.

The SKIF leaders found that the children in school, those at work, and those who lived in the street did not always mix smoothly. The children who were already working, for example, complained that the organization paid more attention to students than it did to them.⁵² Moreover, relations between the school children and the street children were not friendly; the latter tended to be highly competitive as a result of their experiences. In order to survive on the street, many had become aggressive and self-centered. But local SKIF leaders handled potentially explosive differences among the children in a sensitive and appropriate manner. In Baranowicze, for example, where the SKIF had attracted a significant number of street children, it entered into an arrangement with local trade unions under which some of the children were permitted to work in factories or workshops. Working with others in such contexts ultimately contributed to a diminution of their aggressive behavior and helped them to integrate into the SKIF.

Where such arrangements were not possible, suggested one SKIF activist concerned with these issues, SKIF locals themselves ought to not only organize the street children into unions but also encourage them to set standard prices for their wares rather than undercut each other. The SKIF also made efforts to teach street children basic skills—that is, reading, writing, and math.

After SKIF groups had already been established in numerous disparate locations, the Central Committee of the Bund appointed individuals to coordinate this newly created movement. Yankef Patt was named as chairman, and Leyvik Hodes was named the movement's secretary.⁵³

Born in 1890 in Bialystok, Patt had been attracted to the Poalei Zion at the beginning of 1905 and became the leader of the local SS group at the end of that year. He later developed a name for himself as a writer on and for children. From 1921 to 1928, he served as secretary of the TSYSHO.⁵⁴ Beginning with the fall of 1926, Patt also served as editor of the *Kleyne folkstsaytung*—a section of the Bund's Warsaw newspaper devoted to children. Indeed, Patt, who was not directly involved with the SKIF's organizational work on a day-to-day basis, contributed to the development of the SKIF primarily by his role in the newspaper, in which he regularly published reports from SKIF circles, letters from SKIF activists, and material suitable for use at the organization's events.⁵⁵

The task of formulating the principles of the SKIF, and of guiding its work in its first years of existence, fell primarily on Hodes. Born in 1892 in Vitebsker Gubernie, Hodes moved to Vilna in 1908, where he attended a teacher-training institute, and where he eventually became active in the Bundist organization.⁵⁶ In 1923, he moved to Warsaw, where he served for several years as director of a TSYSHO school. During his years in Warsaw, Hodes was among the most prominent leaders of the Bund's left-wing fraction, the so-called *tsveyer*. He became a member of the Central Committee of the Bund in Poland in 1925, wrote for the *Folkstsaytung* (the Bund's most important newspaper), was a coeditor of *Unzer tsayt*, the Bund's theoretical journal, and, in 1930, became one of the editors of *Kegn shtrom*, the organ of the Bund's left wing. Thus the person who had the single greatest impact on molding the SKIF was a Bundist leader of the first rank, with widespread contacts in the movement and with a strong commitment to the internationalist perspective of the left wing of the Bund. In his capacity as secretary of the SKIF, Hodes wrote a number of significant articles on socialist education; translated into Yiddish materials on socialist education produced in Central Europe; and also translated into Yiddish children's literature that had originally appeared in Russian or Polish.

Hodes believed that the SKIF ought to have the same goals as did the socialist children's movements in countries such as Germany and Austria.⁵⁷ From his perspective, as indicated in a piece published two years or so after the establishment of the SKIF, the socialist children's organizations in Western Europe "had the goal of contributing to the formation in children, from earliest youth, of ideals and perceptions in the spirit of the strivings of the working class. These organizations," Hodes wrote, "give themselves the task of planting in young souls the spirit of protest against the injustice of the present day world order; they cultivate the feelings of collectivism and solidarity, plant love and piety towards the heroes and leaders of the workers' movement and strive to forge among the children as their life ideal the ideals of the socialist future."⁵⁸

Just as had socialist children's organizations in Western Europe, Hodes argued in 1936, the SKIF ought to make use of specific attributes of the scouting movement (founded in England by a former military officer at the beginning of the twentieth century) while rejecting its reactionary elements.⁵⁹ He recognized that religiosity and patriotism were key elements of the scouting movement, that such elements tied the scouting movement to the bourgeois system, and that such movements had encouraged chauvinistic and militaristic ideologies. A socialist children's movement such as SKIF, in contrast, Hodes argued, while rejecting these elements, could still make use of some of the scouting movement's techniques. The SKIF, he proposed, ought to counter the spirit of religiosity with the spirit of anticlericalism. Children from more traditional homes participating in SKIF activities should be handled with care and not belittled, but their views should be countered by stressing internationalism, and the spirit of SKIF ought to be that of freethinkers. Similarly, the patriotism of bourgeois scouting should be countered by stressing internationality through, for example, working with the children's movement of the Polish Socialist Party when possible. However, Hodes believed that other aspects of scouting, such as its stress on hikes and camping, could be fruitfully used by socialist educators.[60]

SKIF actualized its principles by naming local groups after socialist leaders, by commemorating significant dates in the history of the workers' movement, by cooperating with the children's movement of the PPS when possible, and by encouraging internationalism, mutual aid, initiative, and administration by the children themselves over their own affairs. It also encouraged its members to keep themselves informed about current events. A report on the activities of the SKIF in Warsaw between July 1938 and May 1939, for example, indicates that SKIF circles in that city had discussed Czechoslovakia, the general strike in France, pogroms in Germany, refugees, and China and Japan, among many other topics.[61] In 1934 SKIF joined the Sozialistische Erziehungs International (SEI), a body made up of socialist children's-oriented organizations from a number of different nations, including those linked to member parties of the LSI. SKIF fostered contacts with the SEI by sending regular reports to it and by inviting one of its representatives to the first and only nationwide SKIF conference, which was held in 1936.[62] The debate within the Bund itself—in the period leading up to 1930—over whether to affiliate with the LSI had been sustained and strenuous. However, there does not appear to have been a comparable debate within SKIF concerning its decision to affiliate with the SEI, despite the prominent role played in SKIF by *tsveyers* such as Hodes (who opposed a link between the Bund and the LSI). The lack of debate on this issue within SKIF may well have been due precisely to the fact that this debate had already occurred in the SKIF's parent-body and been lost by the leftist political faction with which Hodes was associated.[63]

3. Presidium of the first countrywide SKIF conference, Warsaw, October 1936. *Naye folkstsaytung,* November 19, 1937.

SKIF does not appear to have devoted particular attention to debating or criticizing Zionism. To be sure, its leaders took occasional cracks at Zionist youth movements. In an issue of the SKIF periodical *Khavershaft,* published in 1937 in conjunction with the fortieth anniversary of the founding of the Bund, Kalmen Vapner (secretary of SKIF at the time) described the atmosphere in which the SKIF had been created:

> Our camp was small in the first months. We had to overcome many difficulties. The bourgeois, the Zionist, children's organizations dominated the Jewish street. Over the course of years they were driven into the minds of Jewish children and among them many worker children. The ideals of Zionism, that is of nationalism and reaction, taught them attachment to the capitalist world. [The Zionist children's organizations] filled on the Jewish street the same role—of . . . hating other peoples [*felker-has*]; of implanting blind obedience—as did bourgeois scout organizations throughout the world.[64]

This diatribe notwithstanding, SKIF, like the other ancillary organizations of the Bund, was far more concerned with stressing its ties to the socialist movements of other peoples than with critiquing other Jewish organizations. Like the Bund itself, SKIF conceived of itself as first and foremost a socialist group.

Moreover, there may well have been a second—not necessarily explicitly articulated—reason for avoiding potentially acrimonious debates with Zionist children's movements. SKIF, after all, was meant for the young, and it generally strove to make its activities positive, fun, and age appropriate. It made extensive use, for example, of trips, games, music, drama, and athletic activities. The movement would typically organize hikes in good weather and sled-riding or ice-skating parties in the winter.

In addition to working with children in their home cities and towns, the SKIF placed great emphasis on the camps that it created, first during summer vacations and later during winter vacations. From 1931 onward, the SKIF's summer camps were deliberately primitive and took place in scattered forests throughout Poland. The children in these camps slept in tents, cooked in fireplaces, built their own tables and benches out of materials at hand, stood guard at night on a rotating basis, and were encouraged to administer their own affairs insofar as practical. The stark poverty of the SKIF's constituency is underscored by a passing reference that appears in a memoir by Chava Rosenfarb, who attended SKIF-sponsored summer camps in the 1930s. The campers' diet, she notes (at least, at the camp she describes), "consisted of the same food day after day—sticky buckwheat and chunks of black bread."[65] Nevertheless, these camps—eventually known to the children as "socialist children's republics"—were exceptionally popular and made a lasting impact on those who participated in them.[66] Despite the occasional dogmatism of some of its spokesmen, SKIF proved to be very attractive to a segment of the youngest generation of Polish Jewry—indeed far more attractive than its most obvious competitors.

The Pioneer movement—a Communist-oriented children's movement—was already operating in Poland at the time that the SKIF was created, and had adherents in the secular Yiddishist schools in that era, despite the fact that the Communists were forced to operate illegally. In fact, the perceived success of the work of the Pioneer movement was one of the factors that led the Bund to promote the creation of SKIF.[67] The earliest SKIF leaders worried that they would be unable to compete with the Pioneers.[68] Internal SKIF

4. Anna Heller Rozental, a leading member of the Bund, addressing children and youth at a SKIF-sponsored summer camp, 1937. "No Passaran" (They Shall Not Pass), a Republican slogan during the Spanish Civil War, was adopted by the Warsaw Ski-fistn attending this gathering as the name for their portion of the encampment. From the Archives of the YIVO Institute for Jewish Research, New York, RG 1400.

documents, however, suggest that these fears were unfounded, and that the strength of the Pioneers waned as that of the SKIF waxed. These documents note that by the early 1930s, there were apparently no longer strong Pioneer circles in existence in TSYSHO schools comparable to those that had existed in the 1920s.[69]

There were approximately 2,200 children organized in 80 local SKIF organizations in 1930.[70] By 1931, the SKIF had grown dramatically, and claimed to have approximately 3,470 members in 102 local groups. The children's movement of the PPS was known to have had 1,500 members at that time. The children's movements of the Left Poalei Zion *(Yungbor)* and of the Right Poalei Zion *(Fraye skoytn)* were also far weaker than the SKIF. The Fraye skoytn, for one, claimed to have 1,100 members in 1931—a figure that the SKIF believed to be extremely overinflated.[71] On the basis of these figures, the SKIF proclaimed that it had become not only the largest organization in Poland specifically oriented toward the children of the Jewish working class but also the largest socialist children's movement in all of Poland.⁷²

However, the SKIF met strong antipathy from many directions throughout the history of its existence in Poland. The government, anti-Semitic sectors of the population, and the Communists posed particular (not necessarily equal) threats. The SKIF's reports to the SEI, for example, give an indication of the variety of ways in which the Polish government attempted to hinder its activities. "Our work strides forward," reads a report published in a 1934 organ of the SEI. "As a result, the organs of power of the state are manifesting an ever more lively 'interest' in our work. This found its most blatant expression in the prohibition of the 'International Helper' [a publication of the SEI] in Poland, which the Ministry of the Interior and the official telegraph agency have announced."⁷³ In early 1936, a second report to the SEI indicates, the workers' sports organization in Vilna, under whose auspices the SKIF in Vilna had operated, had been forbidden. The office in Vilna was closed. Work materials, camping materials, and an archive were confiscated, and the SKIF in Vilna was forced to continue its work in private premises rather than in a center of its own.⁷⁴ Skifistn (members of SKIF) hiking in the Polish countryside regularly encountered Poles who directed anti-Semitic comments at them or bombarded them with stones. A one-time Skifist, describing a SKIF-sponsored summer camp he attended in the late 1930s, notes, "The guarding of the camp was arranged by posting groups of two's [sic] along the perimeter. . . . This had to be kept up, especially for the nights. We did have quite a number of hooligans interfering with our campers. . . . Anti-Semitic gangs and even political parties engaged in Jew-bashing activities."⁷⁵

But even in the face of this harassment, the SKIF continued to grow steadily. It had roughly five thousand members immediately following the last set of elections to the Jewish community councils.⁷⁶ It undertook an enlistment campaign, doubled in size, and allegedly had more than ten thousand members (in 154 groups) on the eve of the Second World War, which is to say that it was at the peak of its strength in the summer of 1939.⁷⁷

The SKIF, of course, was only one link in the chain of Bundist cultural and social organizations forged in Poland during the years between the world wars. It, too, contributed to the attempts by the Bund to attain cultural hegemony within Polish Jewry and, like the Tsukunft, also succeeded in instilling a new militant spirit among its adherents.[78] By 1939, moreover, some one-time members of SKIF were likely among those voting for Bundist candidates—and many members of SKIF acted as "foot-soldiers" in Bundist electoral campaigns by posting or distributing campaign literature, and by encouraging voters to turn out on election day.

■ ■ ■

As the data provided above suggest, the Kleyner bund, which operated over a swath of the Russian Empire, and the Polish SKIF, which operated in an overlapping but somewhat different geographic area, differed sharply from one another. The Kleyner bund operated illegally. SKIF did not. The Kleyner bund was organized primarily from below, and by children. SKIF was organized from above, and by adults. The Kleyner bundistn (initially) had difficult relationships with their Bundist counterparts. SKIF, in contrast, was encouraged and supported by the Bund. The Kleyner bund was composed in large part of apprentices. SKIF was apparently composed primarily of schoolchildren. The Kleyner bund was interested, first and foremost, in political and economic activities. SKIF devoted a great deal of attention to educational, cultural, and recreational activities as well as to specifically political ones. Bundist children's groups in the Czarist Empire were often exclusively male. SKIF groups were coeducational. Kleyner bund groups had precious little contact with Russian or other organized non-Jewish socialist children. SKIF affiliated with an international socialist children's movement and is known to have sought contact with Polish socialist children. The Kleyner bund, finally, died out within a few years of its formation. SKIF, however, was a large movement, and was still growing when World War II began, thirteen years after its creation. The leaders of the Polish Bund seem to have attempted to learn from the mistakes made by their predecessors—and made a series of conscious decisions that help to explain why the SKIF was so much larger and more successful than the Kleyner bund had been.

Morgnshtern

A Bundist Movement for Physical Education

THE FACT THAT A GROUP of Polish Bundists saw fit to establish the Workers' Society for Physical Education "Morgnshtern" *(Arbeter-gezelshaft far fizishe dertsiung "morgnshtern" in poyln)* can be explained, at least in part, by situating the creation of this organization in the context of the history of Jewish movements devoted to sports and physical education in Eastern Europe.[1] There were several different sports movements in interwar Poland affiliated with specific Jewish political parties, all created within a short time span. The founding of Morgnshtern was one example of a more general phenomenon: the emergence of explicitly Jewish sports movements on the Jewish street.

■ ■ ■

Large-scale Jewish sports movements tended to emerge marginally later in Congress Poland than in Jewish communities in German-speaking Europe.[2] The propensity of orthodox Jewish authorities to frown upon activities perceived as distracting from the study of religious texts, and the restrictions on Jewish organizational life imposed by the czarist regime, hindered the emergence of these sports movements on a mass scale in Congress Poland in the first years of the twentieth century. There may well have been local Jewish sports clubs in specific towns or cities.[3] There were not, however, unified Jewish sports movements per se operating over a broad geographic area.

The German occupation of Congress Poland during the course of the First World War created a dramatically freer atmosphere for the Jewish population and allowed Jewish communal and cultural groups far greater leeway than they had previously experienced. One result was the creation of these explicitly Jewish sports groups—often known as *Maccabi* groups—in Warsaw, Vilna, and Plock (echoing the earlier creation of Maccabi groups in Central European cities).[4] The Lodz-based Jewish sports club *Bar-Kochba*, which allegedly affiliated with the Maccabi world union at a later point in time, also dated from this period. In 1921, a network of Maccabi clubs in Poland was officially established.

Maccabi was a sizeable and vibrant movement in Poland throughout the interwar period. However, it was widely thought of, by the 1920s if not earlier, as particularly attractive to middle class and wealthy elements of the Polish Jewish community, to those Jews who spoke Polish, and to those sympathetic to the mainstream General Zionists. This perception helped to spark the creation of a number of new sports movements and clubs, each of which had ties with a specific, different Jewish political party. The movement founded in 1923 and known in Polish as *Gwiazda* (or in Yiddish as *Shtern*), for example, was affiliated with the Left Poalei Zion.[5] Hapoel, which was linked to the Right Poalei Zion, also operated in Poland in the years between the two world wars.[6] There were individual sports clubs, though not full-fledged sports movements, sympathetic to both the Revisionist-Zionists[7] and the *Folkistn*.[8] At least one local sports club—*Skała* (Rock)—consisted primarily of members of the Jewish Section of the Communist Party.[9] To be sure, the range of political opinion among the leaders of the Jewish sports movements was not quite as broad as was the range of perspectives within Polish Jewry as a whole. The orthodox political party Agudes Yisreol, for example, did not create a movement of its own. Nevertheless, there were significant differences among the Jewish sports movements of Poland rooted in the differing ideologies of their leaders or parent parties.

■ ■ ■

Bundist-oriented sports organizations were active in specific cities, such as Cracow, long before the official creation of Morgnshtern.[10] In Warsaw, for example, the gymnastics groups that met in the building of the Society for the Protection of Health (TOZ) in the early 1920s, while formally nonpolitical, were allegedly organized and composed all but exclusively of Bundists and those likely to be sympathetic to that movement.[11] Morgnshtern per se,

5. Morgnshtern membership booklet of Eljasz Kulkes, Vilna, 1927. From the Archives of the YIVO Institute for Jewish Research, New York, RG 29, Folder 86.

however, was not officially established until late in 1926, and did not hold its first Polandwide conference until April 1929. The first Morgnshtern conference—which was held in Warsaw and which was attended by delegates representing approximately four thousand individual members[12]—can legitimately be taken to mark the emergence of Morgnshtern as a full-fledged, Poland-wide organization. It was controlled by Bundists and Tsukunftistn throughout its life span.[13]

Unlike most other organizations promoting sports and athletics, Morgnshtern emphasized activities that large numbers of individuals could engage in simultaneously, rather than either team or individual sports. The Morgnshtern groups active in Poland in the 1930s sponsored a range of activities, notably gymnastics, hiking, cycling, and swimming.[14] These activities were stressed because of their "mass" character and because they did not require a great deal of practice. It was understood from the outset that the workers at whom Morgnshtern aimed had relatively little time to devote to athletics and insufficient disposable income to become involved in sports that required expensive equipment or training.

Initially, the Morgnshtern groups tended not only to promote specific activities but also to de-emphasize certain sports that were widely popular among European workers, including soccer and boxing. In 1929, Bundist delegates to the Congress of the Socialist Workers' Sports International (SWSI) endorsed a proposal to change the rules for soccer in a manner intended to check violence and brutality in the game. "The proposal," as Roni Gechtman has described it, "(presented together with the representatives of Austria and Switzerland) was that in football competitions, the winning team would be decided not only on the basis of goals scored but also through a system of points rewarding 'aesthetic and fair play' and 'nice combinations.'"[15] From the perspective of the Morgnshtern's leadership of those years, soccer was overly oriented toward emphasis on individual accomplishment and toward the glorification of "champions."

■ ■ ■

The significance of the positions taken by Morgnshtern in its formative era, not only on soccer, but also on other matters, is underscored by comparing these positions to the stances taken by Shtern.[16] Just as did the political parties with which they were associated, Morgnsthern and Shtern had a great deal in common.

Though the Bund was staunchly anti-Zionist, both it and the Left Poalei Zion were not only Yiddishist but also Marxist and secularist.[17] Bundists and Left Labor Zionists cooperated, to some degree, in the context of the TSYSHO and at times even entered into electoral agreements with one another. Thus, the fact that Morgnshtern and Shtern had similar emblems,[18] as well as similar names and goals, should come as no great surprise. The likenesses between these two movements are also suggested by the fact that on more than one occasion individuals who had been affiliated with Morgnshtern dropped out and joined Morgnshtern's rivals, the Left Labor Zionists.[19]

One significant similarity between Shtern and Morgnshtern concerns their attitudes toward language. Certain of the sports clubs active on the Jewish street in interwar Poland were ideologically committed to the use of Hebrew. Dr. Pribulski, the long-term head of Bar Kochba, insisted that Hebrew be the language of command for these clubs. In an interview conducted in 1924,

Pribulski explained that his club strove to help create a Jewish sports movement that would operate simultaneously in numerous countries, and he suggested that only Hebrew was suitable to act as a lingua franca for such a movement.[20] He argued that Hebrew was the symbol of Jewish unity and that, in any event, Yiddish was insufficiently standardized to serve as a command language. Both Shtern and Morgnshtern, in contrast, had a pro-Yiddish perspective.[21]

Though Pribulski insisted that his club was apolitical and ought to be opposed on principle to affiliation with any political party, his stance on the language question as well as numerous other issues was perceived by both Morgnshtern and Shtern as an indication that Bar Kochba (and Makabi) occupied a specific—reactionary—niche on the political and social spectrum of Polish Jewish life. A public statement issued by the Lodz branch of Morgnshtern in 1931, for example, condemned Bar Kochba and Maccabi in no uncertain terms. "Under the mask of physical education," this statement reads, "there are produced in the Maccabis, Bar Kochbas . . . slaves for the . . . capitalist order; nationalists are raised there, supporters of militarism, of shiny epaulets and ringing little swords. The bourgeois sports clubs are the nest of hatred against the working class and its ideals of liberation."[22] Just as the working class had to create its own organizations in politics and in the economic arena, the Bundists reasoned, so too was it necessary to create separate socialist sport organizations in order to tear working-class youth away from the injurious influence of bourgeois sport.

The Left Labor Zionists' Shtern certainly would have agreed, for it insisted that "the worker-sportsman struggles for the liberation of the working class; sport is for him not a goal in itself, but a means by which to educate a physically developed and class conscious member of the international family of workers. . . . [T]he chief goal of the worker-sportsman is socialism. An individual victory has value only if it brings something useful to humanity. Private interests must yield to second place; the collective is the essential thing."[23]

Although the Bundist Morgnshtern and the Left Poalei Zion's Shtern had a number of manifest, objective similarities, they also differed significantly from one another—at least initially. One way in which these differences become apparent is by comparing their attitudes toward soccer.

Though there were dissenting voices within the Left Poalei Zion, Shtern promoted soccer from the time of its founding.[24] In 1928, at which time the

Warsaw Shtern claimed to be the single strongest Jewish workers' sports club in Poland, it proudly listed its soccer section first in a public description of its activities and accomplishments, announced that seventy of its three hundred members were involved in the sport, and stressed that the team had had numerous matches not only in Warsaw but elsewhere.[25]

Even in its early years, soccer was by no means absent from Morgnshtern's list of activities. Teams such as Kraft, Veker, and Charney played in Warsaw under Morgenshtern's auspices as early as 1929.[26] But in the 1920s, soccer simply did not receive the kind of support from Morgnshtern that it received from other sports associations.[27] "Sports-business, commerce in football and with ... convictions," the *Yugnt-veker* sneered in 1929, "our sportsmen leave for the 'experts' in the field of political and societal commerce—for the 'Left' Poalei Zion with its Shtern, *mishtayns gezogt* [of whom some think so highly]."[28]

Just as Morgnshtern differed, in the first years of its existence, from its Left Labor Zionist rival in its attitude toward soccer, it also differed from Shtern in its initial position vis-à-vis boxing. Opposition to boxing within the ranks of Morgenshtern ran somewhat deeper in the organization's founding years than did opposition to soccer. The (non-Jewish) Polish workers' sports organization made a formal decision to allow boxing at the end of the 1920s. The first Morgenshtern conference, however, never considered the issue. Moreover, Bundist representatives to the SWSI spoke forcefully against promotion of boxing at several different congresses.[29]

Shtern did not oppose boxing even in the 1920s and enthusiastically endorsed it at some points in its history. The Warsaw local of the Left Labor Zionist sports movement is known to have had twenty-five members in its boxing section in the late 1920s and to have competed with boxers from the Polish workers' clubs.[30] By 1933, Shepsl Rotholts, a member of the Warsaw Shtern, was the best boxer in his weight class in all of Poland.[31] The supporters of boxing within Shtern's ranks insisted that the sport did not foster brutality, bloodthirstiness, chauvinism, or egoism, as their socialist opponents claimed. Labor Zionists making such claims, one supporter of the pugilists alleged, erred because of the way that bourgeois sports were conducted. As a part of the proletarian movement, Shtern had a Marxist perspective, this supporter insisted, and a "socialist proletarian ethic." One simply did not find among Shtern's boxers imbued with this ethic, he continued, the attitudes feared by the opponents of boxing. "Every comrade in Warsaw knows that it is precisely the boxing section which has the best comrades and which is most closely tied to our slogans and tasks." Boxing made the youth stronger, ready for struggle, and prepared him to undertake successfully the task he needed to perform: to aid in the victory of the international proletariat over the bourgeoisie. Thus, the misgivings of certain Labor Zionists notwithstanding, if boxing could help to create healthy, enlightened working fighters, it should be supported.[32]

But the rather stark difference between Morgnshtern's approach to boxing and the approach of Shtern blurred markedly over time. By 1937, the Warsaw branch of Morgnshtern—which was by far its largest branch in all of Poland—had an official, active section devoted to boxing, and was competing not only with Shtern and with Polish clubs but even with Maccabi (which was generally despised in Morgnshtern circles as a bourgeois, chauvinistic, and linguistically Polonized movement). The spokespersons for the Morgnshtern boxers insisted that the health concerns raised earlier by opponents of the sport had proven to be unfounded. They also pointed out—in what may have been a political analogy—that boxing was first and foremost a defensive sport, but that it teaches an "important truth about life, that one can best defend oneself if one attacks."[33] Nevertheless, a Bundist source has claimed, the boxing sections in local groups of Morgnshtern were treated like "step children" and "did not play a great role in the work" of the movement.[34]

Morgnshtern and Shtern flung charges at one another throughout the late 1920s and 1930s. Early in January 1929, for example, there were struggles between supporters of the bourgeois parties and supporters of the workers' parties within the Football Association of Warsaw. *Nasz Przegląd*—an "influential pro-Zionist Jewish daily"[35]—apparently criticized the role that had been played by the representatives of Shtern in this struggle, and the Bundist *Folkstsaytung* allegedly endorsed *Nasz Przegląd*'s criticism. A report in the Left Poalei Zion's organ, *Arbeter-tsaytung*, shortly thereafter claimed that one delegate to the Football Association, whom it described as an adherent of the right-wing National Democratic Party and an anti-Semite, had credentials authorizing him to represent the Morgnshtern affiliate in Włocławek. This, according to *Arbeter-tsaytung*, was why the *Folkstsaytung* endorsed the

Morgnshtern: A Bundist Movement for Physical Education | 55

6. The managing committee of the Warsaw Morgnshtern, 1937. From the Archives of the YIVO Institute for Jewish Research, New York, RG 1400.

critique of *Nasz Przegląd*—the Bundists needed to support those with whom they were (purportedly) newly connected, "the Polish anti-Semitic and Jewish bourgeois sports clubs."[36]

In 1930, the *Folkstsaytung* criticized the soccer team of the Warsaw local of Shtern for taking part in a trophy competition sponsored by *Nasz Przegląd* for the title of "best Jewish sports club in Warsaw." The other participants were Maccabi, Bar Kochba, and the Jewish Academic Union.[37] The Bundists publicized Shtern's participation in activities sponsored by the bourgeois and the "yellow" press while questioning its leftist credentials.[38] Shtern suggested in reply that Morgnshtern would also have competed for such a trophy—but that it lacked sufficient ability to do so. Moreover, "the *Folkstsaytung* knows that Gwiazda [Shtern] has won a great deal of sympathy among labor and hundreds of workers for the thought of proletarian sport through its participation and its victories in the struggle over trophies."[39]

When, in 1931, *Nasz Przegląd* organized a competition for the title of best Jewish basketball team in Warsaw, Maccabi, Shtern, the Jewish Academic Union, and Morgnshtern competed.[40] *Arbeyter-tsaytung* took pains to point this out to its readership.

Did Morgnshtern cave in to bourgeois values in making a place for soccer and boxing within its organization? Did it do so by competing for trophies against bourgeois clubs? Possibly. One alternative explanation is that its leadership responded to the desires of its membership. Just as the national program of the Bund in Czarist Russia was allegedly influenced by pressure from below, so too, it would appear, was the program of Morgnshtern in interwar Poland. These changes, however, also made Morgnshtern far more similar to Shtern than had earlier been the case.

In certain respects, Morgnshtern continued to be notably different than its Left Labor Zionist equivalent. Unlike Shtern, which had a women's section (at least in its Warsaw local),[41] Morgnshtern deliberately chose not to create a special commission for women, stressing that it was not necessary because women already played a prominent role in the organization. Approximately half of the members of the Warsaw branch's gymnastics section were female, and so were half of those in the handball group, among others. Moreover, according to a report on its activities in 1938 issued by the Warsaw branch, "Women participate actively not only among the 'sports consumers,' that is, the members, but also among the 'producers,' that is, among the instructors ... and activists of the society."[42]

Morgnshtern's choice of affiliations hints at another continuing difference between it and Shtern. The Left Labor Zionist sports movement was instrumental in the formation of the Polish Workers' Sport Federation (ZRSS), which was dominated by members of the PPS.[43] Though Shtern disagreed with the relatively positive relationships that the ZRSS maintained with both the bourgeois Polish sports movements and the governmental authorities concerned with physical education, and though it also disagreed with the decision of the ZRSS to expel certain left-oriented clubs from the federation, Shtern continued to be active within the ZRSS even after losing critical votes on these issues.[44] Shtern believed in "unified class organizations" and thus felt that it ought to remain in the ZRSS for so long as it continued to have the right to express its opinion within that organization, and for so long as the possibility existed that it could have an impact on that organization's policies.[45]

Unlike Shtern, Morgnstern, though ideologically committed to the principle of uniting the labor movement, was not involved with the ZRSS.[46] The

Morgnshtern: A Bundist Movement for Physical Education | 57

7. Gymnasts of the Warsaw Morgnshtern. From the Archives of the YIVO Institute for Jewish Research, New York, RG 1400.

Bund had a complex and not consistently smooth relationship with the PPS—which was, from the Bundist perspective, too reformist in orientation, too nationalistic, and insufficiently decisive in combating anti-Semitism.[47] In the late 1920s, the possibility of having the Morgnshtern and certain other movements promoting physical education and athletics affiliate with the ZRSS was explored. In the course of these exploratory talks, the ZRSS, in the wake of discussions reminiscent of debates on the so-called "organization" and "national" questions that had rocked the Russian Social Democratic Workers' Party before the First World War, agreed to reorganize itself as a federal organization, which would, presumably, have contained Polish, Jewish, German, and Ukrainian sections.[48] However, Shtern declared that it would only form a Jewish section with Morgnshtern within the ZRSS under specific conditions (which it knew the Bundists would not accept)—and negotiations faltered.

At the next congress of the SWSI, held in Prague in 1929, Morgnshtern demanded that it be seated as an independent delegation representing Jewish workers, and not as part of the Polish delegation (as was Shtern).[49] Though the representatives of the ZRSS vigorously objected, the SWSI ultimately acceded to Morgnshtern's perspective. Throughout the remaining years of its existence, Morgnshtern proudly broadcast that it was "the Jewish section of the Workers Sports International"[50] and, as such, fielded its own delegation to the Second International Workers Olympics, which was held in Vienna in July 1931.[51]

Shtern, in contrast, pointedly declined to take part. Shtern had been represented by the ZRSS at earlier events of the Workers Sports International, such as the Fifth International Socialist Sports Congress.[52] However, it refused to participate in the Second Workers Olympics, purportedly because it did not want to be associated with sports groups indirectly affiliated with the LSI (which the Left Poalei Zion considered to be opportunistic and conservative, and which the Bund joined in 1930, after sustained debate).[53] In this area as well, the distinctions between Morgnshtern and Shtern diminished over time. In 1937, Shtern sent a sizeable delegation to the Third Workers Sports Olympics, which were held in Antwerp.[54] Morgnshtern intended to participate, but the Polish government refused to grant its members the visas that they would have needed in order to travel to Belgium.

Both Morgnshtern and Shtern were subjected to political repression. Between 1929 and 1934, divisions of Morgnshtern in thirty-two different Polish cities were closed, for varying lengths of time, by order of the government.[55] In 1933, when Shtern was organizing its first nationwide gathering, train discounts usually granted to participants in such events were denied at the last moment—an apparent attempt to diminish the size of the gathering, seemingly motivated by Shtern's radical socialist ideology.[56] A report from Brisk indicates that the quarters of the Shtern in that city were searched and sealed in 1937.[57]

Anti-Semitism also affected the Jewish workers' sports movements. In the wake of an incident that took place at a soccer game in 1930, a number of Polish papers—*Kurier Warszawski*, *Gazeta Warszawska*, and *Przegląd Sportowy*—published attacks on Shtern that the *Arbeter-tsaytung* described as incitements to a pogrom.[58] There were, similarly, systematic, anti-Semitic attacks on Shtern in Pruszków, in which, *Arbeter-tsaytung* sadly admitted, Polish workers participated.[59]

■ ■ ■

Though there is a fair amount of information available on the *activities* of local branches of Morgnshtern, there is relatively little detailed data available on the demographic composition of the bulk of these branches. In this sense, the information available on the Morgnshtern branch that operated in Vilna, which was created in 1927, is exceptional.[60] A questionnaire completed by the Vilna Morgnshtern some nine years after its establishment notes that it had 152 active members at that time, of whom 50 were men and 102 were women, and also had 38 passive members.[61] In addition, the branch had a group for children with 68 participants. Vilna Morgnshtern's members worked as tailors, metal workers, construction workers, seamstresses, and in other working class jobs.[62] The questionnaire reveals that the club's income was derived from dues, from events, and from fund-raising, and that no subsidies were received at that time from the city, from the Jewish community, from Morgnshtern's national body or other sources.[63] Activities—of which gymnastics was far and away the most significant—were conducted in Yiddish.[64] Vilna Morgnshtern had a reading room, a sports library, and engaged in cultural as well as in physical activities. It fostered, for example, a mandolin orchestra, a chorus, and a drama circle. By 1933, Morgnshtern boasted that it had become the second largest Jewish sports group in Vilna.[65] In the mid-1930s, Vilna Morgnshtern claimed that it was still growing and that its competitors had shrunk.[66] However, it seems never to have become as large as Vilna Maccabi.[67]

■ ■ ■

Was the relative strength of Morgnshtern and Maccabi in Vilna typical of their relative strength elsewhere in Poland? I think not.[68] Neither membership in Morgnshtern nor membership in the other Jewish sports movements of Poland was stable. Large numbers of individuals moved in and out of these movements as a result of internal migration, illness, entry into military service, and for other reasons.[69] In addition to the factors that had an impact on membership in Morgnshtern, membership in the Zionist and Labor Zionist sports movements may well have been affected, to a limited degree, by *aliya*. A small number of one-time activists in these movements emigrated from Poland to Palestine before the beginning of the Second World War.[70]

The flux in its membership notwithstanding, the nationwide Morgnshtern movement grew substantially during its first decade. The organization had 2,500 members in 1927, 4,000 members in 1929, 4,500 in 1933, and 5,000 in

1934.[71] A Bundist source boasts that it had as many as 8,000 members in 1937, and that it was operating in 160 locations at that time.[72]

However, local branches of Morgnshtern were harassed by Polish authorities and forced by the Polish government to shut down, even more regularly in the late 1930s than they had been earlier in that decade. As a direct result, Morgnshtern's countrywide membership declined very sharply between 1937 and the beginning of World War II. There were no Morgnshtern organizations in Aleksandrów Kuj., Baranowicze, Białystok, Kołomyja, Kowel, Równe or Vilna, among other locations, in the spring of 1939.[73] Whether or not Morgnshtern had had 8,000 members in 1937, its total membership was back down to just over 5,000 in the summer of 1938.[74] In May 1939, when it held its third countrywide conference, delegates representing only 4,500 members, and 35 local organizations, were able to attend.[75]

But Morgnshtern continued to grow in the Polish capital city (where it was sometimes subjected to close scrutiny, but seems never to have been forcibly dissolved) in the years immediately preceding the war.[76] In its formal report on activities for the year ending February 1, 1936, for example, the Warsaw branch of Morgnshtern indicated that it had 956 active members.[77] A year later, this same branch had increased its membership to 1,500 and claimed that it had thereby become the single largest local sports organization—Jewish or Polish, socialist or not—in all of Poland.[78] By February 1938, the total membership of Morgnshtern's Warsaw branch had grown yet again—to 1,855.[79] It is all but certain that Morgnshtern increased its strength in Warsaw not only in absolute terms but also relative to its Jewish rivals. The number of activists in the Warsaw Shtern, for one, dropped off from more than 700 in February 1937 to over 400 in January 1939.[80] The experience of Morgnshtern in Warsaw suggests that it had considerable power to attract new members where it was in a position to do so.

Only a very small proportion of Morgnshtern members were also formal members of the Bund per se.[81] However, all of Morgnshtern's members, whether members of the Bund or not, were regularly exposed to Bundist ideas and encouraged to vote for Bundist candidates. Indeed, from the perspective of Morgnshtern's leaders, increasing support for the Bund was surely one of their movement's underlying objectives. It is at least plausible—though admittedly not demonstrable—that some individuals who had previously not had ties to the Bund became more likely to vote for it as a result of participation in Morgnshtern's activities. The increasing membership of Morgnshtern as a whole in the years 1926–37, and its continued growth in Warsaw in the years immediately thereafter, suggest the possibility that the electoral successes of the Bund in the late 1930s were connected to the somewhat earlier rise of Bund-affiliated organizations (such as Morgnshtern).

4

The Medem Sanatorium

THE MEDEM SANATORIUM, an institution for children at risk of contracting tuberculosis, was the crown jewel of the Bundist network in the interwar years.[1] The educational principles on which the sanatorium operated were similar to those of the TSYSHO, with which it was affiliated. TSYSHO, however, was not founded as a Bundist entity, and originally included within its leading circles many educators who were adherents of other parties as well as a number of Bund members.[2] In its early years, TSYSHO was, in the words of Ezra Mendelsohn, "riddled by political conflicts among Bundists, Zionist socialists, Folkists, and even Communists. Its leaders endlessly debated such questions as whether or not its goal was to produce 'class-conscious socialists' and whether or not to allow the teaching of Hebrew."[3]

The Medem Sanatorium, however, while closely identified with the TSYSHO, was firmly controlled by Bundists throughout its history, and was never wracked by the kind of internal wrangling over ideological issues which afflicted the TSYSHO at some points in time. Thus, close examination of the sanatorium reveals more about the educational program of the Polish Bund, and possibly about the prospects of that program, than does scrutiny of the TSYSHO. In this regard, it is of interest that the Medem Sanatorium developed a stellar reputation and—despite its manifest and continuing Bundist orientation—ultimately proved to be attractive not only to Bundists but also to some Jews who were religiously observant and/or relatively well-to-do. The quality of the care, the paucity of comparable institutions serving Jewish children, and the progressive pedagogical approach of the educators affiliated with it led families unlikely to support the Bund to send their children to this

Bundist-run facility. The extraordinarily positive experiences of these children, in turn, may well have led their parents, in certain instances, to reassess preexisting attitudes. Though the number of individuals involved with the sanatorium at any given time was never large, the institution was even more successful in certain respects than the Tsukunft, SKIF, and Morgnshtern, and is likely to have contributed to the Bund's improved image in the late 1930s.[4]

■ ■ ■

There were several attempts made to create institutions devoted to the needs of Polish Jewish children in frail health in the early 1920s. In 1921, for example, the Dinezon Committee—a grouping made up both of Bundists and non-Bundists that was at the forefront of the initiative to create Yiddish secular schools in Poland—established a summer colony for children threatened by tuberculosis in Otvosk, a *shtetl* near Warsaw renowned for its clean air.[5] A board of directors (a majority of which had ties to the Bund) ran the colony, which operated in rented quarters.[6]

It was anticipated that the colony would have room for one hundred children and that each child accepted into the institution would remain for an entire summer.[7] While preliminary results were excellent—the health of the children accepted into the colony improved rapidly during the course of their stay—the doctors associated with this effort maintained that the children needed longer-term care, and that they ought not to be sent back as rapidly as had been initially anticipated to their home environments. A decision was therefore reached to transform the colony into a permanent institution.

The colony had received funds from two Jewish organizations based in the United States, People's Relief and the American Jewish Joint Distribution Committee, but it did not have the financial means to sustain itself on a long-term basis. After failing to pay its rent for several months in a row, it was evicted.

The initiators of the colony, however, appealed to Vladimir Medem, a Bundist leader who had very recently immigrated to New York and who had demonstrated considerable sympathy for the initiative to create Yiddish-language schools. Medem, in turn, spearheaded a fund-raising effort in America and succeeded in raising several thousand dollars. Those funds, which he sent to the then newly established TSYSHO, made it possible to purchase a piece of property in Miedzeszyn, in a forested area near Warsaw.

But the major building on that property was in need of renovation before it could be used for the purpose for which it had been bought. In addition, it was soon apparent that the most significant building on the property would need to be supplemented with at least one additional building. For several years after the initial purchase, construction proceeded by fits and starts.[8] A dedication ceremony at the institution—which was named for Medem following his death in 1923—was held in the summer of 1924. There were apparently a few children on the premises in the summer of 1925.[9] However, the Kindersanatorie u. n. vladimir medem, widely known as the Medem Sanatorium, was not formally and fully opened until January 1926.

Though the sanatorium was built under TSYSHO's auspices and cooperated closely with that group, it had a governing board of its own, and was both legally and financially independent of the overarching school organization. A majority of the Executive Committee of the sanatorium's governing body—a group that met every two weeks—was made up of Bundists.[10]

Yekutiel Portnoy, known as Noyakh (1872–1941), was the de facto chairman of the Bund and also the chairman of the sanatorium's Executive Committee and of its larger administrative board.[11] Portnoy not only chaired the executive meetings but also kept in close contact with the sanatorium's leading staff members, thereby ensuring that it was run with a Bundist perspective.[12]

Unlike Portnoy, Shloyme Mendelson (1896–1948), who was the vice chairman of the Executive Committee,[13] was a prominent educator as well as a political activist. He had been a leader of the Folkspartay at one point in his career but left that organization in 1921, when he became one of the founders of the TSYSHO and an elected member of its governing body.[14] He continued to play exceptionally prominent and visible roles in the TSYSHO for the rest of the interwar era.

Mendelson drew closer to the Bund over a period of years and became a formal member of the party in 1928. A decade later, he became a member of its Central Committee. He was also elected, on Bundist electoral lists, to both the Warsaw City Council and the organized Jewish community council of Warsaw. Mendelson took his position on the Executive Committee very seriously and devoted a great deal of energy to the institution. Indeed, no important decision at the sanatorium was made without consulting with Mendelson.[15]

However important the role of the sanatorium's lay leadership may have been in the running of the institution, the tone was set primarily by the professional staff. Shloyme Gilinski, the beloved director and primary educational administrator as well as the secretary of the sanatorium's presidium, and Yoysef Brumberg, who served as manager for some of the relevant period, were especially important in this regard.

Shloyme Gilinski (1888–1961) was born in Ligmian, in the Vilna region. He spent his childhood in a *shtetl*, Duksht, and received a traditional yeshiva education in Vilna. He became attracted to socialist ideas around 1903, was active in the SS during the 1905 revolution, and was editor of *Undzer veg*, an organ of the United Jewish Socialist Workers' Party (the Fareynigte) immediately following the First World War. Gilinski was an early advocate of the use of Yiddish as an instructional language in Jewish schools, studied pedagogy and psychology first in Warsaw and later in Berlin, and, after the creation of the TSYSHO, worked for that organization (as, for example, an inspector who visited individual classrooms on behalf of the school network in order to get a sense of the teachers' performance). He became a member of the Bund in 1921 and closely identified with the movement in Poland. He was elected to the Warsaw City Council on Bundist tickets in 1927 and 1938; was elected, as a Bundist, to the organized Jewish community council of Warsaw (the *kehile*) in 1936; and served as a member of the Warsaw Committee of the Bund, all while continuing to hold his position at the sanatorium.[16] Within the Bund, Gilinski was a *tsveyer*, that is, an adherent of the party's left-wing faction.[17] There can be no question that he strove to teach socialist values in the sanatorium throughout his years of affiliation with it.

From 1930 until the beginning of the Second World War, Yoysef Brumberg (1897–1965) served as Gilinski's right-hand man. Brumberg, who had been born in Lodz, completed a gymnasium in Moscow and studied in universities in Petrograd and in Vilna.[18] He was also among the founders of a Yiddish secular gymnasium in Swiencian. At some point in the early 1920s, he joined a student club dominated by Communists (though he himself was not a Communist or sympathetic to them) but later received a tip that Polish authorities intended to arrest the club's members.[19] It eventually became clear that he needed to leave the country in order to avoid arrest. With the financial support of the Bund, Brumberg ultimately moved to Palestine. He was employed in Tel Aviv in a number of working-class positions and also wrote for the Warsaw-based Bundist daily, the *Folkstsaytung*. After approximately five years had passed and the danger of arrest by the Polish police had diminished, Brumberg returned to Poland to take on a position at the sanatorium, where he eventually served in many capacities.

When Gilinski found it necessary, as was regularly the case, to leave the sanatorium—whether to fill his political obligations in Warsaw or to conduct work on behalf of the sanatorium that could not be done on-site—the institution was run by Brumberg.[20] Like Gilinski, Brumberg was involved simultaneously in work on behalf of both the sanatorium and the Bund. He was elected to the Warsaw City Council on the Bundist ticket in 1938.

The members of the sanatorium teaching staff in the interwar years, who, in almost all instances, lived at the institution while working in it, tended to be well trained and experienced.[21] A significant proportion of the teachers, both men and women, had attended the Yiddishist- and secularist-oriented Yiddish Teachers Seminary, which opened in 1921, and which operated in Vilna until 1931.[22] Many of the teachers are also known to have taught in other TSYSHO-affiliated institutions.[23] Not surprisingly, not only Shloyme Gilinski and Yoysef Brumberg, but also a number of the rank-and-file teachers at the Medem Sanatorium, including Hershl Grinboym, Zisl Gutman, Yoysef Kats, and Yankl Trupianski, were either members of the Bund or very sympathetic to it.

The Medem Sanatorium also had a medical staff made up of both doctors and nurses. For the entire period from 1926 to 1939, the chair of the Sanatorium's Doctors' Council was Ana Broyde-Heler, a long-term member of the Bundist movement who was widely known for her work in the fields of public health and children's medicine.[24]

One of the ways in which Bundist influence over the sanatorium manifested itself was via the active functioning at the institution of SKIF groups, in which, according to a leading Bundist educator of that era, "the children were taught and raised in a Bundist-party spirit."[25] Participation in SKIF was by no means obligatory. However, the children were encouraged to see membership in SKIF as a privilege that they should strive to earn. The SKIF groups were not led by the teaching staff, but rather by representatives of the SKIF (apparently selected by the group's central body).

To be sure, there were some children in the sanatorium who had had exposure to organized children's movements other than SKIF. Not only SKIF members but also individual members of the Yungbor (the children's group of the Left Poalei Zion) played significant roles at the sanatorium.[26] But there were no Yungbor groups at the sanatorium, and the range of "politically correct" perspectives was not a broad one. All children staying at the sanatorium were given what was determined to be a socialist education regardless of their background or prior affiliations.[27] May Day was celebrated as an important holiday. Bundist figures, moreover, were apparently extolled over others. In 1928, when Central Committee member Beynish Michalewicz passed away, a ceremony in his honor was held at the sanatorium.[28] I do not know of Jewish political figures from other political parties who were accorded similar treatment.

■   ■   ■

On one occasion, the sanatorium's close identification with the Bund led to an ugly and deeply worrisome incident. Previously, relations between the members of the Communist Party of Poland and the Bund had been extremely hostile. Communists had made repeated attempts to break up meetings in which Bundists participated and had physically attacked individuals who did not accept the Communist party line. In June 1927, for example, Communists had stormed a meeting in Warsaw of Jewish divisions of the union of transport workers and had shot at members of the presidium.[29] During the school year 1929–30, Communists engaged in a sustained campaign to disrupt an evening school for young workers that operated in Warsaw under the auspices of the Tsukunft. Communists threw stones through classroom windows while classes were in session; they also threw stones at both teachers and students leaving the school.[30] The ongoing war by Communists on Bundists and their institutions ultimately expanded to the sanatorium.

In addition to teachers and medical personnel, the sanatorium employed a number of people who were responsible for cleaning, cooking, and comparable duties. Some of the individuals employed in those capacities were members of a Communist-dominated trade union. A dispute involving certain of these staff members, dating from 1929, in the course of which several workers were fired, eventually led personnel affiliated with the Communist-dominated union to go on strike.[31] The sanatorium continued to function during the strike by having teachers, doctors, and volunteers take the roles formerly played by the striking workers. The dispute festered, and in February 1931, some one hundred to two hundred armed men attacked the sanatorium, cut its telephone wires, damaged its electrical generator, destroyed a great deal of property, beat members of the staff, and fired off a number of shots. Some of these shots hit buildings in which children were taking shelter.[32] When the Bundist movement in Warsaw was informed of what had taken place (apparently by a staff member who succeeded in fleeing the premises and making a phone call from a nearby town), it rapidly sent a group of trade unionists and parents to Miedzeszyn to help defend the institution and its inhabitants. For several weeks, a group of these defenders patrolled the sanatorium's property, performed the duties of those on strike, and escorted staff members who needed to leave the premises. Though Communists organized demonstrations against the sanatorium, there were no further attempts made to physically attack it.[33]

■ ■ ■

The sanatorium accepted children between the ages of six and sixteen.[34] Children initially remained, on average, for ten weeks. In specific cases, however, children were allowed to remain for significantly longer periods or were permitted to return for repeat visits. Some children stayed at the sanatorium many times over a period of years. Among the repeat visitors were children known to have had personal or family connections to the Bundist movement. However, it is not known precisely how decisions as to which children to accept were made, or whether preference was generally given to those whose parents were members of the party.

The bulk of the children who were brought to the sanatorium were not necessarily seriously ill but were considered to be at risk of contracting tuberculosis. Though children who manifested symptoms of disease—for instance, children who developed a temperature after arrival—were permitted to remain at the sanatorium under close medical supervision, many were not sick but undernourished, in a physically weakened state, or recovering from an illness.

Most of the children served by the institution—which, though located in a pine forest, was only twenty kilometers or so from Warsaw—came from the Polish capital. Indeed, over 90 percent of the 2,278 children who had stayed at the sanatorium prior to September 5, 1930, lived in Warsaw.[35] The number of those from other parts of Poland, including from relatively distant areas such as Vilna, grew steadily over time. By 1938, the institution had served 1,126 children who lived outside of the capital city.[36]

In order to give both the medical staff and the pedagogical staff a clearer idea of the children's home conditions, a bilingual (Polish/Yiddish) questionnaire was created beginning with the period 1932–33. The notion of conducting research of this kind was developed in consultation with Fishl Shneyerson, a child psychologist. Each questionnaire included not only items concerning such matters as the education, health, characteristics, and medical history of the child, but also items concerning the education, profession, and affiliations of the child's parents, and the economic and social conditions in which they lived.[37] House visits were made to children who had been accepted by the sanatorium prior to their arrival at the institution, when possible, and the questionnaires were typically completed by the sanatorium staff member who made these visits. Though blank questionnaires are extant, examples of completed documents have not survived.[38] Nevertheless, some data apparently derived from the questionnaires is still recoverable.

Approximately 80 percent of the parents of children at the Medem Sanatorium were blue-collar workers or employees of some kind, including those who worked in their own homes.[39] Others were professionals, including teachers, journalists, doctors, and artists. At least in later years, the institution housed some children who came from wealthy backgrounds, including a few from the families of merchants or traders. Children from such homes, however, were exceptional cases.

A clear majority of the children grew up in extremely poor homes and in overcrowded conditions. A survey dealing with the period from 1926 to 1936 noted that 1,341 of the children were from families in which six people lived in one room, and 1,180 were from homes in which seven people lived in a room. There were 671 children who lived in families in which eight people lived in a room, and 868 cases in which the number of inhabitants per room was greater than eight. More than 78 percent of the children did not have a bed of their own in their homes.[40] More than 45 percent of the children from Warsaw lived in housing that lacked electrical lighting, running water, and internal plumbing facilities.[41]

While the sanatorium was meant first and foremost for Jewish children, it admitted others. At one point, according to a source published in 1932, twenty-two of the children—13 percent of all of those at the sanatorium at that moment—were from Christian working-class families.[42] During the first years of its existence, the sanatorium was the only institution in Poland serving children with incipient tuberculosis. Progressive Polish doctors such as Professor Michalewicz, who was director of the Children's Clinic at the University of Warsaw, rector of the university, and close to the PPS, took to recommending that Polish families whose children would benefit from a stay at the sanatorium apply for admission. When, as was regularly the case, the families resisted this advice, Michalewicz overcame their doubts by pointing out that the only suitable alternatives were located in Switzerland.[43]

The first non-Jewish Polish children to come to the sanatorium were from families affiliated with the PPS. In addition to wanting to help children in need, regardless of their background, the Bundists in charge of the institution had an additional reason for wanting to find space for the children of Polish socialists: Both the sanatorium and the Bund itself were in need of the political support provided by Warsaw City Council members elected on the PPS ticket and were thus eager to keep in their good graces. Though the problem of incorporating non-Jewish, Polish-speaking children into a Yiddish-speaking milieu was quite a thorny one, the sanatorium took measures to alleviate would could have become an alienating experience for the Poles, and generally succeeded in making the children's stays psychologically positive and medically beneficial. In any event, the number of Polish children served was quite small. Only 121 of the approximately seven thousand children who had stayed in the sanatorium in its first eleven years were non-Jews.[44]

In Poland during the mid- and late 1930s, moreover, when new institutions with similar medical goals were created for Polish-speaking children, and as the level of anti-Semitism intensified, the number of Poles who came to stay each year apparently diminished. Specific members of the Polish radical intelligentsia—for example, Wanda Wasilewska and Władysław Broniewski—sent their own children to the Medem Sanatorium because they agreed with its progressive pedagogical approach.[45] On one specific occasion, the sanatorium took in the children of Polish coal miners in order to express political solidarity with the Polish workers' movement.[46] However, the phenomenon of Polish children attending the Medem Sanatorium seems to have been less prevalent at the end of the sanatorium's history than in its earlier years.

An analysis of the educational backgrounds of the sanatorium attendees between 1926 and 1937 revealed that 38 percent of the children had attended secular, Yiddish-language (TSYSHO) schools; 41 percent had attended schools run by the Polish government in which Polish was the language of instruction; 7 percent had attended religious schools of one kind or another (*khedorim,* Tarbut schools, *gmina* schools, etc.); 12 percent were of preschool age; and 2 percent of the school-age children had not attended any school at all. If one excludes from the total those too young to have attended school, 43 percent of the children—a plurality—had been enrolled in secular, Yiddish-language educational institutions before coming to the sanatorium.[47] Thus, the population that attended the sanatorium was by no means representative of Polish Jewish children of the interwar era.

■ ■ ■

The educational program of the sanatorium was not set in stone. On the contrary, openness to experimentation appears to have been one of its hallmarks. Gilinski was reportedly especially attracted to the ideas of the German pedagogue Berthold Otto and, under the influence of Otto's work, generally emphasized the importance of encouraging conversations.[48] Gilinski was also a great advocate of creativity, and was open to suggestions derived from works by other progressive educators or suggested by the teachers themselves. In many ways, the sanatorium's educational philosophy came to have similarities to the Dalton System, first developed in the United States at the beginning of the twentieth century, which stresses the simultaneous importance of freedom, of independence, and of cooperation.

Over time a number of broad principles appear to have been widely accepted by the sanatorium's staff. One was the significance of learning through playing. A second was the significance of encounters with natural phenomena. A third was that the children should govern themselves insofar as practical. The sanatorium prided itself on advocating the equality of children and adults not only in word but also in deed, and on developing children's inner skills.

The sanatorium came to serve as a laboratory school for the TSYSHO, and techniques successfully used there were sometimes adapted for use in

Yiddish-speaking secular schools in Warsaw and elsewhere. Both the goals of the Medem Sanatorium and the methods that it used differed markedly from those used in most schools of that era, including most Jewish schools in interwar Poland. Whereas many traditional Jewish schools, for example, made use of threats and corporal punishment, the sanatorium pointedly avoided directly punishing children for misdeeds. Discipline was maintained by fostering a positive relationship between the staff and the children, and among the children themselves.

The curriculum of the sanatorium did not, generally, revolve around extended or formal courses. To be sure, the staff gave lessons in Yiddish language and literature, in the natural sciences, in dance, and on other topics. Yoysef Kats, for one, was known to enjoy discussing works by Peretz, Mendele, Sholem Aleichem, Sholem Asch, and other Yiddish writers with the children.[49] However, both the fragile health of those who stayed at the sanatorium and the relatively short duration of a typical stay militated against participation in traditional courses by those in residence.[50] An exception was made, to some extent, for those children who had missed a great deal of school because of their health. Children in that category were tutored in order to make it possible for them to keep up with their classmates and to pass relevant exams.[51] At least one individual who stayed at the sanatorium a number of times over a period of years reported that he had completed school assignments while in residence at the institution, sent them to the teachers in the school he had been attending, and was allowed to graduate with his class—a graduation to which he traveled directly from the sanatorium.[52]

But these situations were far from the norm. The educational goals of the institution—such as encouraging respect for other people—were generally accomplished not so much by formal instruction as by example and by hands-on activity.[53] Emphasis was placed on the performance of plays, singing, drawing, dance, and the production of arts and crafts projects, and on physical activity (especially gymnastics and walks on the grounds of the sanatorium). At least one of the plays written by those associated with the sanatorium and first performed by its resident children—*Lialkes*—became quite well known in broader circles and was performed by others in Warsaw, in Bialystok, and in Brussels. Motl Gilinski and Yankl Trupianski, who created *Lialkes,* once asserted that the decision made by the sanatorium's educators to

8. Costume ball and carnival in the Medem Sanatorium. From *Vi azoy lebt dos kind in medem sanatorium,* Warsaw, 1932.

put particular stress on concerts, performances, and comparable phenomena was linked directly to the fact that many children stayed at the institution for a brief period. In order to have an educational impact on these children, Gilinski and Trupianski note, it was deemed necessary to use "more intensive pedagogical means," and this was why "moments which affect primarily the sphere of feelings" were accented.[54]

According to Khayim Shloyme Kazdan, a leading figure in the TSYSHO during the interwar period, there was "no trace" of religious education in the sanatorium. It did not observe Jewish dietary laws, did not organize prayer services, and did not observe Jewish religious holidays in a traditional manner.[55] If a child from an observant home desired to pray, or if a boy desired to keep his head covered, that child was allowed to do so.[56] However, children from observant backgrounds who stayed at the sanatorium seem to have been more likely to adapt themselves to the mores of the institution than to have shaped it in accord with their own preexisting beliefs and practices.

But the sanatorium did not simply ignore all Jewish holidays and traditions. It marked Passover, in its own way, and observed the custom of leaving a cup of wine on the table for Elijah the Prophet on the night of the first *seder*.[57] On at least one notable occasion, a special meal was served on the eve of Yom Kippur, Shloyme Gilinski described to the children the ways in which it was observed in various households, and a story about the holiday by a prominent writer was read aloud. Some of the older children, who rejected religiosity and who were unhappy with Gilinski's decision to note the holiday, questioned him about his decision during the course of the next day. Gilinski reportedly replied to objections by indicating that in order to say "no" to religion, one must first understand the "yes."[58]

The institution's leadership sustained influence over one-time residents by sponsoring reunions and by organizing groups in Warsaw for sanatorium alumni. Special attempts were made to attract to these activities those former residents of the sanatorium who attended public schools rather than TSYSHO-affiliated institutions.[59] Beginning with the autumn of 1937, the Medem Sanatorium also ran a satellite operation in Warsaw known as the Sanatorium Home. It was meant primarily for those children who had been in the sanatorium, had returned to their families, but who needed additional help because of their poor health and because of the poor conditions of their home environments. These children were encouraged to come to the Sanatorium Home after the conclusion of their school day, where they received food, medical and dental attention, advice on matters related to hygiene and education, aid with their homework, and other kinds of support.[60] Khane Zakheym, who had been a teacher at the sanatorium from 1932 to 1936, served on the staff of the Sanatorium Home, thereby providing the children with much-needed continuity.[61] There were more than one hundred children aged eight to fourteen who participated in its activities in 1938. Because of its success, it did not have room for all those who wished to participate. Indeed, on the eve of the Second World War, the sanatorium's administration decided to attempt to accommodate the needs of additional children by creating four more such "homes"—another in Warsaw, and the remaining three in Lodz, Bialystok, and Lublin.

■   ■   ■

The Medem Sanatorium attracted visitors from near and far and elicited positive commentary published in fifteen languages. Prominent Yiddish writers—Sholem Asch, Moyshe Nadir, H. D. Nomberg, Daniel Charney—were among those who came to experience the institution.[62] Somewhat less expectedly, the sanatorium was also visited, and extolled, by Jewish and non-Jewish educators and others with no obvious ties to the Bund, to the socialist movement, or to Yiddish culture. Adolphe Ferrière, for one, a Swiss writer affiliated with the International Bureau of Education and the Jean-Jacques Rousseau Institute, visited in 1930 and was strongly impressed. Works on the sanatorium are said to have appeared in twenty different countries.[63]

■   ■   ■

The cost of maintaining the Medem Sanatorium was a constant source of worry for its board of directors.[64] Subsidies were obtained from governmental and municipal bodies when possible. The fact that the city government of Warsaw provided material support in the early years of its existence was directly tied, during that period, to the participation of influential Bundists in the Warsaw City Council. Henryk Erlich, Victor Alter, Shloyme Gilinski, and other vigorous advocates of the sanatorium's work were elected members of the city council for much of the relevant period, and engaged in lobbying on the institution's behalf—sometimes successfully, and sometimes unsuccessfully.[65] The Bundist city council members, who were always a minority block in that body, were dependent on the votes of others to push through their proposals. They generally received the support of councillors from the PPS on matters related to the sanatorium, and sometimes received additional support from the more liberal representatives of the Sanacja regime.[66] Using similar coalitions and tactics, Bundist political leaders also succeeded, in the early years of the sanatorium's existence, in obtaining money from the public Sickness Insurance Fund. In 1929, the Warsaw city government covered the costs of seventy children at the sanatorium, and the Sickness Insurance Fund covered the costs of an additional fifteen. At that time, "private" patients—that is, children whose stay was covered neither by the municipality nor by the Sickness Insurance Fund—occupied only fifteen beds at the institution.[67] At some points, the Warsaw city government was covering the cost of up to 120 children a month.[68] Children whose tuition was covered by public sources were permitted to remain at the sanatorium as long as their health status required.[69] The municipality and the Sickness Insurance Fund were the most important sources of funding for the sanatorium in the early 1930s. From time to time, during those same years, Bundists also succeeded in obtaining supplementary funds from municipal sources for renovation of the sanatorium, or were permitted to employ city workers on the sanatorium's grounds for specific projects.

In addition to the subsidies obtained from municipal and state bodies, the sanatorium relied on a support group, the Medem Sanatorium Society, which had formal members and which solicited donations from these members and others. The society had six hundred members in 1937.[70]

Tuition was charged to the families of some of the private patients, at differential rates for children in different categories. In 1930, for example, one rate applied to children in TSYSHO schools and another applied to children enrolled in schools of other kinds.[71] Families with greater means were asked to pay a higher tuition.[72] Some private cases received full tuition scholarships. The total amount taken in from tuition payments, in any event, clearly did not cover the institution's expenses.

Beginning in 1934, the city government of Warsaw sharply diminished its support and, some years thereafter, completely eliminated it.[73] The Sickness Insurance Fund ceased sending children to the sanatorium as of July 1, 1935.[74] The Ministry for Social Defense (the health department) also cut its sizeable subsidy.[75] Those close to the sanatorium attributed these changes to a sharp rise in anti-Semitism.[76]

The declining economic situation of Polish Jewry also hurt the institution, despite the fact that it operated more efficiently in its later years. In 1933 the cost of maintaining a child for one month was 180 złoty. In 1938 the cost was only 120 złoty. However, in the period January-February 1938, there were only two children who were paying full tuition.[77]

The Medem Sanatorium attempted to overcome the loss or diminution of municipal and governmental support by increasing the breadth of its fund-raising, seeking out sympathetic sources both in Poland and abroad. In 1935, the New York-based Forward Association—which owned the Yiddish-language *Forverts*—and the International Ladies Garment Workers Union each provided funds for eight children at a time. Both organizations continued to provide support in later years.[78] The Workmen's Circle, a fraternal organization founded in the United States and made up primarily of Jews of East European origin, supported five children in 1938–39.[79] Other American trade unions with large numbers of Jewish members, the Jewish Labor Committee (headquartered in New York), the American Jewish Joint Distribution Committee, the Federation of Polish Jews in America, Polish Jewish trade unions affiliated with the Bund, other Bundist institutions, and wealthy individuals were among those making significant financial donations at one point or another.[80] Additional money was raised from sources in Western Europe, Mexico, South Africa, and Australia.[81]

The leaders of the sanatorium hoped to use *Mir kumen on,* a high-quality film about the institution directed by Aleksander Ford and completed in 1936, as a fund-raising tool, and invested a considerable amount of energy in its production.[82] The film, however, was officially banned in Poland because of its political tenor. Thus, while it could be (and was) used to raise money in Europe and in America in the latter part of the 1930s, it was not of much help in raising funds within Poland itself.[83] By the fall of 1938, Gilinski reported, every month was bringing new deficits, and the institution did not have the means to pay its debts.[84]

However difficult the economic straits of the sanatorium were in 1938–39, it did not shirk from taking on additional costs. Shortly after Gilinski had underscored the sanatorium's financial difficulties, the institution added to its financial burden by reaching out to Polish Jewish refugee children who had been recently forced to leave Germany. A report released in July 1939 suggests that eighty-five such refugees were being cared for either in the sanatorium or in the Sanatorium Home in Warsaw.[85] The sanatorium's leaders recognized that large numbers of refugee children did not meet the medical criteria for admission to the sanatorium but needed a place to live and had no viable alternatives open to them. They therefore leased two houses and used them as homes for an additional 150 Jewish children who had been obliged to leave Germany.[86] Weeks before the beginning of the Second World War, the need for the sanatorium was quite probably greater than it had ever been. Its reputation was superb; it was expanding its capacity as fast at it could, but it was also under enormous financial strain, which threatened its ability to function.

■ ■ ■

In a study of Jewish education in interwar Poland published in 1998, Shimon Frost describes what he calls the decline of TSYSHO schools in Poland, and asserts that this alleged tendency "began earlier and proceeded faster than in other sectors of the Jewish school system."[87] Ezra Mendelsohn, striking a similar tone, asserts that "the extremely high pedagogical level of the [TSYSHO] school system, which was generally acknowledged, could not conceal its failure to attract the young generation. This failure, partly financial and partly ideological, certainly calls into question the viability of what may be called the Yiddishist program for Polish Jewry."[88]

Though TSYSHO did not and could not extend its reach beyond a certain point, and though it is a matter of fact that only a small fraction of the Jewish children in Poland ever attended TSYSHO schools, the TSYSHO-affiliated Medem Sanatorium did not undergo a decline of any kind in the interwar years and was by no means a failure. On the eve of the Second World War, with its popularity still increasing, it actively planned to expand its capacity.

One indication of the sanatorium's success is that although it was regularly enlarged, it could not fully meet the demand for its services. The institution began with only 14 children and had the capacity to care for no more than 70 children at one time when it was first opened.[89] In 1932, it was able to accept 115 children in the winter and 160 in the summer.[90] By the mid-1930s, it accepted 130 children during the winter months and up to 200 during the summer.[91] The sanatorium made room for 225 children in the winter of 1939 and was preparing itself to accept 300 in the summer.[92] It also maintained a waiting list.⁹³ By 1938, a total of 76,000 children who were in need of a space at the sanatorium had been "qualified" by doctors and thus had their names registered—but only 7,500 had actually stayed there.⁹⁴ Demand was so great that it sometimes took up to two years before a space became available.⁹⁵ Many children deemed to be in medical need of a stay at the sanatorium were never accommodated at all. In specific tragic cases, space for a particular applicant only became available after the child had died.

Though there were periods during which the material resources of the institution made growth impossible, and periods during which the sanatorium was forced to cut back despite a pressing need for its services, the total number of children that passed through its doors grew considerably from the time of its establishment to the late 1930s. The institution served 302 children in 1926, 545 in 1927, and 602 in 1928. It continued to attract more children each year in the period ending with 1933, when it served 772 children. The number of children who attended the institution in a given year dropped below that height in 1934–36.⁹⁶ The decrease in the total number of children served each year in the mid-1930s, however, was in no way whatsoever a reflection of a decrease in the institution's popularity within the Jewish population but was, rather, directly connected to the sharp diminution in financial support.⁹⁷ The total number of children served by the institution per year rose significantly once again in 1937 (though Polish governmental and municipal sources never did bring their support back to the pre-1934 levels).⁹⁸ This increase seems to reflect both the fact that the sanatorium located alternative sources of support, to some extent, and that it found it necessary to serve more children even if it did not know how it would cover the costs of so doing.

In 1938, responding to deteriorating economic conditions, which had had a deleterious impact on the health of poor Jewish children, the sanatorium's administration began a campaign to build a new pavilion that would enable it to increase yet again the number of children served at any given time. The plan called for increasing capacity to a point at which 230 children could have been served at once in the winter months, and 350 children could have been served during the summer.⁹⁹ An anonymous gift in the amount of twenty thousand złoty was received, apparently from Doctor Simkhovitsh, a prominent physician, and the sanatorium purchased additional land, adjacent to its existing grounds, to position the new pavilion.¹⁰⁰

Noyakh Portnoy, the chairman of the sanatorium's board, is said to have hoped to eventually increase capacity by a large multiple.[101] Expansion was limited, however, by lack of the material resources that would have made additional growth possible. Despite these limitations, at least seventy-seven hundred children passed through the sanatorium in the period 1926–39.[102] This total suggests that the institution was successful.

■ ■ ■

Another indication of the institution's success is the respectful attention and praise it received from sectors of the Jewish population that were ideologically opposed to the Bund. *Moment,* a well-known and widely circulated Warsaw-based Yiddish-language daily not inclined to be sympathetic to Bundist institutions, wrote about the sanatorium in December 1937: "It is a great consolation, joy, and delight in today's sad times to see the joyful, Jewish, positive work that is being done in this magnificent institution. . . . May the people who are doing this holy work be blessed."[103] To be sure, the program of the sanatorium was not beyond reproach from certain perspectives. In 1937, representatives of the press participated in an organized tour of the facility and noted that, while it was certainly a model institution, it ought to have taught the children some Hebrew and something about the Land of Israel. Even the representative of the Zionist *Haynt* on this tour, however, was led to note that the sanatorium was more luxurious, magnificent, clean, and orderly than institutions run by allegedly bourgeois groups. One cannot complain if the Bund runs the sanatorium in accord with its principles, the *Haynt* reporter concluded, but rather, if one wants to complain, one can direct criticism to Jewish bourgeois circles and ask them why they do not take pains to create a comparable entity for Jewish children from "national" or traditional Jewish families.[104]

In 1938, the orthodox Horev schools for boys and Beys Yankef schools for girls decided to create a sanatorium for Jewish children that would function in accord with Jewish religious law. The schools sent a delegation of three to observe the functioning of the Medem Sanatorium. The ideological chasm between Agudes Yisroel, which played a role in the Horev and Beys Yankef school systems parallel to that played by the Bund in the Medem Sanatorium, was vast, and much of what went on in the sanatorium was likely to have been seen as abhorrent by rigorously observant Jewish educators. Nevertheless, the orthodox educators clearly hoped to learn from the secularists how to create a successful sanatorium and obviously believed that the Medem Sanatorium was worth a visit that spanned several days.[105]

Some adult Jews not committed to the secularist, Yiddishist, anti-Zionist, and socialist platform of the Bund may even have become more sympathetic to Bundist approaches as a result of the highly positive experiences that their children had had with the Medem Sanatorium. Though not going so far as to claim that the Medem Sanatorium influenced political opinions, Kazdan reports that the institution had "a great influence in an educational sense" on the parents of those who stayed there.[106] He refers explicitly to new ideas that the children brought home with them as to "hygiene, culture, aesthetics, language, [and] behavior with people" and adds that often energetic children sparked "a whole revolution in the house. The parents grew culturally together with the children." Children of the intelligentsia, from assimilated circles, or from wealthier backgrounds who returned to their families very enthusiastic about their experiences sometimes introduced into their households a new and more positive relationship to the Yiddish language, to its culture, and to the Yiddish secular school system.

No evidence exists that Ezra Mendelsohn's contentions—that the TSYSHO was unable to attract the younger generation or that the school system suffered from a failure of its ideology—could be fairly applied to the TSYSHO-linked Medem Sanatorium. In fact, it is possible that its accomplishments reflected so well on the institution's Bundist sponsors that these successes ultimately contributed, albeit only indirectly and only to a small degree, to the political victories of Bundist candidates.[107]

5

The Bundist Women's Organization

JEWISH WOMEN PLAYED leading roles in the Bund's formative years and participated in that party in relatively large numbers during the years of the Russian Empire. However, the Bund had somewhat less success in mobilizing women in independent Poland between the two world wars than it had had during the czarist era. Unlike the movements previously discussed, Yidisher arbeter froy (YAF), the Bundist women's organization, did not attract a large membership during the interwar years. The failure of YAF to draw in a mass membership reveals that Bundist counterculture had its limits, and also suggests that the Bund was unable to extend its reach beyond a certain point.

■ ■ ■

In the czarist era, the Bund had no trouble attracting Jewish women into its ranks. The Bund had its roots in organizing work conducted in the Pale of Settlement in the late 1880s and early 1890s. The establishments in the Pale that produced items such as cigarettes, matches, stockings, gloves, and envelopes, as well as the tailoring industry tended to employ high proportions of Jewish women at the end of the nineteenth century.[1] Moreover, the first efforts at organizing Russian Jewish workers took place precisely in those fields in which many of the employees were female. In Vilna during 1887, for example, stocking makers—the most common job held by Jewish women in that region—conducted a strike.[2]

Not only among the stocking makers but also in other trades employing Jewish women, female "half-intellectuals"—those who had received some education but who did not have advanced degrees—proved to be particularly ripe for organizing.[3] Khaim-Yankev Helfand, who was active in the Bund in its early years, has argued that precisely because Jewish men were more likely than Jewish women to have received extended formal training in Jewish rituals and tradition, the women found it easier than did their male counterparts to break with tradition and to join the socialist movement.[4]

A small number of the earliest Jewish socialist women in the Russian Empire were not workers but rather women who had succeeded—against the odds—in obtaining higher education and who had become attracted to radical ideas. Matle ("Pati") Srednitsky (1867–1943), who graduated from gymnasium in Vilna, and who trained as a dentist in Petersburg, and Liuba Levinson (1866–1903), who studied at the University of Geneva, were actively involved in the illegal social democratic circle that crystallized in Vilna in 1889, and that eventually became one of the sparks leading to the formal establishment of the Bund.

The Bund was built on and grew out of both the union organizing work conducted among Jewish females and males, and the early efforts of intellectuals, including Srednitsky and Levinson. At least two women—Marya Zhaludsky, a seamstress and long-term political activist, and Rosa Greenblat, a weaver—were among the thirteen individuals who attended the meeting at which the Bund was founded.[5]

When, in 1898, all three members of the Bund's first Central Committee were arrested, Zhaludsky and Tsivia Hurvitch[6] (b. 1874), a glove maker, were among those who replaced them. The second congress of the Bund, which was held in 1898, was attended not only by Zhaludsky and Hurvitch but also by two seamstresses, Shaine Raizel Segal of Lodz (d. 1905) and Liza Epstein of Kovne, which is to say that women made up at least one-third of the delegates to this congress.[7]

There was no such thing as a separate Bundist women's organization per se during the czarist era. Thus, the roles of women in the relatively early years of the movement's existence—which included acting as speakers at Bundist gatherings, distributing literature, storing illegal literature, and working in the movement's underground printing shops—can be explored only by referring to specific examples.[8] A female was considered less likely to raise the suspicions of authorities than a male. As a result, any number of female Bundists, including Yulia Abramowicz (d. 1916),[9] Gita Lipshits (d. 1917),[10] Sophia Dubnow (1885–1986),[11] and Cipe Edelman,[12] were able to smuggle literature or arms for the party. Anna Heller Rozental (1872–1941) was co-opted onto the first Vilna City Committee of the Bund. Zhenia Hurvitch (Evgeniia Adolovna Gurvich) (1861–1940) was a major figure at the Fifth Congress of the Bund, which was held in Zurich in June 1903.[13] Ruta (Mina) Batkhan (d. 1942),[14] an effective speaker in both Russian and Yiddish, was a well-known Bund representative among Jewish socialists in Dvinsk, Bialystok, and Lodz.[15] Esther (Eza) Lipshits, who had studied in both Berne and Berlin, and who was widely acknowledged to have been exceptionally erudite, became a member of the Lodz Committee of the Bund. She was arrested in 1903, tortured in Piotrków prison, and died later that year as a result of her treatment while incarcerated.[16]

During the 1905 revolution, Bundist women came to the fore at several different points. Anna (Gaponsha) Lipshits (ca. 1881–1926), for one, served as a member of the Odessa Committee of the Bund, and was among the most popular speakers during the Potemkin uprising.[17] Bundist women were killed in the course of street demonstrations that took place during this tumultuous period. Fruma (Vera) Grabolski (ca. 1881), a member of the Bund's Warsaw Committee at the time of the Revolution of 1905, died as a result of wounds she received during a mass protest organized by the Bund that was attended by thirty thousand people. Sonie Glikman Peysakhzon was trampled to death in Pinsk by the horses of Czarist Cossacks who were breaking up a demonstration in which she was a participant. Esther (Hinda, a.k.a. Tamara) Riskind (ca. 1877/80–1905), a leader of the Bund in Bialystok at the end of the nineteenth century, Gitl Zakhaym, a twenty-one-year-old Bundist, and Ester Vaysvol were also killed in the course of 1905.

Bundist self-defense groups came into being during that era and included women. Nadia (Frume) Kenigshats Grinfeld (1887–1918), for example, who had already established a reputation as a Bundist speaker in the prerevolutionary period, was the head of such a group in Odessa.[18]

The defeat of the Revolution of 1905 resulted in a dramatic contraction in the size of the Bund (and of all other socialist organizations operating in the Russian Empire). There were four major responses to this new situation. A relatively small number of individuals (including a few women) remained actively involved with Bundist affairs. Malke Lifshits (Esther Frumkin) (1880–1943) was among them. She wrote regularly for Bundist periodicals and was a delegate to both the Bund's Eighth Conference in 1910 and the Ninth Conference of 1912.[19] Esther, as she was known in the movement, was among the most prominent Bundists, male or female, during these years. Sophia Dubnow, who was five years younger than Frumkin and not as prominent a figure in those years, wrote on literary themes for the Russian-language Bundist press and, delegated by the party to conduct work in conjunction with other revolutionary movements, agitated among Russian soldiers in Grodno in or around 1906.[20] She continued both her political activities and her affiliation with the Bund throughout the subsequent period. Roza Eichner (d. 1943)[21] led circles of workers in Lodz, the downhill slide of the movement in the post-1905 era notwithstanding.[22] Many Bundists emigrated from the Russian Empire during this period, often to the United States. Others, representing a third response to the defeat of the revolution and the oppression that accompanied it, became politically inactive. Zhaludsky, for one, withdrew from involvement with the Bund in 1908. A fourth category was made up of those who were forced to halt activities because they were imprisoned. Rosa (Fride) Levit, active in the Bund in Lodz in 1907, was eventually arrested and incarcerated. She returned to active engagement in Bundist affairs—which included serving as one of the seventeen voting delegates at the Ninth Conference of the Bund—after her release.[23] Gina (Genie) Birentsvayg Medem (1888–1965), who was also active in and around Lodz until she was arrested in November 1907, left Poland for Switzerland after serving a prison sentence.[24] She married the Bundist theoretician Vladimir Medem, who discouraged his wife from returning to Poland in order to continue her political activities. In 1913, however, Gina insisted on returning to the empire and did, in fact, do so.[25]

According to one memoir, love was initially thought of in Bundist circles as a weakness that interfered with the revolutionary movement, and Bundists who married were looked on as former revolutionaries.[26] However, this attitude appears to have shifted somewhat in later years. Indeed, any number of female Bundists married, either formally or informally, and chose politically compatible male counterparts as their mates. Pati Srednitsky was already romantically involved with Arkady Kremer—often called the "Father of the Bund"—in the 1890s. Anna Heller married Pavel Rozental—a leading Bundist—around 1899. Marya Zhaludsky, similarly, married Dovid Katz (a member of the Central Committee of the Bund from 1898 to 1901 and one of the most important Bund activists until 1908). Liza Grinblat Amsterdam apparently became particularly active in the Bund in the wake of the death of her husband, the Bundist Avrom Meyer Amsterdam.[27] In 1911, at which time civil marriages were not recognized under the laws of the Russian Empire, Henryk Erlich and Sophia Dubnow were married by a rabbi in a synagogue in Petersburg, the fact that neither was religiously observant notwithstanding. Their wedding ceremony was apparently minimalistic.[28] The Bundists tended to insist on marrying without the aid of matchmakers or the use of dowries, on marrying for love, and on modest weddings, with small numbers of guests, and without *klezmorim* (musicians) or *batkhonim* (wedding entertainers).[29]

In specific cases, activity in the Bund was accompanied by revolutionary asceticism—which, I suspect, had more to do with indigenous Russian revolutionary traditions than with the Bundists' commitment to Marxism. Liuba Levinson, who was sent into exile with her husband, Isai Aizenshtat, gave birth during the course of her sentence. At the conclusion of her term, she decided to separate herself from her child in order to be able to devote herself to the movement. Levinson brought her baby to New York, intending to leave the child with her sister, but died before she could return to Europe.[30]

The Bund was reinvigorated during the revolutionary upsurge that took place during the course of the First World War. Esther Frumkin rose through the ranks during this era and in April 1917 was elected to the Central Committee at the Bund's Tenth Conference. She attempted to steer a centrist course following the Bolshevik Revolution but ultimately sided with the left-wing majority when, in 1920, the Bund split into two distinct organizations, one Communist (the Kombund) and the other Social Democratic. Not long thereafter, the Kombund was absorbed into the Communist Party and the Social Democratic Bund declared illegal—thereby bringing the history of the Bund in Russia to a close.[31]

The conditions under which the Bund operated in the Russian Empire made it inadvisable to maintain lists of members. There are no definitive statistics on the total number of women involved or on the percentage of female Bundists in the empire. According to one scholarly estimate (which appears to refer to the Bund in its Russian period), however, approximately one-third of all members of the Jewish workers' movement were female.[32] If this estimate is correct, it would suggest that the proportion of women in the Bund during the czarist years was higher than the proportion of women in those contemporaneous radical movements in the Russian Empire that were not explicitly Jewish, such as the Russian Social Democratic Workers' Party.[33] This is all the more remarkable because the Russian radical movement had a higher rate of participation by women than did other movements, in Russia or elsewhere.

Bundist women in the Russian Empire were not interested in forming groups made up exclusively of women, or which worked primarily on causes of particular interest to women, and seem to have believed that struggle for the general goals of the movement was of greater importance than struggle for their specific needs. Precisely because they were Marxists, Bundists of the czarist era would have been likely to argue that the oppression of Jewish working-class women was a result of the existing relation of production, and that the only way to overcome this oppression was by bringing into being a socialist society. Sheyne-Feygl Szapiro Michalewicz (Dina Blond),[34] who led the YAF in the interwar years, reports that in the early years of the Bund, "Jewish women were fighters for others. There was no difference between them and the men."[35]

The first individual known to have proposed that Bundist women make demands on behalf of their own needs, Khaim-Yankev Helfand, was male and did not make this suggestion until 1915.[36] One document indicates that there was a "women's division" of the Bund created in 1917—but no information on its work has thus far come to light.[37]

■ ■ ■

Helfand's suggestion was ultimately taken up by the Bund in interwar Poland, where the party generally operated under conditions quite different from those under which it had operated in the Russian Empire. The single most important change in conditions involved the fact that the Bund had been illegal for most of the period during which it conducted work in Czarist Russia, and that it was, though subject to harassment by the government, a legal political party in independent Poland. As a result, it no longer had as much need for individuals to take on roles that had earlier been played to a significant degree by women. There was, for example, rarely need for the Bund to maintain illegal print shops in interwar Poland, and rarely need for it to smuggle contraband into or out of the country.[38]

There were few women in the Polish Bund's countrywide leadership. The one major exception to this generalization is Pesl Katelianski, a.k.a. Sara Szweber (ca. 1875–1966), a leading trade unionist and a member of the Central Committee. She helped to develop the Bund's political tactics during the interwar period. In 1938 she was the single female among the sixteen Bundists elected to the city council of Warsaw.[39]

Though Szweber was the only woman to hold a significant position on the Bund's countrywide governing body in Poland, a number of women played major roles on a local level. Esther Alter Iwińska (d. 1963)—whose brother, Victor Alter, was one of the Polish Bund's most widely known figures, and who had been active in Bundist affairs since the beginning of the twentieth century—was elected to the Warsaw city council on the Bundist ticket in 1919 and in 1927.[40] Esther Beyla (Bela) Szapiro (ca. 1891–ca. 1941) was head of the Bund in Lublin—a city of considerable importance—and served on its city council.[41] Similarly, Anna Heller Rozental served for a portion of the interwar years as head of the Vilna Bund.[42] Roza Eichner, a member of the Bund's City Committee in Lodz, was elected to Lodz's city council in the elections immediately preceding the beginning of the Second World War, as were seven male Bundists.[43] Lastly, Rifke Antman (b. 1908) was elected to the city council of Bialystok on the Bundist list in 1938.[44] Nevertheless, the total number of women who played prominent political roles in or on behalf of the Bund either on the nationwide or on the regional level during the years between the two world wars was small. One Bundist, writing in the Bundist press in 1939, estimated that approximately 10 percent of those who had participated in party conferences or affiliated trade unions at which he had been present were female.[45] A list of activists who had served as contacts for the Polish Bund in the pre–World War II era, created in 1950, contains 293 names. Fewer than twenty on the list are female.[46] To be sure, the proportion of women in the party as a whole was larger than the proportion of activists or party leaders. But the proportion of female members of the Polish Bund—no more than 26.6 percent in 1930—appears to have been significantly smaller than that of the Russian Bund. Somewhat comparable non-Jewish parties—such as the Social Democratic Party of Germany and the Communist Party of Germany—had even lower proportions of female members during this period.[47] This fact notwithstanding, the percentage of female members in the

Polish Bund was neither large nor close to the proportion of women in the Jewish population.

■　■　■

In the mid-1920s, the same period in which activists in the Polish Bund created the SKIF and the Morgnshtern, the Central Committee of the Bund initiated the establishment of YAF and hoped that it would organize Jewish working-class women and, in particular, the wives of Jewish working men.[48] It was admitted from the outset that the Bund believed such an organization to be necessary because it thought that too few women were actively engaged in the party: "The separate women's organization had to be created," proclaimed the woman who headed YAF shortly after its establishment, "because the female worker still participates too little in the general movement" *("Di bazundere froyen-organizatsie hot . . . gemuzt bashafn vern tsulib dem veyl di arbeterin bateylikt zikh nokh tsu venik in der algemeyner bavegung").*[49]

The decision to form an organization of and for Jewish working women, made in 1925,[50] originally encountered sharp opposition from women already active in the Bund, many of whom saw no need for it.[51] However, the opposition of these female Bundists was overcome.

Sheyne-Feygl Szapiro Michalewicz (1887–1985), known in the Bundist movement as Dina Blond, served as the chair of the new organization.[52] Born in Vilna, Blond became an activist in the Bund immediately after the Russian Revolution of 1905. She was also active in trade union activities in the period preceding the First World War. Blond moved to Warsaw in 1920, where she continued to live until the beginning of the Second World War. She was married to Beynish Michalewicz (Yoysef Izbitski) (1876–1928), one of the most prominent leaders of the Bund and an activist in the TSYSHO. Blond wrote for many periodicals, at various points, including *Di tsayt, Lebnsfragn, Arbeter-luakh, Foroys*, and for the Warsaw-based Bundist daily newspaper. She was exceptionally active as a translator of literary works—from Russian, Polish, English, and German into Yiddish. While serving as the head of YAF, Blond also served as a member of the Warsaw City Committee of the Bund, and as editor of two features in the *Naye folkstsaytung*, one known as the "Women's Corner" *(Froyen-vinkl)* and the other devoted to the international socialist movement.[53] Blond was, in other words, a prominent figure not only in YAF but also in the party itself.

Cipe Edelman served as YAF's secretary from the time of the organization's creation until her death in November 1937.[54] She was, in addition, a member of YAF's central administrative body.[55] Born in 1887 into a wealthy family in Homel, Edelman became involved in a Bundist self-education circle when she was fourteen years old. She participated in a Bundist self-defense group in 1902, was arrested, and fled to Warsaw. She was involved with Bundist activities in Kiev during the Revolution of 1905, returned to Warsaw after its collapse, and remained active in the Bund, in Warsaw and elsewhere, throughout the following years. Edelman is known, for example, to have acted as a liaison among local Bundist groupings during the First World War. Although reportedly among the most dedicated members of YAF, Edelman was by no means as influential a member of the Bundist movement as was Blond.[56]

Roza Eichner, who was born in Minsk in a well-to-do family, and who was already active in the Bund in the era of the Revolution of 1905, lived in Lodz in the interwar era, and was chair of the branch of YAF that operated in Lodz, a Bundist stronghold.[57] She was, simultaneously, involved with the Lodz branch of SKIF, the Yiddish secular schools of that city, and the Bundist organization itself. Eichner was elected, at one point, to the Lodz City Committee of the Bund, and, at another point, to the city council of Lodz.

Ruta Batkhan Berman (1884–1942), like the other leading members of YAF described earlier, was involved with the Bund in the czarist era.[58] She worked in TSYSHO schools from 1923–26 and, in later years, spoke regularly at YAF's public meetings.[59]

Not all YAF members were of the older generation of Bundist activists. Rena Hister Hertz, a child of strictly orthodox parents, who received a traditional education, and who was, at various points in time, a member of the Central Committee of the Tsukunft, an employee of the Association of Jewish Cooperatives, and a student at Warsaw's Free University, was significantly younger than the women mentioned above and was particularly active in YAF in the late 1930s.[60] Gitl Skutelski and Ruta Rutman Perenson (1905–43)[61]—the latter of whom was, in the 1920s, a student in the drama school run under the auspices of the Kultur-lige—are also known to have been involved with YAF.[62]

In a statement issued in 1926—"What does the Society Jewish Worker-Woman (YAF) want?"—the new organization reported that it had three goals:

(1) lifting the intellectual and moral position of its members; (2) interesting its members in the life of the community; and (3) providing its members with a useful way to entertain themselves in their free time.[63] The organization proclaimed that it was creating libraries, reading rooms, and educational societies, and that it was organizing courses, excursions, choruses, and concerts in furtherance of its goals. It underscored that the underlying purpose of these activities was to enable Jewish working-class women to stand on their own and to realize their own significance and role in life.

In 1927, in the midst of an electoral campaign for the Vilna city council, the local branch of YAF issued a flyer encouraging Jewish working women to vote for the Bundist list and demanding that the city council create free day-care centers operating in the Yiddish language, build inexpensive housing for working people, and create jobs for the unemployed.[64]

Both before and after this appeal, YAF devoted considerable energy to the creation of day-care and other facilities for the young children of working mothers, popularly known in some circles as *yasles*.[65] It succeeded in establishing such institutions under its own auspices in several cities. A "nutrition center" for the preschool-age children of poor and unemployed parents was opened in Lublin as early as the summer of 1926.[66] There were three YAF-run day-care centers operating simultaneously in Vilna in the late 1930s.[67] In late 1938, YAF reached out to those Polish Jewish families who had been forced to leave Germany, and provided care and supervision to their children from 8 A.M. to 4 P.M. The children received three meals a day, and also received scholarships if needed.[68]

YAF also undertook to organize summer day camps for children, and is known to have initiated such an effort in Warsaw in the summer of 1927, at which up to two hundred children participated. Five hundred took part in the summer of 1928. The organization instituted a sliding scale for tuition for these camps, did not charge unemployed families, and was already operating at a deficit just one year into its existence.[69] In the late 1920s, the Warsaw YAF received a small subsidy from the municipality for its summer camps, which, like the subsidies for the Medem Sanatorium, was obtained as a result of the political activities of the Bundist members of the Warsaw city council.[70] The members of YAF transformed the sessions at which it oriented the parents of camp participants into political events.

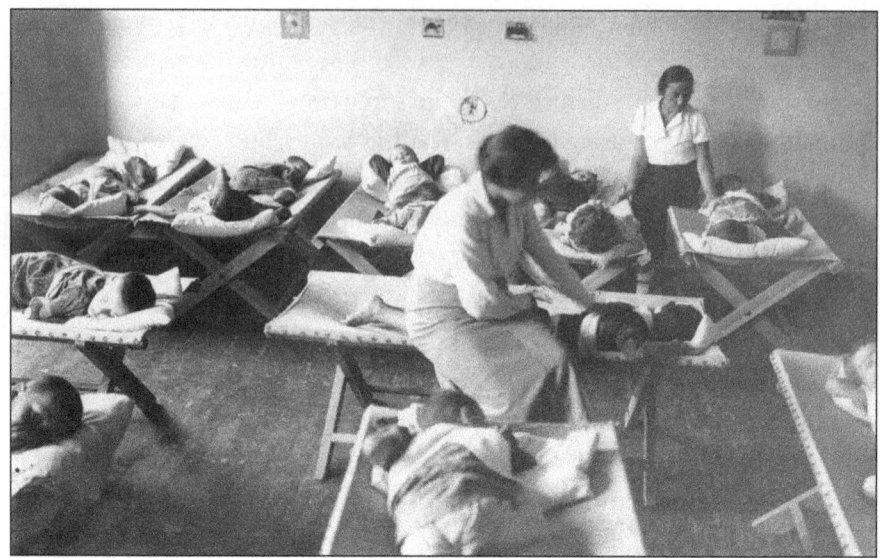

9. Naptime at the A. Litvak Day Care Center, which was run by YAF, Vilna, 1934. From the Archives of the YIVO Institute for Jewish Research, New York, RG 120, PO 5373

But YAF, it should be underscored, was interested in far more than day care. YAF advocated dissemination of birth control information by creating a section devoted to "Propaganda for Conscious Motherhood" in Warsaw in 1932.[71] YAF also supported campaigns for equal pay for women, conducted numerous meetings at which general political affairs and/or questions considered to have been of special interest to women were discussed, organized International Women's Day celebrations,[72] participated in May Day rallies, and attempted to mobilize its constituency on behalf of Bundist candidates in city council and Sejm elections.[73] Late in its history, the Lodz YAF also created a retreat space for women in the countryside, at which working-class women could take vacations.[74] The Bialystok branch organized excursions—and combined politics with recreation by including a moment of silence for the fallen defenders of the Spanish Republic during one such trip.[75]

By March 1927 there were YAF-affiliated groups in nine Polish cities.[76] A year later, YAF reported that the total size of its membership had increased by 30 percent, and that it had created a special section devoted to the defense of Jewish working-class children.[77] An unpublished memorandum written by

Bundists in New York in 1937 asserted that YAF had branches throughout Poland.[78] YAF, however, remained a small group. In 1929, its total number of members was 616.[79] Moreover, the number of YAF members who formally joined the Bund was smaller still. The Warsaw branch of YAF boasted considerable growth in the 1930s.[80] In mid-1935, the Vilna YAF publicly noted that it had around one hundred members.[81] But in Vilna—and apparently in the other Polish cities as well—YAF found it hard to build its membership. At the beginning of 1939, the Bund's Warsaw branch had 3,159 members, sixty-two of whom were also members of the Warsaw YAF.[82] Though YAF as a whole may well have grown in the late 1930s—a published report of the Lodz YAF written in 1938 indicates that a recruitment drive had brought ninety-three new members into its local branch[83]—and though the total number of members of YAF on the eve of the Second World War was all but certainly a large multiple of the number of YAF members who were in the Bund, it is telling that YAF, unlike SKIF or Morgnshtern, never published a periodical of its own, is only known to have organized a Poland-wide conference of female Bundists on one occasion—and that it convened that meeting only after the Central Committee of the Bund in Poland had declared that the organizing of a countrywide secretariat for YAF was a party priority.[84]

One reason why the Bund had more difficulty in organizing women in interwar Poland than it had had in Czarist Russia revolved around the constituency which YAF approached. The women who the Bund succeeded in organizing in the Russian Empire, and who had made up a significant portion of its rank-and-file membership during that era, were generally young, single, and employed. YAF, however, targeted a somewhat different sector of the female population: those who were married, who were mothers, and/or did not work outside the home. Though it made use of volunteer organizers who went from household to household, YAF's activists found that the women they approached, who were generally very poor and had little exposure to the culture of the world at large, were often overburdened or had difficulty grasping the organization's purpose.[85]

But mothers and home workers were not the only groups of women that YAF (and the Polish Bund) had trouble attracting in significant numbers. In the months immediately preceding the beginning of the Second World War, leaders of the Bund and of YAF debated the reasons why there were so few women in leading positions in the party.[86] The Bundist educator Khayim Kazdan created a stir by asserting in the pages of the *Naye folkstsaytung* in 1939 that the fact that women were underrepresented in the Polish Bund could be attributed to the degree to which Polish Jewish women had become assimilated.[87] Polish Jewish women, Kazdan claimed, were more assimilated both linguistically and culturally than were their male counterparts. Many Jewish women, he continued, educated in Polish schools, did not read Yiddish, and were indifferent to the Jewish sphere. They were, therefore, he implied, not as inclined to become active in a Jewish political party as were their male peers.

YAF activists, however, while agreeing with Kazdan's assertion that there were relatively few women in the Polish Bund's leading entities, offered quite different explanations for why and how this situation had come about. In an article entitled "Where Are the Women?" Dina Blond replied to Kazdan by arguing that the characteristics needed by leaders of a legal political party such as the Polish Bund—for instance, ambition and a willingness to put oneself forth—did not reflect the "essence" of women as much as did the characteristics needed by party workers when, in the czarist years, the Bund had been an illegal movement.[88] Blond pointed out, in support of her contention, that there were not only very few women in leading positions in the party, but also very few women in the highest-ranking positions within the Bund's youth movement.

Ruta Batkhan Berman also took part in this public discussion and contended that over the course of generations, women had come to underestimate themselves and, conversely, had come to believe too much in the abilities of their male counterparts. She also noted that women sensed that male comrades did not have much faith in the abilities of women, and that this reinforced their feeling of inferiority.[89] To Berman, it was precisely because of this problem that YAF was needed. When women are in their own organization, she argued, they feel themselves to be among equals, and this begins the process of increasing belief in oneself. Over time, she concluded, as a result of their experience in YAF, women would take more active roles than they had taken in the past.

Other readers of *Naye folktsaytung* also chimed in.[90] One reader from Lodz was critical of Kazdan's reasoning and proposed that the roles played by women in the Bund ought to be explained not so much by purported assimilation as by economic and political factors.[91] This reader noted that although changed economic conditions made it necessary for women to earn money, men had not changed their sense of women's responsibilities. Thus, the burdens on women had increased: They needed to work both in their homes and outside of them. But, this reader asserted, the general rate of participation of women in meetings and gatherings was—nevertheless—not lower than was the rate of male participation. How then could the low proportion of female leaders in the movement be explained? Over hundreds of years, Jewish women had lived in an intellectual ghetto. Neither the milieu in which they lived nor the women themselves had believed that women were called to take part in the life of society. The psychology of women had not changed since that era—and as a result, Jewish working-class women were still restrained, modest, and bashful. The reader continued: "She does not have a great belief in her own forces and therefore cannot break a path through to the foremost positions of party life." Moreover, since men had not changed, they continued to believe that they, and not women, were called to lead party life.

A second reader, who was thirty-one, childless, born in Poland, and apparently a widow, noted that at one time she had been employed while her partner had not, and that during that period her partner had cleaned their home while she was at work. They had gone together to various kinds of events, had read together, and shared thoughts with one another. The writer of this letter, understanding that her situation differed from that of women with children, noted that in households in which children were present, things could be arranged so that the woman went out sometimes and the man at other times. She commented that those male comrades who said that women did not want to interest themselves with societal work had probably chosen women "whose heads are filled with all kinds of foolishness"—and she blamed the male comrades for such a state of affairs. If, she underscored, a man always left his wife alone with the children in order to go off to the union or to socialize with friends, if a man did not read the newspaper with his wife, if he did not explain to her the source of her troubles, who could be surprised by his wife's turn to religiosity as a mechanism by which to ease her pain?[92]

This discussion within Bundist circles exposed significant differences of opinion concerning both the nature of the role played by women in the Bund and how that role could be explained. The matter was unresolved at the time that the Second World War began.⁹³

However, it seems to be the case that all those involved in the Bund generally agreed that the proportion of women in party leadership was lower than was their proportion in the population, and most acknowledged that YAF had not broken through to a mass audience.

■ ■ ■

Even in the late 1930s, YAF was not the only Bundist-oriented organization that remained small. The loosely structured Bundist organization for university students—known as *Ringen* in Yiddish and as *Ogniwo* in Polish—was very small throughout the years of its existence, including the period when the Bund itself was growing in strength.⁹⁴ However, the failure of Ringen to attract large numbers of members and the failure of YAF to do so are of dramatically different significance.

Not many Polish Jews had an opportunity to attend an institution of higher education in the 1930s.⁹⁵ Those Jews who did attend universities in Poland in the interwar years, moreover, were likely to have been fluent speakers of Polish (in a period when many Polish Jews were not), were more acculturated than were most Jewish workers, and were also more likely to come from bourgeois households than from poor or working-class families.

One of the manifestations of the rise of anti-Semitism in Poland in the 1930s was the imposition of measures designed to limit the numbers of Jewish students able to attend Polish universities. Agitation on behalf of a *numerus clausus* (a quota on the number of Jews admitted), the introduction of segregated seating for Jewish students in university classrooms, and repeated violent attacks by right-wing Polish students on their Jewish classmates, all had an impact on the numbers of Jews who attended universities in Poland in the years immediately preceding the beginning of the Second World War.

Arcadius Kahan—the son of the Bundist leader Virgily Kahan—who attended university in Vilna in the 1930s, reports that "the overall enrollment of Jewish students" at Stefan Batory University "reached its highest point around 1929–30, when 882 students declared Yiddish and eight students declared Hebrew as their mother tongue out of a total of 3,336 students at the university." However, "The subsequent years witnessed a lessening in the number and share of Jewish students, declining to six hundred out of about four thousand by the late 1930s."⁹⁶ There were similar declines in the enrollment of Jewish students in other Polish universities during this period. The proportion of Polish university students who were Jewish decreased from 24.3 percent in the academic year 1921–22, to 14.9 percent in 1934–35, and decreased yet again to 9.9 percent in 1937–38.⁹⁷ There were, in total, only 4,113 Jewish university students in Poland in the last school year preceding the beginning of the war.⁹⁸

To be sure, some young Polish Jews who were raised in bourgeois families, such as Abraham Chwoinik, whose father was the owner of a successful leather factory, were active in Ringen.⁹⁹ In addition, a small number of individuals who grew up in Bundist homes succeeded in being admitted to Polish universities. Alexander and Victor Erlich (both of whom served briefly, at various points, as chairmen of Ringen), the sons of Henryk Erlich and of Sophia Dubnow-Erlich, are prominent cases in point.¹⁰⁰ Neither Chwoinik nor Alexander Erlich nor Victor Erlich, however, was typical of Polish Jews of his generation.¹⁰¹ In the Polish context, Ringen had no chance of attracting large numbers of members and did not expect to do so. The Warsaw City Committee of the Bund was sufficiently interested in Jewish university students to delegate a representative to the Ringen circle, which was active in the Polish capital city in the 1930s.¹⁰² Nevertheless, Jewish university students were never part of the Bund's core constituency.¹⁰³

But the same cannot be said about Jewish working-class women. The latter were an essential and substantial portion of the population needed by the Bund to achieve its electoral and other goals. Thus the fact that Ringen did not grow at a rate comparable to the rates attained by the Tsukunft or Morgnshtern, and that it remained small in size throughout its years of existence, is neither surprising nor important in assessing the prospects of the Polish Bund. The fact that YAF's trajectory was more like that of Ringen than like that of the Tsukunft, however, is rather revealing. YAF's lack of success underscores that the Bund could not break through on all fronts, and strongly suggests that there was a ceiling beyond which the Bund was unable to climb. Bundist counterculture had its limits.

Conclusion

THE JEWISH WORKERS' BUND, which was supported by only a limited proportion of Polish Jewry at the beginning of the 1920s, grew in power quite markedly over the course of the interwar period. The augmentation in the Bund's power was both presaged and fostered by an increase in the size of certain of the movements most closely affiliated with the Bund, notably the Tsukunft, SKIF, and Morgnshtern. The increase in the sizes of these movements began in the 1920s and seems, in some especially notable cases, to have gained momentum over time. The Tsukunft, among the most important of the movements in the Bundist constellation, had some three thousand or so members in 1924, five thousand members in 1925, close to ten thousand adherents in 1930, and over twelve thousand members in 1939.[1] SKIF, which was not established until the mid-1920s, grew from an entity with twenty-two hundred members in 1930, to one of almost thirty-five hundred in 1931, and five thousand in the mid-1930s.[2] It claimed to have more than ten thousand members on the eve of the Second World War.[3] The Bundist movement for physical education, founded in the same year as was SKIF, had approximately twenty-five hundred members in 1927 (six months after the creation of its central coordinating body), four thousand members in 1929, forty-five hundred in 1933, five thousand members in 1934, and may have had as many as eight thousand in 1937.[4] The Medem Sanatorium, finally, increased the maximum number of children it was able to serve at any one time from seventy in the mid-1920s to 160 in 1932 and to two hundred in the mid-1930s. It expected that it would serve up to three hundred children at a time in the summer of 1939—and was filling only a small fraction of the requests made for admittance.[5] The sanatorium also sharply increased the total number of clients it served each year between its opening and its eventual closing.

There is concrete evidence that young people regularly graduated from SKIF into the Tsukunft, and that significant numbers of Polish Jewish youth graduated from the Tsukunft into the Bund.[6] There were reportedly more than one thousand one-time Tsukunftistn entering the Bund every year in the period leading up to the Second World War.[7] By 1939, one-time members of the Tsukunft were playing leading roles in its parent party. No fewer than five of the sixteen Bundists elected to the Warsaw city council in the last election to be held before the war—Jerzy Gliksman, Yoysef Gutgold, Zalmen Likhtnshteyn, Emanuel Scherer, and Nakhman Shafran—had been active in the Tsukunft at various points in time. At least one of the Bundists elected to the Lodz city council in 1938, Hersh Mayzner, had also been a Tsukunftist during an earlier period in his life.[8]

The electoral victories obtained by the Bundist party in the period 1936–39 came in the wake of successes achieved over a longer time span by a number of movements and institutions closely affiliated with that party. It is by no means the case that the successes of Bundist peripheral organizations were the primary cause of the eventual political successes of the Bund. But the growth of certain of these peripheral organizations in the 1920s and early 1930s was an indicator of the potential of Bundist institutions and may have directly contributed to the victories achieved by the party's candidates in the years immediately preceding the start of World War II.

Thus, some of the arguments made by Ezra Mendelsohn and Antony Polonsky appear to be open to reconsideration, such as the one suggesting that electoral victories by the Bund in city council and Jewish communal elections in the late 1930s ought not to be taken as suggestive of longer-term trends.[9] The success of Bundist candidates in 1936–39 was not an aberration. It was not even particularly surprising given the growth in the breadth of constituent components of the Bundist constellation that had gone on over a number of years preceding 1936. The increases in the size of the party's children's movement, youth movement, and physical education movement led to an increase in the total number of people who had had positive experiences in its entities (either directly or via members of their families) and helps to explain why more people voted for Bundist candidates in city council and Jewish community council elections in the late 1930s than in earlier years.

The fact that the Tsukunft, SKIF, and Morgnshtern all underwent growth spurts beginning in the 1920s undermines the hypotheses of some of those who attributed the Bund's electoral successes primarily to political events that took place in the late 1930s. The increasing intensity of anti-Semitism (and the Bundist response to that challenge), on the one hand, and disillusionment with the Zionist movement on the other, may well have led some voters to the Bund. But the 1938 dissolution of the Communist Party of Poland cannot explain the increases in the Bund's electoral strength in 1936.

The alternative explanation of the rise in the electoral power of the Bund provided by Pickhan—that is, that changes in the socioeconomic structure of Polish Jewry led to an increase in the size of the Jewish trade unions, and that the increased power of these unions, in turn, provides an indication of a major change in consciousness (ultimately beneficial to the Bund)—is far more credible than are explanations revolving around current events. Pickhan focuses on an alleged threefold increase in the total of Polish Jewish trade union members from 1930 to 1939.[10] However, Shmuel Zygielbaum, a prominent Bundist who served at one point as secretary of a major Polish Jewish trade union confederation, the National Council of Professional Class Unions in Poland (Land-rat fun di profesionele klasn-fareynen in poyln),[11] and whose most important piece on Jewish trade unions in Poland, written in 1939, is cited extensively by Pickhan, notes that the Land-rat did not steadily increase in size in the 1920s and early 1930s.[12] Indeed, Zygielbaum points out that the total membership of the Polish Jewish trade unions—which, he states, had already reached fifty thousand at one relatively early point after the establishment of the independent Polish state—dipped under that figure during the worst periods of the "critical years" that began in 1928–29.[13] Zygielbaum suggests that the Land-rat, the only Polish Jewish trade union movement closely aligned with the Bund, did not begin a rapid increase in its size until 1935–36.[14] Similarly, Sara Szweber, another prominent Bundist who had also served as secretary of the Land-rat at one time, indicated in 1937 that a series of splits and attempted splits engineered by Communists in 1924–26 and again from 1928–35 helped to explain why the Land-rat had trouble amassing additional members in the 1920s and in the first half of the following decade.[15]

The growth of the Jewish trade union movement from 1935–36 until September 1939 was certainly very impressive. The Land-rat represented slightly fewer than seventy-two thousand Jewish members in 1937 and had more than ninety-nine thousand in 1939.[16] Bundists dominated many of its individual unions.[17] However, the rise of the Tsukunft, SKIF, and Morgnshtern were *harbingers* of a Bundist upswing. The most significant increases in the size of the union movement occurred more or less *simultaneously* with the rise in the voting strength of the Bund, not (as Pickhan seemingly would have it) before that rise in voting strength had manifested itself.[18]

If, however, the successes of the Tsukunft, SKIF, and Morgnshtern (and of Bundist-oriented trade unions) suggest that in the late 1930s the Bund had reason to think that it would continue to grow over time, the failure of the YAF ought to have given it pause. The Bund and its peripheral organizations fostered values and ideas that differed sharply from those fanned by Catholic-dominated Polish institutions and by Polish Jewish religious authorities. Bundists in Poland succeeded to a notable degree in wooing children and youth and in fostering a distinctive counterculture. But the counterculture did not appeal to everyone. YAF's inability to attract substantial numbers of Jewish working women indicates that the growth of the Bund as a political force—despite the upsurge in the sizes of Tsukunft, SKIF, Morgnshtern, and the Land-rat—was likely to have reached a ceiling at some point. The reach of Bundist counterculture went only so far.

Contrary to the contentions of Bernard Johnpoll and Antony Polonsky, the politics of the Bund were not "the politics of futility."[19] Claims made by some Bundists, particularly in the post-World War II era, that the Jewish population of Poland chose the Bund as its *sheliakh-tsibur* (emissary on behalf of the community) or that the Bund "was chosen by the majority of Jews to lead the fight of and for the Jewish masses" overstate the case.[20] However, it is not true that the Bund failed as a political party in interwar Poland. It achieved notable victories not only in cultural and educational fields but also on the political front, and its electoral victories increased in intensity and in frequency as the interwar period went on. And yet the Bund did not attain hegemony across the board. Its counterculture was, at the end of the day, only partially successful.

Notes

Glossary

Bibliography

Index

Notes

Introduction

1. The Bund has received a fair amount of attention from the scholarly world. There have been any number of studies devoted to the Bund's development in Russia and a somewhat more modest number of academic works focused on the Bund in interwar Poland. Particularly notable academic books dealing with the Bund in the Czarist Empire include Ezra Mendelsohn, *Class Struggle in the Pale: The Formative Years of the Jewish Workers' Movement in Tsarist Russia* (Cambridge: Cambridge Univ. Press, 1970); Henry J. Tobias, *The Jewish Bund in Russia: From Its Origins to 1905* (Stanford, Calif.: Stanford Univ. Press, 1972); Jonathan Frankel, *Prophecy and Politics: Socialism, Nationalism and the Russian Jews, 1862–1917* (Cambridge: Cambridge Univ. Press, 1981); Moshe Mishkinsky, *Reshit tenuat ha-poalim ha-yehudit be-rusyah: megamot yesod* (Tel Aviv: Ha-kibutz Ha-meuchad, 1981); Yoav Peled, *Class and Ethnicity in the Pale: The Political Economy of Jewish Workers' Nationalism in Late Imperial Russia* (New York: St. Martin's Press, 1989); Joshua D. Zimmerman, *Poles, Jews, and the Politics of Nationality: The Bund and the Polish Socialist Party in Late Tsarist Russia, 1892–1914* (Madison, Wis.: Univ. of Wisconsin Press, 2004), and Claudie Weill, *Les cosmopolites: Socialisme et judéité en Russie (1897–1917)* (Paris: Éditions Syllepse, 2004). Books that discuss the Bund in the era of the Bolshevik Revolution include Zvi Gitelman, *Jewish Nationality and Soviet Politics: The Jewish Sections of the CPSU, 1917–1930* (Princeton, N.J.: Princeton Univ. Press, 1972) and Arye Gelbard, *Der jüdische Arbeiter-Bund Russlands im Revolutionsjahr 1917*, Ludwig Boltzmann Institut für Geschichte der Arbeiterbewegung, Materialen zur Arbeiterbewegung, vol. 26 (Vienna: Europaverlag, 1982). Books focusing on the Bund in interwar Poland include Bernard K. Johnpoll, *The Politics of Futility: The General Jewish Workers Bund of Poland, 1917–1943* (Ithaca, N.Y.: Cornell Univ. Press, 1967); Zvi Barzilai, *Tenuat ha-bund be-polin ben shete milhamot ha-olam* (Jerusalem: Carmel, 1994); and Gertrud Pickhan, *"Gegen den Strom": Der Allgemeine Jüdische Arbeiterbund "Bund" in Polen 1918–1939*, Schriften des Simon-Dubnow Instituts Leipzig, vol. 1 (Stuttgart, Munich: Deutsche Verlags-Anstalt, 2001). Two edited volumes—Jack Jacobs, ed., *Jewish Politics in Eastern Europe: The Bund at 100* (New York: New York Univ. Press, in

association with the Jewish Historical Institute, Warsaw, 2001), and Zvi Gitelman, ed., *The Emergence of Modern Jewish Politics: Bundism and Zionism in Eastern Europe,* Pitt Series in Russian and East European Studies (Pittsburgh, Pa.: Univ. of Pittsburgh Press, 2003)—contain chapters on both the Russian and the Polish periods of the Bund's history, as do Henri Minczeles's *Histoire générale du Bund: un mouvement révolutionnaire juif* (Paris: Denol, 1999) and Yosef Gorny's *Converging Alternatives: The Bund and the Zionist Labor Movement, 1897–1985* (Albany, N.Y.: State Univ. of New York [SUNY] Press, 2006).

2. Pickhan, *"Gegen den Strom,"* 206.

3. See, for example, Antony Polonsky, "The Bund in Polish Political Life, 1935–1939," in *Jewish History: Essays in Honour of Chimen Abramsky,* ed. Ada Rapoport-Albert and Steven J. Zipperstein (London: Peter Halban, 1988), 571–72; and Antony Polonsky, "The New Jewish Politics and its Discontents," in *Emergence of Modern Jewish Politics,* ed. Gitelman, 36–37.

4. In the elections of 1919, in which Bundist candidates won precisely 16,366 votes in Congress Poland, candidates of the Temporary Jewish National Council (which was dominated by General Zionists) received around 180,000 votes, candidates running on an Orthodox list won 97,000 votes, Folkist candidates received 59,000, and those of the Poalei Zion, 27,000 (Ezra Mendelsohn, *Zionism in Poland: The Formative Years, 1915–1926* [New Haven: Yale Univ. Press, 1981], 108–9). Though schisms within the Folkist and Poalei Zion parties eventually sapped their electoral strength, both the General Zionist movement and Agudes Yisroel (representing an Orthodox constituency) won seats in other specific Sejm elections as well. See M. Balberyszki, "Volkism and the Volksparty," in *Struggle for Tomorrow: Modern Political Ideologies of the Jewish People,* ed. Basil J. Vlavianos and Feliks Gross (New York: Arts, Inc., 1954), 241–42; Mark W. Kiel, "The Ideology of the Folks-Partey," *Soviet Jewish Affairs* 5, no. 2 (1975): 76; Isaac Lewin, *The Jewish Community in Poland: Historical Essays* (New York: Philosophical Library, 1985), 200–214; Gershon C. Bacon, "Agudat Israel in Interwar Poland," in *The Jews of Poland Between Two World Wars,* ed. Yisrael Gutman, Ezra Mendelsohn, Jehuda Reinharz, and Chone Shmeruk (Hanover, N.H.: Univ. Press of New England, 1989), 24 and passim.

5. J[acob] S. Hertz, "Der bund in umophengikn poyln, 1918–1925," in *Di geshikhte fun bund,* ed. [Sophia] Dubnow-Erlich, J[acob] S. Hertz, Kh[ayim] Sh[loyme] Kazdan, and E[manuel] Scherer [Sherer] (New York: Farlag unzer tsayt, 1972), 4:30–32; Johnpoll, *Politics of Futility,* 85.

6. Mordekhay V. Bernshteyn, "Der 'bund' in poyln," in *Yorbukh,* ed. Shimen Federbush (New York: Velt federatsie fun poylishe yidn, Amerikaner ekzekutiva, 1964), 1:184; Johnpoll, *Politics of Futility,* 128–29; Hertz, "Der bund in umophengikn poyln, 1918–1925," 4:36. One scholar comments "The electoral system strongly favoured the Zionist parties, for, in the constituencies where Jewish lists obtained one or more seats, Zionist sympathizers were more numerous than in the country as a whole. This is clearly demonstrated by the 1922 (and later) election results." Joseph Marcus, *Social and Political History of the Jews in Poland, 1919–1939,* Studies in the Social Sciences (Berlin, New York: Mouton Publishers, 1983), 263. See Mendelsohn, *Zionism in Poland,* 218, for the votes received by other Jewish lists in this election.

7. Bernshteyn, "Der 'bund' in poyln," 184–85; Johnpoll, *Politics of Futility,* 154–56; J[acob] S. Hertz, "Der bund in umophengikn poyln, 1926–1932," in *Di geshikhte fun bund* (New York: Farlag unzer tsayt, 1981), 5:18–21.

8. Bernshteyn, "Der 'bund' in poyln," 185; Johnpoll, *Politics of Futility,* 167. The Bund boycotted Sejm elections in 1935 and 1938, as did a number of other parties. Jacob S. Hertz, *Di geshikhte fun bund in lodz* (New York: Farlag unzer tsayt, 1958), 385, 426; Johnpoll, *Politics of Futility,* 205, 223; Celia S. Heller, *On the Edge of Destruction: Jews of Poland between the Two World Wars* (New York: Columbia Univ. Press, 1977), 350; Pawel Korzec, *Juifs en Pologne: La question juive pendant l'entre-deux-guerres* (Paris: Presses de la foundation nationale des sciences politiques, 1980), 240–41.

9. *Der yidisher arbeter-klas in yor 1936* (Lodz: n.p., 1937), 224–25. My estimates of the Jewish population of Warsaw, and of other major cities in Poland, are derived from Marcus, *Social and Political History,* 468.

10. The Bundist list won 30 percent of the vote in Grodno, 30.5 percent in Piotrków and "about a third" in Lublin (Robert Moses Shapiro, "The Polish *Kehillah* Elections of 1936: A Revolution Reexamined," *Polin* 8 [1994]: 215). As Shapiro points out, the Bund was not equally successful in every city and town, winning only one council seat in both Kalisz and Tomaszów Mazowiecki. In contrast, in some of the cities in which the Bundist list did not win a plurality, such as in Vilna, it substantially increased the number of voters it attracted. The Bund received 566 votes (and three seats) in Vilna in 1928. It received 1,157 votes (and five seats) in 1936 (*Der yidisher arbeter-klas,* 222).

11. Emanuel Melzer, *No Way Out: The Politics of Polish Jewry 1935–1939* (Cincinnati: Hebrew Union College Press, 1997), 97. Agudes Yisroel's proportion of the vote in the ninety-seven locations in question (excluding Warsaw) was twenty-one. The General Zionists obtained 17 percent of the vote. The Bund obtained 8.8 percent (p. 198).

12. *Der yidisher arbeter-klas,* 227–31; Melzer, *No Way Out,* 97; Polonsky, "The Bund in Polish Political Life," 562–63; Shapiro, "The Polish *Kehillah* Elections of 1936," 217–19.

13. Seventy-four and one-half percent of those eligible to vote cast ballots in this election. Shapiro, "The Polish *Kehillah* Elections of 1936," 219.

14. Barbara Wachowska, "Łódź Remained Red: Elections to the City Council of 27 September 1936," *Polin* 9 (1996): 102.

15. Daniel Blatman, "The Bund in Poland, 1935–1939," *Polin* 9 (1996): 78. A summary of recent election results prepared under the auspices of the Bund's Central Committee in 1937 and including both elections to city councils and to *kehiles* underscored the disparity between the results obtained by both the Bund and the Right Poalei Zion. According to this summary, the Bund had outperformed the Right Poalei Zion in eighteen of the most important Jewish settlements in Poland—Bialystok, Cracow, Czstochowa, Grodno, Kutno, Lemberg, Lodz, Lomża, Lublin, Mezrich, Pinsk, Piotrków, Radom, Siedlce, Tarnów, Vilna, Warsaw, and Włocławek—and had obtained results comparable to those of the Right Poalei Zion in a nineteenth location, Kalisz. "Tsentral-komitet fun 'bund' in poyln," *Memorandum tsum yidishn arbeter-komitet in amerike* (New York: Bundisher klub in nu york, 1937), 4–5.

16. Melzer, *No Way Out*, 108. Sixteen of the seventeen individuals elected on this slate were Bundists. Hertz, *Di geshikhte fun bund in lodz*, 429.

17. Nachman Libeskind, "Far velkhe parteyen hobn yidn in lodz geshtimt bes di valn tsum shtotrat un seym in 1919–1938?" *Undzer tsayt*, nos. 7–8 [692–93] (July–Aug. 2000): 27. The Bundist slate in the 1919 Lodz city council elections, the first such election in Lodz after the creation of the independent Polish state, won five mandates. The Bundists won three mandates in 1923 and five in 1927 (Pawel Samuś, "The Bund Organization in Lodz, 1898–1939," in *Jewish Politics in Eastern Europe*, ed. Jacobs, 106–7). The slate headed by Bundists elected five Bundists and one Labor Zionist in 1936 (Libeskind, 28). Thus, the results obtained in 1938 were better, from the Bund's perspective, than any previous results. One authoritative source indicates that there were not seven (as reported by Libeskind) but rather eight Bundists elected to the Lodz city council in 1938: Shmuel Milman, Shmuel Zygielbaum, Khayim Leyb Poznanski, Roza Eichner, Sergey Nutkevitsh, Yoysef Morgentaler, Meir Mermelshtayn, and Hersh Mayzner. Hertz, *Di geshikhte fun bund in lodz*, 427–28.

18. Blatman, "Bund in Poland," 79.

19. On Lwów, see Marcus, *Social and Political History*, 468.

20. Blatman, "Bund in Poland," 81.

21. Johnpoll, *Politics of Futility*, 195.

22. Marcus, *Social and Political History*, 283.

23. Ezra Mendelsohn, *The Jews of East Central Europe between the World Wars* (Bloomington: Indiana Univ. Press, 1983), 78.

24. Ezra Mendelsohn, *On Modern Jewish Politics* (New York: Oxford Univ. Press, 1993), 77.

25. Celia Heller, in her 1977 study of Polish Jewry between the two world wars, also argued that the votes won by Bundist lists should not be interpreted as necessarily indicating agreement on the part of Jewish voters with Bundist positions. Heller, *On the Edge of Destruction*, 282–83.

26. Blatman, "Bund in Poland," 59.

27. Ibid., 60–61.

28. Pickhan, *"Gegen den Strom,"* 206.

29. Polonsky, "The Bund in Polish Political Life," 572. Ezra Mendelsohn, very similarly, has noted that "one basic characteristic of Jewish politics in Poland was the oscillation between the extremes of euphoria and despair, a kind of 'manic-depressive' quality" and has explicitly suggested that this "cycle of euphoria and depression" explains the course not only of the ups and downs of the Polish Zionist movement (and of other Polish Jewish political movements) but also of the Bund. Ezra Mendelsohn, "Jewish Politics in Interwar Poland: An Overview," in *The Jews of Poland*, ed. Gutman et al. (see Introduction, note 4), 10, 11–12.

30. Scholars of the Social Democratic Party of Germany have tended to argue that German social democrats of the Wilhelmine era supported a subculture rather than a counterculture. See, as one example among many, Gary P. Steenson, *"Not One Man! Not One Penny!" German Social Democracy, 1863–1914* (Pittsburgh: Univ. of Pittsburgh Press, 1981), 113. They

have pointed out that the "complex of alternative organizations" affiliated with the German social democratic party—which included organizations for youth and for women—"were separate but not remarkably different" than those created by nonsocialists: "The people in them were Germans, they were subject to many of the same pressures and prejudices as their non-socialist counterparts, and these things account for similarities along a broad front" (Steenson, *"Not One Man!"* 112–13. But whatever may have been the case in Germany, Polish Bundists—like the Austro-Marxists of the First Republic—aspired to create more than a subculture, and perceived the ancillary organizations they established or fostered as differing significantly from the organizations created by their political opponents. Just as the Austro-Marxists attempted, from the end of the First World War until February 1934, "to develop a comprehensive proletarian counterculture, going beyond piecemeal cultural reform efforts of socialist parties in other countries" (Helmut Gruber, *Red Vienna: Experiment in Working-Class Culture 1919–1934* [New York: Oxford Univ. Press, 1991], 5), so too did the Polish Bund. The Bundists of interwar Poland, in sum, were eager to establish not a subculture but a counterculture. Cf. Roni Gechtman, "Yidisher Sotsializm: The Origin and Contexts of the Jewish Labor Bund's National Program" (Ph.D. diss., New York Univ., 2005) 17: "The Polish Bund created a whole subculture of working-class, secular Yiddishist institutions that represented an impressive 'national-cultural autonomy in the making.'"

The Bund was by no means the only Jewish political tendency in Poland determined to create a counterculture. Zvi Gitelman points out that "both the Bund and the Zionists modernized Jewish life. . . . Each movement built schools, published newspapers, sponsored theaters, inspired music, and undertook other cultural activities, all of which were designed to articulate, promote and disseminate the ideals of the movement. . . . Each created a kind of counterculture and counter community to the historically dominant religious culture and communities of Eastern Europe. . . . This was especially true of the Bund." See Introduction, note 1 of Zvi Gitelman, "A Century of Jewish Politics in Eastern Europe: The Legacy of the Bund and the Zionist Movement," in *Emergence of Modern Jewish Politics*, 18.

1. The Youth Bund Tsukunft

1. I delivered a paper containing the argument I make in this chapter in April 2007 at the conference on "Jewish Politics in Central and Eastern Europe: From Shtadlanut to Mass Parties," sponsored by the Center for Studies of the Culture and History of East European Jews, Vilnius, Lithuania, and have benefitted from the comments I received from other participants at that event.

2. N. A. Tan, "Di 'tsukunft' un der 'bund,'" *Yugnt-veker* 6, no. 20 (Oct. 15, 1927): 28–30; idem, "Tsvantsik yor," *Yugnt-veker* 10, no. 12 (June 1, 1931): 4–6. It is highly likely that these two articles were written by Nakhman Shafran, a founding member of the Tsukunft who was known in the movement as Natan (J[acob] S. Hertz, "Nakhman [Natan] Shafran," *Doyres bundistn*, ed. Jacob S. Hertz [New York: Farlag unzer tsayt, 1968], 3:44). The prehistory and early history of the Tsukunft are also discussed in J[acob] S. Hertz, *Di geshikhte fun a yugnt:*

Der klayner bund—yugnt-bund tsukunft in poyln (New York: Farlag unzer tsayt, 1946), 121–55, and in Moshe Kligsberg, "Di yidishe yugnt-bavegung in poyln tsvishn beyde velt milkhomes (a sotsiologishe shtudie)," in *Shtudies vegn yidn in poyln 1919–1939: Di tsvishnshpil fun sotsiale, ekonomishe un politishe faktorn inem kamf fun a minoritet far ir kiem*, ed. Joshua [Shikl] Fishman (New York: Yidisher visnshaftlekher institut—YIVO, 1974), 190–91. Hersh Mendel, referring to the period 1911–13, writes:

> It is generally the case that young people first join the youth movement and only from there go on to become members of the party. It was exactly the opposite with me. After I had already been a member of the [Bund] for some time, I was invited to a conference of . . . the Tsukunft. In those days, the Tsukunft was not yet a purely Bundist organization; people from other tendencies within the socialist movement also belonged to it. In 1913, when I did time in prison with Shafran, who later became a noted Bundist, he was still one of the Bund's opponents. He made a point of saying that he would either join the PPS-Left or the Social Democratic Party of Poland after his release from jail. He gave absolutely no thought to working inside the Bund. Yet he was one of the leaders of the . . . Tsukunft. Most of the leaders of the Tsukunft, however, were Bundists at the time. (Hersh Mendel, *Memoirs of a Jewish Revolutionary,* [London: Pluto Press, 1989], 64)

3. The emergence of the Kombund in Poland is discussed by P[inkus] Minc (Alexander), *Di geshikhte fun a falsher iluzie (zikhroynes)*, vol. 103, Dos poylishe yidntum (Buenos Aires: Tsentral-farband fun poylishe yidn in argentine, 1954), 80–84; idem, *The History of a False Illusion: Memoirs on the Communist Movements in Poland (1918–1938)*, trans. Robert Michaels (Lewiston: Edwin Mellen Press, 2002), 68–69. See Johnpoll, *Politics of Futility*, 184; Hertz, "Der bund in umophengikn poyln, 1918–1925," 107–8. In September 1922, the Kombund was dissolved, and many of its members joined the Communist Workers' Party of Poland.

4. The International Information Bureau of Revolutionary Socialist Parties, also known as the Paris Bureau, was initiated by the French Marxist Paul Louis. Its secretary was the Russian-born Angelica Balabanoff. Angelica Balabanoff, *My Life as a Rebel* (Bloomington: Indiana Univ. Press, 1973), 309. See Johnpoll, *Politics of Futility*, 184; Hertz, "Der bund in umophengikn poyln, 1926–1932," 53–54.

5. The history of the Bund's relationships to both the Comintern and to the LSI is reviewed, from a Bundist perspective, by Emanuel Nowogrodzki, *The Jewish Labor Bund in Poland: From its Emergence as an Independent Political Party Until the Beginning of World War II 1915–1939* (Rockville, Md.: Shengold Books, 2001), 28–79. See Mario Kessler, "The Bund and the Labour and Socialist International," in *Jewish Politics in Eastern Europe*, 183–94.

6. The Warsaw Committee of the Komtsukunft was made up of Kh. Kaplan, Mendl Skrobek, Itsik Kovner, Benyomin ("Yanek") Goldflam, Gitele Rapoport, Aleksander Zatorski, Hershl Goldfinger, Yankele Bibleyzer, Adek Likhtenboym, Efrayim Pinkert, and Haline Fefer. Hershl Goldfinger, "Fun shmoln gesl oyfn breytn trakt," in *Unter der fon fun k.p.p.*, ed.

H[ershl] Goldfinger, M[ikhael] Mirksi, Sz[imon] Zachariasz (Warsaw: Książka i Wiedza, 1959), 110. See Jakub Wajsbrot, "'Jugunt-bund "Cukunft" in Pojłn'/ Młodzieżowa organizacja bundowska 'Przyszłość' w Polsce od zarania do 1939 r." (Warsaw: N.p., 1962), 42–46, typescript, Archiwum Akt Nowych, Warsaw, 76/II-87.

In addition to those one-time members of the Tsukunft who affiliated first with the Komtsukunft and later with the communist movement, there was another group of Tsukunftistn who associated themselves with the communist movement via a slightly different road. In 1919, a group emerged in the Warsaw Tsukunft that argued that a youth movement ought not to be identified with a party because young people were insufficiently astute to differentiate appropriately among party platforms. This group ultimately broke from the Tsukunft and created an independent youth organization, but purportedly it soon thereafter liquidated itself and entered the communist youth association (which was affiliated with the Communist Youth International). J[acob] S. Hertz, "Ideyishe erlikhkayt," in *Yid, mentsh, sotsialist. I. artuski ondenk-bukh* (Tel Aviv: Farlag "lebns-fragn," 1976), 45.

7. "Der 4-ter tsuzamenfor fun yugnt-bund 'tsukunft,'" *Yugnt-veker* 4, no. 8 (Nov. 20, 1925): 9. Thirty two of the delegates to the Tsukunft's fourth conference voted in favor of a resolution endorsing the Bund's affiliation with the Paris bureau. Thirty delegates endorsed the general principles of the Communist Youth International.

8. "Yugnt-bund 'tsukunft' in poyln" (ca. 1928), Bund Archives, RG 1400 (hereafter referred to as Bund Archives), MG 9-258, YIVO Institute for Jewish Research, New York (hereafter referred to as YIVO Archives).

9. The members of the Bund disagreed strongly about whether to join the LSI. The members of the Tsukunft, in turn, were also divided over this issue. As a result of the Bund deciding to join the LSI, seventy or so Tsukunftistn broke away from the Tsukunft in 1930 and created an organization of their own, the Left Tsukunft. "Tsu ale mitglider fun 'tsukunft,'" flyer, Warsaw, Aug. 9, 1930, Bund Archives, MG 9-290.

In the period leading up to the Tsukunft's sixth conference, the Tsukunft's Central Committee considered two very different resolutions on the question of affiliation with the Socialist Youth International. Nine members ultimately voted in favor of a resolution that advocated joining that international body. Four voted in favor of an alternative resolution that was critical of the Socialist Youth International (Yugnt-bund "tsukunft" in poyln. Tsentral komitet, Tsirkular 3/36, Warsaw, Feb. 15, 1936 [Bund Archives, MG 9-265]). The resolution in favor of joining the Socialist Youth International was ultimately passed by the delegates to the Tsukunft's sixth conference by a vote of forty-nine for, thirty-one against, and one abstention. "Der 6-ter tsuzamenfor fun yugnt-bund tsukunft in poyln," *Yugnt-veker* 15, no. 9 (Apr. 15, 1936): 4.

The fact that the Tsukunft affiliated with the Socialist Youth International six years later than the Bund had affiliated with the LSI should not be taken as suggesting that the views of the Tsukunftistn differed sharply from those of the Bundists. The fifth conference of the Tsukunft took place in 1929, before the Bund had resolved to join the LSI. The sixth conference, therefore, was the first time that the Tsukunft's most authoritative body met following the Bund's decision.

10. "Der 6-ter tsuzamenfor fun yugnt-bund 'tsukunft' in poyln," *Yugnt-veker* 15, no. 11 (May 1, 1936): 6. Jacob S. Hertz, a leading figure in the Tsukunft in the interwar years, asserts that the Tsukunft had approximately 250 local organizations on the eve of the Second World War. There were additional locations in which Tsukunft locals had existed at one time or another, but in 1939, the organizations in these locations were no longer active. Hertz, *Di geshikhte fun a yugnt*, 507.

11. Jacob Lestschinsky, *Di yidishe arbeter-yugnt in poyln*. N.p, 1929. Lestchinsky, a key figure in the Zionist Socialist Workers' Party in the czarist era, was one of the founders of the United Jewish Socialist Workers' Party, the Faraynikte. Though the entry on Lestschinsky in the *Leksikon fun der nayer yidisher literatur* (vol. 5, col. 384) declares that he was close to the Bund in the mid-1930s, a polemical article by Henryk Erlich dating from 1935 (and written after Lestschinsky had published a piece critical of the Bund) notes that the Bund was always too "left" and too little "national" for Lestschinsky. H[enryk] Erlich, "Der 'forverts' un der 'bund,'" in *Der "forverts" un der "bund"* (New York: Bundisher klub in nu york, 1935), 18].

12. P. Shvarts, "Vos dertseylt unz di ankete fun yugnt-bund 'tsukunft'?" *Yugnt-veker* 9, no. 14 (July 1, 1930): 10.

13. The proportion of girls and of young women who reported that they prayed (5 percent of those surveyed) was far smaller. Lestschinsky, *Di yidishe arbeter-yugnt in poyln*, 18.

14. The younger the age of the respondent, moreover, the greater the differential. Of the 3,889 completed surveys, 328 were submitted by children younger than fourteen. Four surveys were completed by children under twelve who were part of the workforce.

These young respondents, I would note here, were certainly not in Tsukunft. The Sotsialistisher kinder farband (SKIF), the Bundist-oriented movement for children that was organized in 1926, was meant for those between the ages of twelve and sixteen. Once the SKIF was established, the Tsukunft tended to think of itself as a movement for those Jewish working youth who were too old to be *Skifistn* (members of SKIF).

Nevertheless, if we focus for a moment on the younger respondents to the Tsukunft's survey, those not likely to have been in the Tsukunft at the time that they filled out the questionnaires, we find data which may be even less hopeful from the perspective of the Tsukunft than the general results I have already cited. Seventy out of every one hundred of the younger respondents who lived in *shtetlekh* reported that they prayed, as did 82 percent of those who lived in large cities. In sum, the overwhelming bulk of those very young Jewish workers who replied to this survey were, to some extent, at least nominally religiously observant in the mid-1920s.

There are a number of plausible explanations as to why the youngest respondents were more likely than others to report that they prayed. The most probable, I suspect, is that while both younger and older respondents were likely to have been raised in more-or-less observant households, members of the younger demographic group were less likely to rebel against their parents than were older teens.

15. Shvarts, "Vos dertseylt unz di ankete fun yugnt-bund 'tsukunft'?" *Yugnt-veker* 9, no. 10 (May 1, 1930): 9.

16. Ibid., 8.

17. Lestschinsky notes that wages were generally lower among the very youngest Jewish workers than among somewhat older adolescents; that those young Jewish workers who worked in the large cities of Poland tended to earn significantly more than did those in small villages; that some jobs (such as those in textiles and printing) paid, on average, far more than others (such as those involving cleaning or jobs for house servants); and that boys generally received wages one- and-a-half times larger than did girls. Lestschinsky, *Di yidishe arbeter-yugnt in poyln*, 8–11.

18. P. Shvarts, "Vos lernt unz di ankete fun yugnt-bund 'tsukunft'?" *Yugnt-veker* 9, no. 12 (June 1, 1930): 7.

19. A. Y[ugnt] B[undist], "Avek mitn khuliganizm!" *Yugnt-veker* 2, no. 1 (Feb. 1, 1923): 9–10.

20. "Demoralizirte," *Yugnt-veker* 5, no. 1 (Jan. 1, 1926): 30.

21. "Yugnt-bund 'tsukunft' in poyln."

22. "Der 4ter tsuzamenfor fun yugnt-bund 'tsukunft,'" *Yugnt-veker* 4, no. 8 (Nov. 20, 1925): 6.

23. Pickhan, *"Gegen den Strom,"* 89.

24. *Arbeter tashn kalendar 1930.* Sots[ialistisher] yugnt-bibliotek, 7, n.p., 34. The same source claims that regarding the membership, 55 percent at that time was male, 91 percent were workers, and 4 percent were students. A survey done of the delegates to the fifth countrywide conference of the Tsukunft, held in 1929, provides additional demographic information on the Tsukunft's leading activists at that time. The survey was completed by seventy-nine of the ninety-three delegates to the conference. Seventy-three of those who replied were male, and six were female. Fifty-one respondents classified themselves as "workers," eleven as office or other kinds of employees, one as an agricultural worker, two as teachers, and six as professionals. Eight of those who replied seem to have been employed by the movement, in one way or another. Forty-seven had studied in a *kheder,* fifteen in a *talmud toyre,* twelve in a modern folk school run under Jewish auspices, seventeen in a state-sponsored school, seven in a trade school, fifteen in a middle school, four in either a university or a polytechnic school, seven in a yeshiva, and a small number of others in educational institutions of other kinds. Seventy-six could speak and write Yiddish, sixty-four could speak and write Polish, twenty-two had such abilities in German, fourteen in Hebrew, thirteen in Russian, and four in other languages. Some of the delegates to the conference of the Tsukunft had belonged to other movements before becoming Tsukunftistn. Of these, five had been in Hechalutz, one in Hashomer Hatsair, three in the Poalei Zion, three in the communist youth movement, and two in Fraye Yugnt (Hertz, *Di geshikhte fun a yugnt,* 283).

25. "Der yugnt-bund 'tsukunft'—oyfn 5tn ort in sots. yugnt internatsional," *Yugnt-veker* 16, no. 9 (Apr. 1, 1937): 3.

26. "Der 6-ter kongres fun sots. yugnt-internatsional," *Yugnt-veker* 18, no. 16 (Aug. 15, 1939): 3. Several post–World War II writers have reported that the Yugnt-bund tsukunft's membership ultimately reached as high as fifteen thousand (Yankef Kener, *Kvershnit [1897–1947]: Fragmentn fun zikhroynes, epizodn, geshikhtlekhe momentn, gedenkverter vegn umgekumene kedushim, martirer un kemfer* [New York: Tsentral komitet fun linke poyle-tsien in di fareynikte shtatn un kanade, 1947], 164; Bernshteyn, "Der 'bund' in poyln," 208). These estimates all but certainly exaggerate the size of the Bundist youth movement.

27. See, for example, the unpublished manuscripts submitted to the YIVO autobiographical contest of 1939 by "Tsukunftistka," who became a member of the Bundist youth movement in Maków-Mazowiecki after having earlier been a member of Hashomer Hatsair (YIVO Archives, RG 4-3749), and by Judka Fiksenbaum, who came to the Bundist movement from Betar (YIVO Archives, RG 4-3514).

28. Hertz, *Di geshikhte fun a yugnt*, 472. Shtral formally liquidated itself in 1938 (Michael Astour, *Geshikhte fun der frayland-lige un funem teritorialistishn gedank*, intro. L. M. Fruchtbaum [Frukhtboym] [Buenos Aires: Frayland lige, 1967], 1:102). See Kligsberg,"Di yidishe yugnt-bavegung in poyln," 236.

29. Aharon Shapiro, *Mentsh un goyrl* (Tel Aviv: Farlag i. l. peretz, 2002), 24.

30. Agudes's distress is mentioned by Pickhan, *"Gegen den Strom,"* 272.

31. Hertz, *Di geshikhte fun a yugnt*, 468. Levi Mendelson, one of the Arkadi Group's more notable speakers, is known to have studied at the yeshiva in Lublin (Aharon Shapiro, *Mentsh un goyrl*, 26] and may well have been the person responsible for attracting others who had also studied there. Writing more than half a century after the founding of the Arkadi Group, Mendelson mistakenly indicated that the group was established in the winter of 1934–35. L[evi] Mendelson, "Nokh vegn der arkadi-grupe in varshe," *Lebns-fragn* 38, no. 445–46 (May–June 1989): 11.

32. Shapiro claims that there was in fact an Arkadi Group in Lublin (Aharon Shapiro, "Zikhroynes fun der arkadi-grupe," *Lebns-fragn* 37, nos. 433–34 (May–June 1988): 8). In contrast, Mendelson notes that attempts made by himself and another member of the Warsaw Arkadi Group to establish comparable groupings in Lublin and in Zamość came to naught, reportedly because potential local recruits declined to remain involved when the organizers' activities became known to local circles affiliated with Agudes Yisroel. Mendelson, "Nokh vegn der arkadi-grupe in varshe," 11.

33. Nowogrodzki, *Jewish Labor Bund in Poland*, 292.

34. A. Bundist [Yehoshua Perle], "Mit khasidishn bren . . . (oyfn banket fun der arkadi-grupe)," *Naye folkstsaytung*, Jan. 5, 1938, 5.

35. Mendelson, "Nokh vegn der arkadi-grupe in varshe"; Bundist [Perle], "Mit khasidishn bren . . . "

36. "Fun unzer bavegung in galitsie," *Yugnt veker* 17, no. 24 (Dec. 15, 1938): 5.

37. In addition to *Yugnt-veker* and *Wolna Młodzież*, there was a third periodical issued in 1938–39 under Bundist auspices and directed at some members of Tsukunft: *Naye kultur:*

Tsaytshrift far fragn fun sotsialistisher oyfklerung un dertsiung. Five issues of the periodical appeared between the end of 1938 and the summer of 1939. Published jointly by the Central Committee of the Tsukunft and that of the SKIF, *Naye kultur* was meant for leaders and activists of both of these movements.

38. L. B., "Di 'tsukunft'-prese in poylish," undated clipping from *Yugnt-veker,* [1939], Bund Archives, MG 9-325.

39. Israel Oppenheim, *The Struggle of Jewish Youth for Productivization: The Zionist Youth Movement in Poland,* East European Monographs 273 (New York: Columbia Univ. Press, 1989), 69.

40. Astour, *Geshikhte fun der frayland-lige,* 1:139.

41. "Der 6-ter tsuzamenfor fun yugnt-bund tsukunft in poyln," *Yugnt-veker* 15, no. 9 (Apr. 15, 1936): 2; "Barikht fun v.k. fun y.b. 'tsukunft' fun merts 1935 yor biz yanuar 1937 y.," p.1, Bund Archives, MG 9-270; *Tsvey yor arbet un kamf: Barikht fun der varshever organizatsie fun yugnt-bund "tsukunft" in poyln. 1.I.1937—1.III.1939,* 1, Bund Archives, MG 9-269; "Konferents fun der varshever organizatsie fun yugnt-bund 'tsukunft,'" *Naye folkstsaytung,* May 1, 1939, 14.

42. The Tsukunft in Lodz, created in December 1918 (A. Wolf [Jasny] [Wolf Yasni], "20 yor 'tsukunft' in lodz," *Yugnt-veker* 18, no. 14 [July 15, 1939]: 10) seems not to have gone through the process of dramatic growth that characterized the history of the Tsukunft's Warsaw branch in the late 1930s. The Tsukunft in Lodz claimed to have three hundred members in 1929 ("Azoy zeen mir oys," *Lodzer sotsialistishe yugnt-shtime* [Jan. 11, 1929]: 7), more than 550 members in mid-1932 (Leybl, "'Royte' bloferayen vegn lodz," *Yugnt-veker* 11, no. 9 [Apr. 15, 1932]: 11), and boasted that it had eight hundred members in 1934 (A. Wolf [Jasny] [Volf Yasni], "15 yor 'tsukunft' in lodz," *Naye folkstsaytung,* Feb. 2, 1934, 7)—but claimed only seven hundred members in April 1939 (David Reyzman, "Bay der lodzer arbeter-yugnt," *Yugnt-veker* 18, no. 9 [May 1, 1939]: 15).

43. Pickhan, *"Gegen den Strom,"* 129.

44. *Tsvey yor arbet un kamf,* 1.

45. Bernshteyn, "Der 'bund' in poyln," 208. One specific, documented, example of the Tsukunft acting as a feeder group for the Bund involves the Tsukunft study group known as Prometheus, which met in Warsaw. A core member of the Prometheus circle who survived the Second World War has reported that "With time, the Prometheans got older and went from being members of the Tsukunft to being members of the Party: the students became members of the Bundist academic group Ringen, the workers entered the party groups for members of their trade, and little by little the meetings of the Promethean circle ceased" (Shoshke Erlich, "Dzielna 22," in *Leon oler: Zayn lebn un tetikayt* by Leon Oler [New York: Farlag unzer tsayt, 1973], 83–88. I have adapted, but not made full use of, the published English-language version of this passage: Shoshke Erlich, "Dzielna 22," in *Leon Oler: The Life of a Jewish Socialist,* by Leon Oler, ed. [Sofia] Dubnow-Erlich, trans. Hinda Oler Gutoff [Brookline, Mass.: n.p., 2006], 67–71). Not all of the members of the Promethean circle, Erlich adds, became party members. A majority of one-time Prometheans, however, did in fact remain affiliated with the Bund.

46. Hertz, *Di geshikhte fun a yugnt*, 344.

47. Chone Shmeruk, "Hebrew-Yiddish-Polish: A Trilingual Jewish Culture," in *The Jews of Poland* (see Introduction, note 4), 287. In 1931, Tsukunftistn led a campaign urging people to have themselves listed both as "without religion" and as having Yiddish as their mother tongue. Thus, some members of the Tsukunft may not have been included in the category of individuals of the Mosaic faith.

48. When, in 1939, the Tsukunft had 12,300 members, its size relative to the size of Polish Jewry was in all probability somewhat smaller. Though there are no official census figures for 1939, one scholar has estimated that the Jewish population was at least 3,460,000 at the point that the Second World War began (Marcus, *Social and Political History*, 173). If so, the Tsukunft had appromixately 28 members per 10,000 Jews in Poland at that point in time.

49. Hashomer Hatsair purportedly had 4,700 members in 1919 (Ezra Mendelsohn, *Zionism in Poland*, 130), but allegedly had 15,000 to 20,000 members in the prewar years (Kener, *Kvershnit*, 179). Another source suggests that Hashomer Hatsair had 21,000 members in Congress Poland in 1938 (N. Kantorowicz [Kantorovitsh], "Die tsienistishe arbeter-bavegung in poyln," *Yorbukh*, 152).

50. On one occasion, the *Yugnt-veker* denounced Hashomer as reactionary, nationalistic, and as "ostensibly revolutionary, in fact petty bourgeois," and also denounced Hashomer's periodicals as "full with typically petty bourgeois pretensions to socialism" (M. Z., "Der 'shomer-hatsair' demaskirt zikh," *Yugnt-veker* 12, no. 14 [July 1, 1933]: 7). However, the Bundist youth periodical did not devote sustained attention to critiquing Hashomer.

51. Mendelsohn, *Zionism in Poland*, 147; Kener, *Kvershnit*, 174, 202. According to the *Yugnt-veker*, the Central Committee of Yugnt had ceased to exist by the summer of 1938. L., "Der 'proletarisher'-tsienizm hot nisht kayn yugnt," *Yugnt-veker* 17, no. 14 {July 15, 1938]: 11.

52. Mendelsohn, *Zionism in Poland*, 328; Kener, *Kvershnit*, 178. Frayhayt was merged with Hekhalutz Hatsair in 1938 (Kligsberg, "Di yidishe yugnt-bavegung in poyln," 219). The figure of 7,000 members refers to the size of the Frayhayt prior to this merger. Afterward, the new, unified organization was known as Dror (N. Kantorowicz, "Die tsienistishe arbeter-bavegung in poyln," 144). Kantorowicz's claim that it had about 20,000 members is not corroborated. For additional detail on Frayhayt and on Hekhalutz Hatsair, see Leyb Shpizman, ed., *Khalutsim in poyln* (New York: Forsh-institut fun der tsionistisher arbeter-bavegung, 1959), 1:497ff.

53. In 1925, Herman Kruk, who was active in the Bund at that time, helped to establish a central cultural department for the Tsukunft. "The department's goals were to encourage young workers to undertake programmes of self-education and to offer them direction in their studies. One of his projects as secretary of the cultural department was the creation of *vander-bibliotekn* (mobile libraries), collections of books that were sent to various Bund-related organizations around the country in order to make educational materials more readily available to their members" (Ellen Kellman, *"Dos yidishe bukh alarmirt!* Towards the History of Yiddish Reading in Inter-War Poland," *Polin* 16 [2003]: 236). Kellman's fine article also contains material on other libraries run under Bundist auspices in Poland. These libraries were, obviously,

components of the Bundist counterculture to which my book is devoted. However, I will refer interested readers to Kellman's piece rather than rehearse the ground she has so ably covered.

54. Algemeyner yidisher arb.-bund "bund" in poyln, "Barikht tsum VItn tsuzamenfor 14, 15, un 16-II-1935, 1929–1935," Bund Archives, MG 2-443D, 61-65; *Tsvey yor arbet un kamf*, 7.

55. Leonard Rowe, "Jewish Self-Defense: A Response to Violence," in *Shtudies vegn yidn in poyln 1919–1939*, 147. Tsukunft-shturem was sparked by, and modeled on, the self-defense group of the Social Democratic Workers' Party of Austria, the Schutzbund, to which Blit was exposed at a meeting he attended in Vienna in 1929, and with which Blit maintained contact after he returned from Austria to Poland (Rowe, "Jewish Self-Defense," 143).

56. Kligsberg, "Di yidishe yugnt-bavegung in poyln," 137–228.

57. Pickhan, *"Gegen den Strom,"* 206.

58. A. Goldshmid, "Dos seksuele lebn fun der yugnt," *Yugnt-veker* 11, no. 17 (Aug. 15, 1932): 9.

59. A. Goldshmid, "Dos seksuele lebn fun der yugnt," *Yugnt-veker* 11, no. 18 (Sept. 1, 1932): 9.

60. S[ophia] Dubnow-Erlich, "Tsu a nayem lebns-shteyger," *Yugnt-veker* 13, no. 1 (Jan. 1, 1934): 6–7.

61. Bertell Ollman, *Social and Sexual Revolution. Essays on Marx and Reich* (Boston: South End Press, 1979), 161; Gruber, *Red Vienna*, 162.

62. Myron Sharaf, *Fury on Earth: A Biography of Wilhelm Reich* (New York: Da Capo Press, 1994), 142.

63. Sharaf, *Fury on Earth*, 134–35.

64. Gruber, *Red Vienna*, 162.

65. Victor Erlich, "Life with Grandfather," in *The Life and Work of S. M. Dubnow: Diaspora Nationalism and Jewish History*, ed. Sophia Dubnow-Erlich (Bloomington: Indiana Univ. Press, 1991), 250, 253.

66. He had moved from Vienna to Berlin in 1930, and had conducted work on sexual issues within the Communist Party of Germany, but he was expelled from that party early in 1933. Ollman, *Social and Sexual Revolution*, 192–93.

67. Sophia Dubnow-Erlich, *Bread and Matzoth*, trans. Alan Shaw (Tenafly, N.J.: Hermitage Publishers, 2005), 221–22. Tadeusz Boy-Żeleński (1874–1941) was the pseudonym of a prominent Polish gynaecologist, journalist, translator, and outspoken supporter of the legalization of abortion.

68. S[ophia] Dubnow-Erlich, "Di naye seksuele etik," *Yugnt-veker* 13, no. 2 (Jan. 15, 1934): 5.

69. S[ophia] Dubnow-Erlich, "Di seksuele oysleyzung fun der froy," *Yugnt-veker* 13, no. 7 (Mar. 15, 1934): 5. For additional information on Dubnow-Erlich's attitude toward prostitution, see S[ophia] Dubnow-Erlich, "Di yugnt un prostitutsie," *Yugnt-veker* 13, no. 21 (Oct. 1, 1934): 8–9.

70. Idem, "Egoizm un altruism in seksueln lebn," *Yugnt-veker* 13, no. 8 (Apr. 1, 1934): 4.

71. Idem, "Seksuele problemen in der sovietisher literatur," *Yugnt-veker* 13, no. 9 (Apr. 15, 1934): 8.

72. Idem, *Bread and Matzoth*, 223.

73. Ibid., 224.

74. Ibid., 225. The article to which Dubnow-Erlich is referring in this passage, "Dos perzenlekhe lebn un di svive," *Yugnt-veker* 14, no. 6 (Mar. 15, 1935): 4–5, was written as a result of Dubnow-Erlich's direct encounters with a seventeen-year-old girl, Gutka, who was active in the Tsukunft, had become pregnant, and had sought help from Dubnow-Erlich. Dubnow-Erlich had introduced Gutka to a physician, who had performed an illegal abortion. In the wake of the termination of her pregnancy, Gutka had become depressed and had also begun to fend off the young comrade who had impregnated her (and who wanted to continue to have a sexual relationship with Gutka). The other members of Gutka's Tsukunft branch, apparently aware of what had occurred, allegedly "bombarded her with reproaches and advice" (Dubnow-Erlich, *Bread and Matzoth*, 224). Gutka turned once again to Dubnow-Erlich and asked to be taken under her wing. Dubnow-Erlich, attempting to defend Gutka, made it clear that she believed that it was not permissible for the group to interfere in the personal life of one of its members in such a case. "The intervention of societal opinion in such cases is not normal," Dubnow-Erlich underscores in the piece sparked by Gutka's plight (though the piece protected Gutka's privacy by not revealing either her name or the local group with which she was affiliated). Significantly, at least one local youth leader ardently defended Dubnow-Erlich's perspective after having read her piece in *Yugnt-veker* (Dubnow-Erlich, *Bread and Matzoth*, 225).

75. Nina Tennenbaum Becker, "Leon Oler, Teacher and Spiritual Leader," in Oler, *Leon Oler: The Life,* 59–60. I have compared this translation with the Yiddish original: Nina Tennenbaum Becker [Tenenboym-beker], "Der lerer un der gaystiker firer," in *Leon oler: Zayn lebn,* by Oler, 74–75. The fact that Alexander (Olek) Erlich was a member of Oler's study group is mentioned by Henry Greenbaum, "To the memory of a Teacher and Friend," in *Leon Oler,* 151 (Henry Greenbaum [Henri Grinboym], "Tsum ondenk fun a lerer un fraynt," in *Leon oler,* 178).

76. Interview of Shoshke Erlich conducted by Ellen Kellman, Apr. 18, 1986. My thanks to Professor Kellman for providing me with a copy of this interview.

77. Kligsberg, "Di yidishe yugnt-bavegung in poyln," 137–228; Michael C. Steinlauf, "Jewish Politics and Youth Culture in Interwar Poland. Preliminary Evidence from the YIVO Autobiographies," in *Emergence of Modern Jewish Politics,* 95–104.

78. Autobiography of S. Frejlich, Autobiographies of Jewish Youth in Poland, RG 4-3601, YIVO Archives, 131, 156.

2. SKIF: The Bundist Children's Movement

1. Early versions of portions of this chapter were delivered as papers at a conference entitled "Polish Jewry 1918–1939: Life-worlds, Self-understanding and Political Conduct," sponsored by the Simon-Dubnow-Institut für jüdische Geschichte und Kultur, Leipzig, Germany, on December 13, 1999, and on February 28, 2000, before the seminar on Jews in the Russian Empire, École des Hautes Études en Science Sociales, Paris. My thanks to the participants in these events for their feedback.

2. A. Vayner (Abrashe), "Der kleyner bund," *Yugnt-veker* 24 (Nov. 1, 1937): 13.

3. Hertz, *Di geshikhte fun a yugnt*, 20 (citing Papiernikov's Russian-language study on the history of the youth movement in Poland, which was published in Kharkov in 1925).

4. A. Litvak [Khayim-Yankef Helfand], *Vos geven: Etiudn un zikhroynes* (Vilna: Farlag fun b. kletskin: 1925), 212.

5. There were regional conferences in certain areas such as Minsk and Kovne (J[acob] S. Hertz, "Di ershte ruslender revolutsye," in *Di geshikhte fun bund*, 2:440).

6. "Yidn in youston gibn op koved a yidisher kultur-tuerin tsu ir 100stn geboyrnyor," *Forverts* (May 4, 1990): 16.

7. Litvak, *Vos geven*, 218.

8. See Henry J. Tobias and Charles E. Woodhouse, "Revolutionary Optimism and the Practice of Revolution: The Jewish Bund in 1905," *Jewish Social Studies* 47 (1985): 135–50, on the mood in the Bund during this era.

9. *Di letste pasirungen* 1, no. 12 (July 4, 1905): 4.

10. Litvak, *Vos geven*, 214.

11. Ish Katan, "Kinder-shpilen fun 'kleynem bund,'" *Der arbayter* (May 2, 1908): 4.

12. Hertz, "Di ershte ruslender revolutsye," 442.

13. A. K. Elenboygn, "Lublin in unzer tsayt," *A[rbeter] r[ing] lubliner young men's br. 392. 25 yoriger yubileyum 1909–1934* ([New York?]: Tsentrale yidishe bibliotek un prese arkhiv, [1934]), 24.

14. Moyshe Faynkind, "Khane sore gants," *Yugnt-veker* 14, no. 16 (July 15, 1935): 10.

15. Litvak, *Vos geven*, 219.

16. Ibid., 220.

17. Yankl Levin, *Fun yene yorn. "Kleyn bund"* (Minsk: Beltrespetshat, 1924), 25.

18. Litvak, *Vos geven*, 217.

19. Moise Katz [Moyshe Kats], *A dor, vos hot farloyrn di moyre: Bleter zikhroynes fun arum 1905* (New York: Moyshe kats yubiley-komitet, 1956), 247.

20. Hertz, *Di geshikhte fun a yugnt*, 49.

21. Levin, *Fun yene yorn*, 39.

22. Hertz, *Di geshikhte fun a yugnt*, 57.

23. *Posledniia izvestiia* 254 (Oct. 17, 1905), as cited in Hertz, *Di geshikhte fun a yugnt*, 33. Cf. Vayner, "Der kleyner bund."

24. The composition of the Kleyner bund in Polotsk, where the group was made up of twelve- to fifteen-year-old boys, some of whom were students and others workers, is discussed in Neytn Rozen, "Iberlebungen fun a 'kleyenem bundist' (derinerungen fun vilne, vitebsk un polotsk)," *Unzer tsayt* 12 (Dec. 1943): 31.

25. W[iktor] Szulman [Viktor Shulman], *Bletlekh geshikhte fun der yidisher arbeter-bavegung* (Warsaw: Farlag "di velt," 1929), 92–95. Membership figures from Warsaw provide a telling indicator of the extent to which the Bund declined. In 1906, the Bund in Lodz had had sixteen-hundred members eligible to vote for delegates to the Bund's Congress. In 1910, there

were no more than one hundred such members, of whom only seventy bothered to exercise their mandate. Henry J. Tobias and Charles E. Woodhouse, "Political Reaction and Revolutionary Careers: The Jewish Bundists in Defeat, 1907–10," *Comparative Studies in Society and History* 19 (1977): 377.

26. Tobias and Woodhouse, "Political Reaction," 393.

27. Tobias, *The Jewish Bund in Russia*, 351.

28. Zvi Gitelman, *Jewish Nationality and Soviet Politics*, 185–89.

29. Hertz, *Di geshikhte fun a yugnt*, 51.

30. Ibid., 58.

31. "Yidn in youston gibn op koved," 16.

32. Litvak, *Vos geven*, 218.

33. B. Charney Vladeck [Vladek], "Tsvey yinglekh," in *B. vladek in leben und shafen*, ed. Ephim Jeshurin [Yefim Yeshurin] (New York: "Forverts" association, 1936), 156–57; Dovid Kasel, *Meirke fun "kleynem bund,"* Sotsialistishe yugnt-bibliotek, vol. 4 (Lodz: Tsentralkomitet fun yugnt-bund "tsukunft," 1947).

34. Esther [Frumkin], "Forvort," in Levin, *Fun yene yorn*, 8.

35. *Tashn-kalendar mayn khaver 1930*, Skif bibliotek, vol. 2 (Warsaw: 1930). Among those who participated in these meetings were the Tsukunft activists Yoysef Lifshits, Leon Oler, Moyshe Kligsberg, Ruta Berman of the YAF (Jewish Worker-Woman), the teachers Leah Halpern, Gershon Zaltsman, and Yulian Vielikovski, and the Bundists Leyvik Hodes, Yankef Pat, and Abram Stoler (Emanuel Patt [Pat], "Mir zaynen yung un dos iz sheyn: Leyvik hodes un der sotsialistisher kinder-farband 'skif,'" in *Leyvik hodes: Biografie un shriftn* (New York: Farlag unzer tsayt, 1962), 344]. For biographical information on Oler see *Leon oler: Zayn lebn*. On Halpern and on Vielikovski see Kh. Sh. Kazdan, ed., *Lerer-yizkhor-bukh. Di umgekumene lerer fun tsysho shuln in poyln* (New York, [1954]), 128–29, 151–53. For information on Lifshits and Zaltsman, see Hertz, *Doyres bundistn*, 3:80–88, 145–49. On Patt, see Emanuel Patt [Pat], *In gerangl: Yankef pat un zayn dor* (New York: Yankef pat familie fond, 1971). The new organization was initially called "SKIB" (Sotsialistisher kinder-bund) but changed its name shortly after it was created (Hertz, *Di geshikhte fun a yugnt*, 292).

36. Patt, *In gerangl*, 220; "Referat vegn di problemen un tsushtand fun der skif-arbet gehaltn oyf der land-baratung fun di skif-tuer dem 19-tn april 1931," Bund Archives, MG 9-243.

37. In 1928, Hodes indicated that the children belonging to SKIF at that time were between the ages of twelve and sixteen (L[eyvik] Hodes, *Materialn un onvayzungen far der sotsialistisher dertsiung-arbet*, Skif bibliotek, vol. 1 [Warsaw] [1928]: 6). In 1930, an official publication of the SKIF suggests that Skifistn who became fourteen or fifteen were expected to graduate into the Tsukunft *(Tashn-kalendar mayn khaver 1930*, 39). One revealing talk delivered in 1936 notes (disapprovingly) that it had become common in the smaller *shtetlekh* to allow teenagers as old as eighteen to remain in SKIF (A. Kdusman, "Skif arbet in kleynem shtetl," *Ershter land tsuzamenfor fun "skif" in poyln [varshe, 1–3 oktober 1936]*, Skif-bibliotek, vol. 4 [Warsaw: Farlag skif-bibliotek, 1937], 61). A letter from the leaders of SKIF to the Jewish Labor Committee

in New York written in 1939 claims that SKIF had members as young as nine. Y[ankef] Patt, L[eyvik] Hodes, and K[almen] Vapner to the Jewish Labor Committee, Apr. 20, 1939, Bund Archives, MG 9-243.

38. Hertz, *Di geshikhte fun a yugnt,* 290. On TSYSHO see Kh. Sh. Kazdan, *Di geshikhte fun yidishn shulvezn in umophengikn poyln* (Mexico City: Gezelshaft "kultur un hilf," 1947), and Kh. Sh. Kazdan, "Di shul- un kultur-tetikayt," in *Di geshikhte fun bund*, 4:287–388. The work and ideology of TSYSHO in the early 1920s is also discussed in Mendelsohn, *Zionism in Poland*, 198–205.

39. Y[osl] Mlotek, "Der 'skif' in poyln," *Yugnt-veker* 7 (n.d.): 15 (Bund Archives, MG 9-243).

40. Patt, *In gerangl*, 222.

41. Executive of the Central Committee of the General Jewish Workers' Bund in Poland, "Tsirkular nr. 7," Warsaw, Jan. 1927, Bund Archives. This circular had not yet been fully accessioned, and thus did not yet have a file number, when I made use of it. In an apparently otherwise accurate talk delivered at a countrywide meeting of SKIF activists in 1931 and meant for internal consumption, the claim was made that there had not been a directive of any kind to form SKIF organizations ("Referat vegn di problemen un tsushtand fun der skif-arbet"). The January 1927 circular demonstrates that this claim was incorrect. It is not out of the question that it was made for ideological or political reasons— that is, in order to be able to assert that SKIF grew in response to a need perceived from below (as had the Kleyner bund in Czarist Russia) rather than as a result of a decision made by the Bund's leaders.

42. For Kazdan's considered opinion on the positive relationship between the TSYSHO schools and the SKIF, see Kazdan, *Di geshikhte fun yidishn shulvezn in umophengikn poyln*, 308.

43. F. Melman, "Di arbet fun skif in unzere shuln un tsvishn di shiler fun unzere shuln," *Ershter land tsuzamenfor fun "skif" in poyln*, 17ff. Leah Halpern, a Bundist who participated in the meetings leading to the formation of the SKIF, was the long-term director of the TSYSHO-affiliated Groser-shul in Warsaw.

44. Patt, *In gerangl*, 222.

45. In 1929 there were 17,780 children attending TSYSHO primary schools (folk-shuln) (Kazdan, *Di geshikhte fun yidishn shulvezn in umophengikn poyln*, 186). Forty percent of the TSYSHO schools in Congress Poland were dominated by the Left Poalei-Zion in 1921 (Mendelsohn, *Zionism in Poland*, 205). The number of students in these schools is not known.

46. Heller, *On the Edge of Destruction*, 223.

47. A directive dated December 31, 1931, sent by the SKIF's central office to SKIF locals in the midst of a campaign to enroll new members urges the locals to place particular emphasis on enrolling children in "the state [*powszechne*] schools, traditional Jewish religious schools [*khedorim*], schools of the Jewish community [*gmina-shuln*], etc." ("Arbets-plan farn 'skif' oyf yanuar 1932," Bund Archives, MG 9-243).

48. Hertz, *Doyres bundistn*, 2:399.

49. Executive of the Central Committee of the General Jewish Workers' Bund in Poland, "Tsirkular nr. 7."

50. Hertz, *Di geshikhte fun a yugnt*, 290. Elka Yonas, "Skif-arbet tsvishn arbeter-kinder un gasn-kinder," *Ershter land tsuzamenfor fun "skif" in poyln*, 26.

51. Bernard Goldstein [Goldshteyn], *Tsvantsik yor in varshever "bund" 1919–1939* (New York: Farlag unzer tsayt, 1960), 93–95.

52. Yonas, "Skif-arbet," 23.

53. Emanuel Patt (Yankef's son) was named secretary of the SKIF in 1933. Kalmen Vapner took over Emanuel's role in 1936. See Patt, "Mir zaynen yung un dos iz sheyn," 345. Vapner, born in 1913, joined SKIF in 1927. He was a graduate of the Vilna Real Gymnasium and also had an engineering degree from Cannes. See the entry by M[oyshe?] K[ligsberg?] on Vapner in *Doyres bundistn*, 2:483–85. Emanuel Patt, Yankef Patt, and Hodes all survived the Second World War. Vapner did not (Paie Wapner-Lewin [Vapner-levin], *Mayn flikht tsu dertseyln: Derinerungen fun a lererin in vilner geto* [Buenos Aires: Memoria, 1999], Yiddish section, 100).

54. Patt, *In gerangl*, 221.

55. Kazdan and Hodes edited the *Kleyne folkstsaytung*, which first appeared in October 1926, at later points in its history. The *Kleyne folkstsaytung* generally appeared once a week, within the Friday edition of the *Naye folkstsaytung*. Its articles tended to be very short. Works by prominent adult writers—including such figures as Sholem Asch, Leib Kvitko, Mani Leib, and Avrom Reisen—and by young children appeared in its pages. The supplement also published Yiddish translations of creative works by Polish and Russian writers (P[inkus] Shvarts, "Folkstsaytung," in *Fun noentn over*, vol. 2 [New York: Alveltlekher yidisher kultur-kongres, 1956], 350–53).

56. Sophia Dubnow-Erlich, "Dos lebn fun leyvik hodes," in *Leyvik hodes: Biografie un shriftn*, 9ff.

57. "The Social Democratic youth movement" in the Weimar Republic "consisted of a series of organizations for different age levels: the Nest Falcons (6 to 10), the Young Falcons (10 to 12), the Red Falcons (12 to 14), the Socialist Workers' Youth (14 to 20), and the Young Socialists (18 to 25), the last being for young members of the adult party" (Richard N. Hunt, *German Social Democracy 1918–1933* [Chicago: Quadrangle Books, 1970], 50). A group that also used the name Red Falcons was created in Austria in 1926 under the auspices of the Social Democratic Workers' Party.

58. Hodes, *Materialn un onvayzungen far der sotsialistisher dertsiung-arbet*, 3.

59. Hodes, "Di ideologie fun sotsialistishn scouting," *Ershter land tsuzamenfor fun "skif" in poyln*, 40–47.

60. The SKIF summarized its core principles in twelve so-called commandments, the most revealing of which read: "The Skifist is a member of the family of workers. . . . The Skifist is loyal and devoted to the new Jewish culture," and "The Skifist is a friend and supporter of nature." *Tashn-kalendar mayn khaver 1930*, 35.

61. "1 yor sotsialistishe dertsiungs-arbet fun varsh. 'skif' 1938/39," hectographed, 1939, Bund Archives, MG 9-245.

62. The SEI responded to the SKIF's invitation by sending Willi Hocke, an activist based in Bodenbach, Czechoslovakia *(Die Falken Organisationen in Ost- und Mitteleuropas von 1923*

bis Heute [Brussels: IFM-SEI]). Hocke's remarks at the SKIF conference are summarized in *1-ter land tsuzamenfor fun "skif" in poyln*, 10–12.

63. Mario Kessler, "The Bund and the Labour and Socialist International," in *Jewish Politics in Eastern Europe*, 183–94. Leon Oler, who was active in SKIF affairs, was also a prominent "tsveyer." *Leon oler: Zayn lebn*, 24–25.

64. K[almen] Vapner, "Mir gehern tsum 'bund,'" *Khavershaft* (Nov. 1937): 11.

65. Chava Rosenfarb, "An Oak Has Fallen," in *Bono Wiener Remembered* [Dos bono viner gedenkbukh] (Montreal: privately published, 1997), 24. She immediately adds, however, that "the monotony of the meals went hand-in-hand with a daily dose of laughter and enjoyment."

66. For reports by a prominent adult Bundist on his visits to SKIF camps see Goldstein, *Tsvantsik yor in varshever "bund,"* 240–42, 327–28.

67. Executive of the Central Committee of the General Jewish Workers' Bund in Poland, "Tsirkular nr. 7," Jan. 1927, Bund Archives.

68. Hodes, *Materialn un onvayzungen far der sotsialistisher dertsiung-arbet*, 13–16.

69. "Referat vegn di problemen un tsushtand fun der skif-arbet."

70. *Tashn-kalendar mayn khaver 1930*, 32.

71. "Referat vegn di problemen un tsushtand fun der skif-arbet."

72. Ibid. Although Hashomer was larger than the SKIF, it was considered by the latter to be a bourgeois organization and thus not competing for the same constituency.

73. *Helfer* (SEI) 1934/9 as cited in *Die Falken Organisationen in Ost- und Mitteleuropas von 1923 bis Heute*.

74. *Helfer*(SEI) 1936/5 as cited in ibid.

75. Perec Zylberberg, "This I Remember," published by the Concordia Univ. Chair in Canadian Jewish Studies, volume 2, entry written on July 18, 1993, http://migs.concordia.ca/memoirs/zylberb/zyl_2.html. In 1929–30 Communists in Warsaw repeatedly disrupted the work of the evening school—aimed at children and youth who had been forced to drop out of other schools in order to work—located at Miła 51 (which was not formally run by the SKIF, but which was Bundist-oriented and attracted many twelve- and thirteen-year-olds). Communists massed at the entrance of the evening school, ran into classrooms, yelled out catcalls, broke windows, and harassed students and teachers leaving the courses at the end of the evening. Goldstein, *Tsvantsik yor in varshever "bund,"* 159–60.

76. Kalmen [Vapner], "Unzere groyse nitskhoynes, *Kleyne folkstsaytung*, June 2, 1939.

77. Y[ankef] Patt, L[eyvik]Hodes, and K[almen] Vapner to the Jewish Labor Committee, Apr. 20, 1939, Bund Archives, MG 9-243. In the final period of its existence in interwar Poland, the SKIF organized distinct divisions within itself. The youngest children, aged ten to eleven, were grouped in "Mikhalevitsh's eyniklekh." Those who were eleven and twelve were in the "Yung-falkn." Those older than twelve were in the "Royte falkn." Emanuel Patt [Pat], *Di skif grupn. Loyt dem proyekt, vos iz gevorn ongenumen oyf dem plenum fun der skif-tsentrale dem 15-tn november 1937. Hant-bikhl far skif-helfer* (Warsaw: Farlag skif-bilbiotek, 1938), 1.

78. It is far from coincidental that individuals who had been members of SKIF—for example, Asie Big, Yurek Blones, Yanek Bilak, Stashek Brilianshtayn, Tobtshe Davidovitsh, Gabriel Frishdorf, Dovid Hokhberg, Yisroel Mitlman, Melekh Perlman, Hershl Posesorski, Soreh Rozenboym, and Velvl Rozovski—went on to play significant roles in the resistance movement during the Second World War. The spirit of SKIF encouraged these young men and women to actively resist when possible. For biographical information on Skifistn who were involved in the resistance movement during the war, see Hertz, *Doyres bundistn*, 2: passim.

3. Morgnshtern: A Bundist Movement for Physical Education

1. My thanks to Samuel Kassow, for providing me with access to materials in his possession, and for discussing the history of the Left Poalei Zion with me; to Diethelm Blecking, for providing me with a copy of his work on Jewish sport in Poland between the two world wars prior to publication; and to Roni Gechtman, for sending me a copy of his Ph.D. dissertation, "Yidisher Sotsializm." Blecking's piece has subsequently been published as "Marxism Versus Muscular Judaism—Jewish Sports in Poland," in *Sport and Physical Education in Jewish History: Selected Papers from an International Seminar Held on the Occasion of the 16th Maccabiah. Wingate Institute, Israel July 12–15, 2001,* ed. George Eisen, Haim Kaufman, and Manfred Lämmer (Wingate Institute, Israel: 2003), 48–55. Portions of the relevant chapter of Gechtman's dissertation have appeared as Roni Gechtman, "Socialist Mass Politics though Sport: The Bund's Morgnshtern in Poland, 1926–1939," *Journal of Sport History* 26, no. 2 (summer 1999): 326–52, and as idem, "Playing on the Left Wing," *Jewish Socialist* 47 (winter 2002–3): 24–26. I have benefitted from Gechtman's fine analysis of Morgnshtern—an analysis that largely corroborates my own.

2. I have adapted the section of this chapter devoted to the history of Jewish sports movements in Eastern Europe from Jack Jacobs, "The Politics of Jewish Sports Movements in Interwar Poland," in *Emancipation Through Muscles: Jews and Sports in Europe*, ed. by Michael Brenner and Gideon Reuveni (Lincoln, Neb.: Univ. of Nebraska Press, 2006), 93–105.

3. Minutes of a meeting of the YIVO Branch for the Jewish Sports Movement suggest that the oldest Jewish sports club operating in Poland in the late 1930s had been founded in 1901. However, the minutes do not indicate the location in which this club had been created and thus leave open the possibility that it had been located in part of the Austro-Hungarian Empire rather than the Russian Empire at the time of its establishment. Minutes [of the YIVO Branch for the Jewish Sports Movement], May 5, 1937, RG 29, file 86, YIVO Archives.

4. There is a large literature dealing with the emergence of Jewish sports movements in the German-speaking lands. See Toni Niewerth and Lorenz Peiffer, "'Jüdischer Sport in Deutschland'—eine kommentierte Bibliografie," *SportZeit* 1, no. 2 (2001): 81–106.

5. Shtern traced its ancestry back to a group known as Spartakus, which was established in Warsaw by the Labor Zionist youth organization Yugnt in 1920 (P. Frim, "Fun varshever arbeter sport-klub 'shtern,'" *Di fraye yugnt* 5, no. 2 [Feb. 1928]: 18). The name Spartakus was meant to invoke the memory of the German Marxist group with which Rosa Luxemburg had been closely

identified during the First World War, and which had founded the Communist Party of Germany in 1918. In 1923 the Polish Jewish sports group Spartakus united with a group made up of middle school students that called itself *Gwiazda*—the Polish word for star—and this union began to refer to itself as the Shtern [Star] Workers' Sport Club. The creation of the Shtern club in Warsaw gave an impetus to the establishment of similar groups in other areas of Poland. The Shtern group in Lodz—Poland's second largest city, and a city with a particularly large number of Jewish workers—was organized around 1925 and began to operate around 1926. By 1928, it had a gymnastics section, a soccer section with fifty active members, and a table tennis section. The bulk of the Lodz group's leadership at that time was made up of members either of the Left Poalei Zion or of the youth movement of that party (B. R., "Fun lodzer sport-klub 'shtern,'" *Di fraye yugnt* 5, no. 5 [May 1928]: 17; see "Rirevdike tetikayt fun lodzer sport-klub 'shtern,'" *Arbeter-tsaytung* 5, no. 8 [Feb. 21, 1930]: 10). In the mid-1930s, however, a political dispute within the ranks of the labor zionist movement led to the dismantling of the Shtern branch in Lodz. A new sports club, Typhoon, acted as a de facto replacement for the earlier club. A. Lagerist, "Prekhtiker derfolg funm sport-lager funm lodzer 'tyfun,'" *Arbeter-tsaytung* 10, no. 24 (June 14, 1935): 8; B. Sh., "Unzer sport-bavegung in lodz er reyon," *Arbeter-tsaytung* 10, no. 35 (Aug. 30, 1935): 6; M., "Opklangen fun der 'aktivistisher' provokatsie kegn lodzer 'shtern,'" *Arbeter-tsaytung* 10, no. 40 (Oct. 11, 1935): 7; "Erev dem turn-yontef fun lodzer 'tyfun,'" *Arbeter-tsaytung* 11, no. 6 (Feb. 7, 1936): 6. Reports by local Shtern groups were regularly printed in the labor zionist press.

6. Kantorowicz, "Die tsienistishe arbeter-bavegung in poyln," *Yorbukh*. The leaders of Hapoel were Meyer Peker, Dov and Mietek Zilberman, and Khayim Glavinski.

7. Dovid Rogoff, "Sport in vilne," *Forverts* (Sept. 8, 2000): 20.

8. "An onfrage tsum varshever sport-klub 'samson,'" *Arbeter-sportler* 5 (Nov. 1, 1929): 7.

9. Borukh Yismakh, "Sports Clubs and Self-Defense," in *From A Ruined Garden: The Memorial Books of Polish Jewry*, ed. Jack Kugelmass and Jonathan Boyarin (New York: Schocken Books, 1983), 61. Yismakh's piece was first published in 1964.

10. The group in Cracow, Jutrzenka, was active even before the First World War (Hertz, "Der bund in umophengikn poyln, 1926–1932," 136). In this section, I have drawn on Jack Jacobs, "Creating a Bundist Counter-Culture: Morgnshtern and the Significance of Cultural Hegemony," in *Jewish Politics in Eastern Europe*, 59–68.

11. B. Goldshtayn, *Tsvantsik yor in varshever "bund" 1919–1939* (New York: Farlag unzer tsayt, 1960), 127. The leadership of TOZ was well aware of the Bundist sympathies of those participating in these gymnastics groups. See [Moses Kligsberg], "Der 'morgnshtern,'" unpublished typescript, Moses Kligsberg Collection, RG 719, Box 15, Folder 416, 340, YIVO Archives.

12. Sh. Tsharnetski, "Unzere sportler marshirn faroys (der ershter tsuzamenfor fun unzere sport-organizatsies)," *Yugnt-veker* 8, no. 10 (May 15, 1929): 4.

13. Khayim Pizshits, the long-term chairman of Morgnshtern's central governing body, was a member of the Warsaw Committee of the Bund in the years immediately preceding the beginning of the Second World War (Hertz, "Dr. khayim un renie pizshits," in *Doyres bundistn*, 2:323). Shmuel Kruk (a.k.a. Pinkas Shvarts, a member of the Central Committee

of the Tsukunft), Leon Feiner (a member of the Bund's Central Committee), Leybl Fridman (secretary of the countrywide Morgnshtern and, at one time, secretary of the Tsukunft), Morris Gelborn (who had been secretary of the sport groups that had operated under the auspices of TOZ prior to the creation of Morgnshtern), Zalmen Friedrich (a one-time secretary of the Warsaw Morgnshtern and a writer of the weekly sport page in the *Naye folkstsaytung*), Moses Kligsberg (a chairman of the Warsaw Morgnshtern and a member of Tsukunft's Central Committee), and Shloyme Notkovski (who served, at one point, as secretary of the Warsaw Tsukunft, and who was chairman of the Warsaw Morgnshtern after Kligsberg) were also particularly notable leaders of Morgnshtern (Kligsberg, "Der 'morgnshtern,'" 342).

14. These were not, however, the only activities—or types of activities—conducted under Morgenshtern's auspices. Table tennis and chess, for example, also attracted some support.

15. Gechtman, "Socialist Mass Politics though Sport," 343.

16. The following section of this chapter, comparing the activities and orientations of the Bundist movement for physical education and its Left Labor Zionist equivalent is derived in large part from Jack Jacobs, "Jewish Workers' Sports Movements in Interwar Poland: Stern and Morgnshtern in Comparative Perspective," in *Jews, Sports and the Rites of Citizenship*, ed. Jack Kugelmass (Urbana and Chicago: Univ. of Illinois Press, 2007), 114–28.

17. On the Left Poalei Zion see, above all, Bine Garntsarska-Kadari, *Di linke poyle-tsien in poyln biz der tsveyter velt-milkhome* (Tel Aviv: Farlag i. l. peretz, 1995), and the excellent article by Samuel Kassow, "The Left Poalei Tsiyon in Inter-War Poland," in *Yiddish and the Left*, ed. Gennady Estraikh and Mikhail Krutikov. Vol. 3, European Humanities Research Center Studies in Yiddish (Legenda: Oxford, 2001), 109–28.

18. The emblems of both the Arbeter-gezelshaft far fizisher dertsiung "morgnshtern" in poyln (Robotnicze Stowarzyszenie Wychowania Fizycznego "Jutrznia" w Polsce) and that of the Arbeter-gezelshaft far fizisher dertsiung "shtern" (Robotnicze Stowarzyszenie Wychowania Fizycznego "Gwiazda") featured a line drawing of a naked male figure reminiscent of a Greek statue and engaged in athletic activity. The discus-throwing figure in the Shtern emblem appears in front of belching smokestacks—as does the javelin-throwing figure in Morgnshtern's emblem. Both the Morgnshtern and the Shtern emblem contained the organization's name in Yiddish and in Polish.

19. One case led Morgnshtern to accuse Shtern of using money and promises of posts to lure members. A commission of the Warsaw Workers Sports Association investigated the actions of Shtern in this matter and recommended that it be strongly reprimanded ("'Linker poyle-tsienizm' un sport," *Naye folkstsaytung*, Nov. 3, 1930, 5); Cf."Bundisher onfal oyf unzer sport-bavegung," *Arbeter-tsaytung*, Nov. 7, 1930, 6. Another case involved one-time members of the Warsaw Morgnshtern table tennis section, which apparently had leadership and organizational difficulties in 1937–38 (Arbeter-gez. far fizisher dertsiung "morgnshtern" in poyln. Varshever optaylung. *A yor arbet: Tetikayts-berikht far der tsayt fun II.1 1937 bizn II.1 1938*, 23 [Bund Archives, MG 9-158]). Other former members of Morgnshtern's table tennis section joined the Hashmoneans during this same period.

Table tennis was taken quite seriously during this era. All of the champion players in Poland of the interwar period came from Jewish clubs (Diethelm Blecking, "Der jüdische Sport in Polen zwischen den Weltkriegen," unpublished paper). Its widespread popularity among Shtern members provoked at least some dissent within Labor Zionist ranks. "Our pious grandfathers" were better swimmers than the "ping-pong" players of today, griped a Left Labor Zionist (M. Koyavski, "Shotn-zaytn funm arbeter-sport," *Arbeter-kultur: Eynmolike oysgabe tsum 2tn kultur-kongres. 30, 31 oktober un 1ter november 1931*, 45). The table tennis ("ping-pong") devotees don't get enough fresh air, he continued. They ought to skate or sled instead of devoting so much time to an indoor game. Moreover, he noted, the rise of the so-called sport of ping-pong had been accompanied by a widespread decline in educational and cultural work, by the virtual disappearance of comrades versed in sociology and labor history, and the rise of the "intellectual cripple." "This is not an exceptional occurrence in one city or shtetl. Entire regions of the movement are poisoned by this and similar sport-plagues" (44).

20. I. R-g, "Di yudishe sport-bavegung: A gesprekh mit'n dr' pribulski," *Sport-tsaytung* 2 (July 15, 1924): 4.

21. In 1931, Shtern leaders agreed to demand that all affiliated local sports clubs produce posters and notices in Yiddish (as well as Polish) (*Arbeter-tsaytung* 6, no. 43 [Nov. 6, 1931]: 7). Precisely because Morgnshtern was ideologically committed to Yiddish, it was a concern in the late 1920s that there was not a universally accepted set of Yiddish terms used by its ping-pong players. Morgnshtern took steps to create a list of acceptable terms ("Yidishe terminologie far ping-pong," *Arbeter-sportler* 5 [Nov. 1, 1929]: 7).

22. Arb[eter] gezelshaft far fizisher dertsiung "morgnshtern" in poyln, optaylung in lodz, "Vendung," Lodz, Feb. 1931, Bund Archives, MG 9-159.

23. Shtern membership book of Bolek Lemberger (RG 28, folder 60, YIVO Archives). The book also contains a selection of edifying quotes from Karl Marx and Ber Borochov. For additional insight into the relevant views of Left Labor Zionists toward the goals and tasks of a workers' sports movement see I. A-tsh, "Arbeter-sport," *Arbeter kultur* (Sept. 28, 1928): 4; "Di oyfgabn fun arbeter-sport," *Arbeter-tsaytung* 5, no. 23 (July 11, 1930): 6.

24. Kligsberg, "Di yidishe yugnt-bavegung in poyln," 221–22. There were Poalei Zionists who argued that soccer and boxing were not proletarian sports. The leadership of Shtern, however, replied that there was no such thing as a proletarian sport. "The bourgeois or proletarian character [of a sports movement] depends only on who leads the sport organization and on its goals." *Arbeter-tsaytung* 6, no. 43 (Nov. 6, 1931): 70.

25. Frim, "Fun varshever arbeter sport-klub 'shtern,'" 18.

26. "Varshever turney fun der 'n. folkstsaytung," *Arbeter-sportler* 3 (Sept. 1, 1929): 1.

27. Opposition to soccer was apparently stronger in the Czech workers' sports organization than in Morgenshtern. However, the Czechs too eventually came around and permitted soccer within their ranks. Similarly, there were principled arguments made against soccer by Austrian socialists. Nevertheless, in 1926, the organized workers' soccer organization of Austria formally affiliated with the Arbeiterbund für Sport und Körperkultur in Oesterreich.

The Austrian workers continued to play soccer after that date; they merely forswore matches with bourgeois clubs. Wolfgang Maderthaner, "Sport für das Volk," in *Die ersten 100 Jahre. Österreichische Sozialdemokratie 1888–1988*, ed. Helene Maimann (Vienna, Munich: Verlag Christian Brandstätter, 1988), 175.

28. Tsharnetski, "Unzere sportler marshirn faroys," 4.

29. *Arbeter-gez. far fizisher dertsiung "morgenshtern" in poyln. Varshever optaylung. A yor arbet. Tetikayts-berikht far der tsayt fun II.1 1937 bizn II.1 1938*, 21.

30. Frim, "Fun varshever arbeter sport-klub 'shtern,'" 18.

31. Natan, "Kh. sh. rotholts boks-mayster fun poyln," *Arbeter-tsaytung* 8, no. 17 (Apr. 28, 1933): 5. Rotholts went on to win widely noticed victories over three German boxers. As a result, the Nazis removed these boxers from the German national boxing team. Letter to the editor by Ben Tsheisin, *Forverts*, Mar. 9, 2001, 21.

32. Nekhamia, "Boks un der arbeter-sport (diskusie artikl)," *Arbeter-tsaytung* 8, no. 17 (Apr. 28, 1933): 5.

33. *A yor arbet. Tetikayts-berikht far der tsayt fun II.1 1937 bizn II.1 1938*, 21. See Mik, "Boks derobert birger-rekht," *Der nayer arbeter-sportler* (June 1937): 7.

34. [Kligsberg], "Der 'morgnshtern,'" 341.

35. Heller, *On the Edge of Destruction*, 208.

36. "An endek, an antisemit iz a bafulmekhtiker fartreter fun bundishn sport-klub in vlotslovek," *Arbeter-tsaytung* 4, no. 8 (Feb. 22, 1929): 7.

37. "Fun arbeter-sport," *Arbeter-tsaytung* 5, no. 43 (Oct. 24, 1930): 8; "Bundisher onfal oyf unzer sport-bavegung," 6.

38. "Linker poyle-tsienizm un sport," *Naye folkstsaytung*, Nov. 3, 1930, 5.

39. "Bundisher onfal oyf unzer sport-bavegung," 6.

40. "Fun arbeter-sport in varshe," *Arbeter-tsaytung* 6, no. 11 (Mar. 13, 1931): 8.

41. Frim, "Fun varshever arbeter sport-klub 'shtern,'" 18. In 1933, the Women's Section of the Warsaw Shtern conducted a recruitment campaign ("Verbir-aktsie fun arb. froyen-sportlerins," *Arbeter vort* 11 [May 10, 1935]: 5). Shtern urged women to enter the workers' sports movement because women suffer from "capitalist oppression and exploitation." It encouraged women to "become healthy free people" in part through "the collective creation of the workers' sports movement." "Di arbeter-froy in di reyen fun der arb. sport-bavegung," *Arbeter vort* 11 (May 10, 1935): 5.

42. *Arbeter-gezelshaft far fizisher dertsiung "morgnshtern" in poyln. Varshever optaylung. 1938. Yor barikht*, p. 7, Bund Archives, MG 9-158.

43. A. V. "Di proletarishe sport-bavegung," *Di fraye yugnt* 5, no. 1 (Jan. 1928): 17. Titlman and Yitskhok Gotlib (1902–73) were elected as representatives of Shtern to the managing committee of ZRSS in October 1927. In 1929, Dr. Ber Opnhaym (b. 1892) of the Shtern was elected to the presidium of the third congress of the ZRSS, and served as vice chairman in the presidium ("Arbeter-sport kongres," *Arbeter-tsaytung* 4, no. 6 [Feb. 8, 1929]: 7; "Driter kongres fun arbeter-sport-farband in poyln," *Arbeter-tsaytung* 4, no. 7 [Feb. 15, 1929]: 6). For

biographical information on Gotlib, Opnhaym, and other Shtern activists, such as Dr. Hersh Liberman, see Shlomo Schweizer [Shloyme Svaytser], ed., *Shures poyle-tsien: Portretn* (Tel-Aviv: I. l. peretz farlag, 1981).

44. The governmental agency responsible for physical education also had responsibility for military education and preparation. Shtern leadership worried that the influence of this agency, therefore, might lead to the militarization of the workers' sports movement, and to the "fascistifacation" of young workers. "Der aroystrit fun 'shtern' forshteyer in z.r.s.s. kegn der militarizirung fun di sport-klubn," *Arbeter-tsaytung* 4, no. 35 (Aug. 23, 1929): 7.

45. *Arbeter-tsaytung* 6, no. 43 (Nov. 6, 1931): 7. See A. V-s, "Finf yor arbeter-sport-farband," *Arbeter-tsaytung* 5, no. 10 (Mar. 7, 1930): 6. Relations between the ZRSS and the Shtern deteriorated in the late 1930s. "6ter kongres fun arbeter-sport-farband in poyln," *Arbeter-tsaytung* 12, no. 11 (Mar. 12, 1937): 6, 8.

46. Morgnshtern began negotiations with the Polish workers' sport organization over merger conditions right after Morgnshtern was organized as a countrywide movement (Kligsberg, "Der 'morgnshtern'," 342). A representative of the Morgnshtern, Lucjan Blit, greeted the ZRSS at the third congress of the ZRSS in 1929, pointed to the continuing divisions within Poland among workers' sports movements, and proclaimed that he hoped that these movements would work together for common goals in the near future (Driter kongres fun poylishn arbeter-sport-farband," *Naye folkstsaytung*, Feb. 17, 1929, 4). Blit's greeting was described by a Labor Zionist reporter as having made a "pitiful impression" (N., "Driter kongres fun arbeter-sport-farband in poyln," *Arbeter-tsaytung* 4, no. 7 [Feb. 15, 1929]: 6). A small number of Bundist delegates attended the sixth congress of the ZRSS ("6ter kongres fun arbeter-sport-farband in poyln," 6). None bothered to attend the seventh congress, at which twenty-four of the 140 delegates represented Shtern, and two delegates represented Hapoel. "Der 7ter kongres fun arbeter-sport-farband in poyln," *Arbeter-tsaytung* 14, no. 4 (Feb. 10, 1939).

47. Abraham Brumberg, "The Bund and the Polish Socialist Party in the Late 1930s," in *The Jews of Poland*, 75–82; Piotr Wróbel, "From Conflict to Cooperation: the Bund and the Polish Socialist Party, 1897–1939," in *Jewish Politics in Eastern Europe*, 161–65.

48. A. V., "Di proletarishe sport-bavegung," 17.

49. Gechtman, "Socialist Mass Politics though Sport," 336–37.

50. *Arbeter-gezelshaft far fizisher dertsiung "morgnshtern" in poyln. Yidishe sektsie fun arbeter sport internatsional. Varshever optaylung. Barikht fun der tsayt 1.II.1936-1.II.1937*, Bund Archives, MG 9-158.

51. Goldshtayn, *Tsvantsik yor in varshever "bund" 1919–1939*, 222. See Hertz, "Der bund in umophengikn poyln, 1926–1932," 90–91. The First International Workers Olympics had been held in Frankfurt am Main in 1925, before the creation of Morgnshtern and when Shtern was still in its infancy.

52. "Der 5ter internatsionaler sotsialistisher sport-kongres in prag," *Arbeter-tsaytung* 4, no. 44 (Oct. 25, 1929): 2.

53. "Fun arbeter sport bavegung," *Arbeter-tsaytung* 6, no. 24 (June 12, 1931): 8. A report in the newspaper of the Left Poalei Zion on the Vienna Workers Olympics accused the Olympics' organizers of having transformed the mass of worker athletes into a "golem of clay, without a trace of proletarian soul," pointed out that contingents in the various parades organized in conjunction with the Olympics lacked appropriate political slogans, and claimed that the delegation from Morgnshtern was scarcely in evidence. N. N. "Arbeter-olimpiada in 'roytn' vin," *Arbeter-tsaytung* 6, no. 32 (Aug. 21, 1931).

54. Almost two hundred members of Shtern were in its delegation to the third Workers Olympics (I. Gotlib, "Der yungster tsvayg fun unzer bavegung," *Arbeter-tsaytung* 14, no. 7 [Mar. 3, 1939]: 21). The ZRSS chose not to participate because it objected to the presence of representatives of the Soviet Union ("Z.r.r.s. tsit zikh tsurik fun der arbeter-olimpiade," *Arbeter-tsaytung* 12, no. 26 [June 25, 1937]: 5).

55. Hertz, *Di geshikhte fun a yugnt*, 208.

56. "Der ershter 'shtern' tsuzamenfli," *Arbeter-tsaytung* 8, no. 22 (June 2, 1933): 1.

57. "Farkhasmet dem lokal fun 'shtern,'" *Arbeter-tsaytung* 12, no. 16 (Apr. 16, 1937): 7. A newspaper article dating from 1935, in contrast, suggests that although local units of the Left Poalei Zion had been subjected to legal pressure, Shtern may not have been under quite as much pressure: "In many places the workers' societies for physical culture are the only legal workers' organizations." I. K., "In shelikhes fun klas!" *Arbeter-vort* 8–9 (Apr. 19, 1935): 7.

58. "A reaktsionere hetse kegn dem a. s. k. 'shtern,'" *Arbeter-tsaytung* 5, no. 15 (Apr. 11, 1930): 10.

59. "The management of the Workers Sports Association endeavors to instill comradely relations, but does not always succeed and workers sports competitions are sometimes disrupted by the appearance of anti-Semitism." Melekh, "Antisemitizm in sport," *Arbeter-tsaytung* 10, no. 39 (Oct. 4, 1935): 6.

60. I have adapted this paragraph from my paper, "Jews and Sport in Interwar Vilna," delivered at the conference "Jewish Space in Central and Eastern Europe: Day-to-day History," which was sponsored by the Center for Studies of the Culture and History of East European Jews and held in Vilnius in May 2006.

61. Information in this section is derived primarily from the questionnaire distributed by YIVO's "Optsvayg far der yiddisher sport-bavegung," submitted by the "Arbeter gezelshaft far fizisher dertsiung 'morgnshtern' in poyln, vilner opteylung," and accessioned by the YIVO on January 19, 1936 (RG 1.1, File 600, YIVO Archives).

62. The class composition of the Vilna Morgnshtern differed dramatically from that of Maccabi Vilna's rowing section, first established in 1925, which was, at some points in time, the largest section of the latter organization. At least in its early years, the rowing section was characterized by the fact that it was highly attractive to Jewish professionals. Doctors, lawyers, journalists, and engineers made up a notable portion of its membership ("Brief fun vilna," *Haynt*, June 7, 1926). The employment distribution of Vilna's Jewish community in the 1920s and 1930s is briefly discussed in Arcadius Kahan, "Vilna: The Sociocultural Anatomy of a Jewish Community in Interwar Poland," in *Essays in Jewish Social and Economic History*, ed. Roger Weiss (Chicago: Univ. of Chicago Press, 1986), 151.

63. Vilna Morgnshtern had received subsidies earlier in its history. A published notice points out that the city had lowered the size of Morgnshtern's grant for 1930–31 from 2,000 zl. to 625 zl. *(Arbeter-sportler* 2, no. 5 [10] [June 10, 1930]: 1). I became aware of this and specific other sources dealing with Vilna Morgnshtern as a result of my examination of notes gathered by Yisroel Zajd (Yisroel Zajd Collection, RG 1467, YIVO Archives).

64. At other points in time, Vilna Morgnshtern had sections devoted to table tennis, light athletics, and other activities ("Banayte arbet fun vilner 'morgnshtern," *Naye folksaytung*, Jan. 18, 1932, 5). Though neither soccer nor boxing were emphasized by Vilna Morgnshtern, it did sponsor soccer teams *(Arbeter-sportler* 2, no. 5 [10] [June 10, 1930]: 1).

65. Sh. Khaykin, "Birgerlekher un proletarisher sport in vilne," *Naye folkstsaytung*, Nov. 20, 1933, 7.

66. "Di algemeyne farzamlung fun 'morgnshtern' in vilne," *Naye folkstsaytung*, Mar. 16, 1936, 5.

67. I explore explanations as to why Vilna Morgnshtern remained smaller than Vilna Maccabi in "Jews and Sport in Interwar Vilna."

68. See the questionnaire completed by the Lublin Morgnshtern in 1935 (RG 29, File 86, YIVO Archives) and the ones completed by the Morgnshtern branches in Włocławek and Piotrków in 1936 (RG 1.1, File 600, YIVO Archives).

69. *Naye optaylung. Arbeter gezelshaft far fizisher dertsiung "morgnshtern" in poyln, optaylung in lodz*, March 1939, p. 3, Bund Archives, MG 9-159.

70. "Alg. farz. fun varshever 'shtern,'" *Arbeter-vort* 2 (Jan. 24, 1936): 6.

71. Mor., "Der 'morgnshtern' geyt faroys," *Yugnt-veker* 6, no. 8, (Apr. 15, 1927): 10; Tsharnetski, "Unzere sportler marshirn faroys," 4; *Beckmanns Sport Lexikon A–Z* (Leipzig, Vienna: Verlagsanstalt Otto Beckmann, 1933), col. 1370; Hertz, *Di geshikhte fun a yugnt*, 445.

72. [Bundisher klub in nu york], "Vegn di atakes ofn 'bund' in tsuzamenhang mit dem kempeyn fun yidishn arbeter komitet," [Apr. 1937], 4, Jewish Labor Committee Records, Robert F. Wagner Labor Archives, Wagner 025, Box 9, file 23, Tamiment Library, New York University Libraries, New York (hereafter referred to as Tamiment).

73. "Dem 'morgnshtern'—unzer grus," *Naye folkstsaytung*, May 25, 1939, 6. See "Der ershter sakhakl," *Naye folkstsaytung*, May 29, 1939, 5, which adds that there was not a Morgnshtern local affiliate in Piotrków.

74. Kh[ayim] Pizshits and Z[almen] Friedrich to [Jewish] Labor Committee, July 7, 1938, Bund Archives, MG 9-289.

75. "Farendikt driter land-tsuzamenfor fun 'morgnshtern,'" *Naye folkstsaytung*, May 26, 1939, 11.

76. Morgnshtern had more trouble in Lodz than it did in Warsaw. The Lodz branch was formally established at the end of 1927 (Hertz, *Di geshikhte fun bund in lodz*, 345; Cf. L.-en., "Yidisher arbeter-sport in lodz," *Lodzer sotsialistishe yugnt-shtime* [Jan. 11, 1929], 10). The branch seems to have had 535 dues-paying members in 1935 (Arbeter gezelshaft far fizisher dertsiung "morgnshtern" in poyln, opteylung in lodz, "Kase-barikht far der kadents fun der farvaltung fun yanuar 1935 biz detsember 1935," [Collection of the Algemeyner Yidisher

Arbeyter Bund in Lite, Poylen, un Rusland 'Bund,' folder 326, International Institute of Social History, Amsterdam]). In February 1937, however, Lodz Morgnshtern was forced to close because of purported engagement in illegal fund-raising activities (Hertz, *Di geshikhte fun bund in lodz*, 416). Weeks later, the countrywide organization opened a new Morgnshtern local in Lodz, which, by the end of 1937, had five hundred active members (419). The branch claimed to have increased its membership total to 658 by mid- 1938 *(Tetikayts-barikht.* "Morgnshtern" *optaylung in lodz. 31 mai 1937 bizn 1 marts 1938*, Bund Archives, MG 9-159). In March 1939, it claimed a total of 680 affiliates, of whom 436 were active adult members, 142 were youth members, and 102 were passive members *(Naye optaylung. Arbeter gezelshaft far fizisher dertsiung* "morgnshtern" *in poyln, optaylung in lodz*, March 1939, p. 3, Bund Archives, MG 9-159.

77. Arbeter-gezelshaft far fizisher dertsiung "morgnshtern' in poyln (yidishe sektsie fun arbeter sport internatsional). Varshever optaylung, "Barikht tsu der alg. farzamlung dem 14-tn fevruar 1936 far der tsayt fun 1. II. 1935—1. II. 1936," RG 29, file 86, YIVO Archives.

78. Arbeter-gezelshaft far fizisher dertsiung "morgnshtern" in poyln. Yidishe sektsie fun arbeter sport internatsional. Varshever optaylung, "Barikht fun der tsayt 1.II.1936-1.II.1937," Bund Archives, MG 9-158.

79. Arbeter-gez. far fizisher dertsiung "morgnshtern' in poyln. Varshever optaylung, *A yor arbet. Tetikayts-barikht far der tsayt fun II.1 1937 bizn II.1 1938.*

80. "Yerlekhe alg. farzamlung fun varshever 'shtern,'" *Arbeter-tsaytung* 14, no. 2 (Jan. 27, 1939): 2.

81. On October 1, 1936, there were sixty-three members of the Morgnshtern group of the Warsaw Bund. On January 1, 1939, there were seventy-one men and women who were members. Algemeyner yidisher arbeter-bund "bund" in poyln. Varshever komitet, "In yor fun groysn val-zig. Materialn tsu der shtotisher konferents fun der varshever organizatsie fun 'bund,'" Feb. 1939, Bund Archives, MG 2-293.

4. The Medem Sanatorium

1. I presented a paper on the Medem Sanatorium at a conference on "The Cultural Geography of Modern Yiddish," sponsored by the University of Haifa and held in Haifa in December 2006. I have written this chapter around the core formed by that paper.

2. See Kazdan, *Di geshikhte fun yidishn shulvezn in umophengikn poyln*, 18–371; Nathan Cohen, "The Bund's Contribution to Yiddish Culture in Poland between the Two World Wars," in *Jewish Politics in Eastern Europe*, 114–17.

3. Mendelsohn, *The Jews of East Central Europe between the World Wars*, 64. "Although the Bund was the largest faction in [TS]YSHO, and even though one of its senior leaders always headed it, it never attained a majority there." Gorny, *Converging Alternatives*, 90.

4. To be sure, the Medem Sanatorium was not directly comparable to the SKIF, Tsukunft, or Morgnshtern in certain respects. The sanatorium was a single entity, not an organization or movement.

5. The grouping that established this colony was known as the Dinezon Committee because of the pivotal role played earlier by Yankef Dinezon (ca. 1856–1919) in activities on behalf of Yiddish schools (Kh[ayim] Sh[loyme] Kazdan, *Fun kheder un "shkoles" biz tsysho: Dos ruslendishe yidntum in gerangl far shul, shprakh, kultur* [Mexico City: Shloyme mendelson fond bay der gezelshaft far "kultur un hilf," 1956], 416). The committee's role in the establishment of the colony in Otvosk was mentioned by Vladimir Medem, "Kinder vos zaynen farmishpet tsum toyt," *Forverts,* Apr. 19, 1922, 4.

6. The board consisted of Sh. Abramson, Dr. B. Ayzenshtat, Dr. A. Broyde-Heler, Dr. A. Kruk, Dovid Meyer, and Shloyme Fayvish Gilinski (Sh[loyme] Gilinski, "Medem-sanatoria. Fun oyfbli—bizn heylikn umkum," in *Medem-sanatorie-bukh,* ed. Kh[ayim] Sh[loyme] Kazdan [Tel Aviv: Farlag "Hamenora," 1971], 20). Several of these directors had, or developed, direct ties to the Bund. Dr. Broyde-Heler was already active in the Bund during the years of the First World War (S[ophia] Dubnow-Erlich, "Dr. ana broyde-heler," in *Doyres bundistn,* 2:141). Dovid Meyer was elected to the Central Committee of the Bund in Poland in 1919 (Hertz, "Der bund in umophengikn poyln, 1918–1925," 75). See below for information on Gilinski's ties to the party.

7. Medem, "Kinder vos zaynen farmishpet tsum toyt," 4; Kazdan, "Di medem-sanatorie in miedzeszyn," in *Medem-sanatorie-bukh,* ed. Kazdan, 39.

8. In 1923, while the renovations in Miedzeszyn were still under way, a temporary sanatorium for children was established elsewhere under the leadership of Dr. Kruk (Kazdan, "Di medem-sanatorie in miedzeszyn," 40). Approximately seventy children threatened by tuberculosis were admitted to this provisional entity (Lola Brumberg, "Derinerungen fun a sanitarin," in *Medem-sanatorie-bukh,* 151). Like its predecessor, however, it too was forced to close for lack of funds.

9. Brumberg, "Derinerungen fun a sanitarin," 151.

10. A document written by a trusted leader of the sanatorium and apparently dating from 1937 indicates that the presidium of the sanatorium was made up of four individuals: Yekutiel Portnoy, Shloyme Mendelson, Shloyme Gilinski, and Yoysef Brumberg. The same document lists the members of the sanatorium's managing committee as Portnoy, Mendelson, Gilinski, Brumberg, Dr. Ana Broyde-Heler, Menakhem Rozenbaum, L Klok [*sic*], Yitzkhok Giterman, Leova Neustadt, and Ludwik Honigwil ([Yoysef Brumberg], "Tsu der redaktsie fun yidishn gezelsh. leksikon," 1937, 2 (Bund Archives, M 12-30, item 460). The individual listed as Klok was Lozer Klog, a well-known activist in trade union circles. Klog was elected to the Warsaw City Council on the Bundist list in the last election to precede the Second World War (Hertz, "Lozer Klog," in *Doyres bundistn,* 2:66). Giterman, a leading figure in the Joint Distribution Committee in Warsaw, was not a Bundist (Daniel Blatman, *For Our Freedom and Yours: The Jewish Labour Bund in Poland 1939–1949,* trans. Naftali Greenwood [London; Portland, Ore.: Vallentine Mitchell, 2003], 22, 78). All of the other individuals listed by Brumberg were members of the party. An article written in the postwar era by Menakhem Rozenbaum lists Dr. Natalia Shpilfogel-Likhtenbaum, who was not a Bundist, as a member of the executive of the sanatorium, but does not indicate the years she held such a position (Menakhem Rozenbaum,

"A mitglid fun der sanatorie-farvaltung dertseylt," in *Medem-sanatorie-bukh*, 157]. Cf. the lists of members of the sanatorium's governing bodies given by Kazdan, "Di medem-sanatorie in miedzeszyn," 50, and idem, "Di shul- un kultur-tetikayt," in *Di geshikhte fun bund*, 4:330. Though the lists of members provided by Kazdan in these sources overlap, and also overlap with the list provided by the sources listed above, they are not identical.

11. Portnoy's life and work are discussed in Gertrud Pickhan, "Kossovsky, Portnoy and Others: The Role of Members of the Bund's Founding Generation in the Interwar Polish Bund," in *Jewish Politics in Eastern Europe*, 71–74.

12. The fact that Noyakh took a hands-on role in the running of the sanatorium is evidenced by the fact that he is known, during specific periods of the its history, to have conferred with the sanatorium's administrators by telephone on a daily basis. When he believed it to have been necessary, he had more than one such phone conversation per day. Rozenbaum, "A mitglid fun der sanatorie-farvaltung dertseylt," 157, 159. See Sh[loyme] Gilinski, "Yozef der forzitser fun unzer kinder-sanatorie," *Unzer tsayt* 10 (Nov. 1941): 44–45.

13. Kazdan, *Lerer-yizkhor-bukh*, 558.

14. *Leksikon fun der nayer yidisher literatur*, vol. 6 (New York: Alveltlekher yidisher kultur-kongres, 1965), cols. 43–47; *Shloyme mendelson. Zayn lebn un shafn* (New York: Farlag unzer tsayt, 1949).

15. Kh[ayim] Sh[loyme] Kazdan, "Der shul-un kultur-tuer," in *Shloyme mendelson*, 61.

16. Kh[ayim] Sh[loyme] Kazdan, "Shloyme feyvish gilinski," in *Doyres bundistn*, 3:109–15; *Leksikon fun der nayer yidisher literatur*, vol. 2 (1958), cols. 216–18.

17. Emanuel Patt [Pat], "Gilinski mayn lerer, mayn khaver, mayn patsient," in *Medem-sanatorie-bukh*, 287. Details on the perspective of the *tsveyer* may be found in Leon Oler, "Di linke rikhtung in bund fun poyln," in *Khmurner-bukh* (New York: Farlag unzer tsayt, 1958), 9–44, and in Abraham Brumberg, "The Bund: History of a Schism," in *Jewish Politics in Eastern Europe*, 81–89.

18. *Leksikon fun der nayer yidisher literatur*, vol. 1 (1956), col. 455.

19. Abraham Brumberg, "Mayn foters 10 yor in der medem-sanatorium," in *Medem-sanatorie-bukh*, 304.

20. Kh[ayim] Sh[loyme] Kazdan, "Yoysef brumberg," in *Medem-sanatorie-bukh*, 299–301.

21. Among those who taught at the sanatorium at various points in time in the 1920s and/or 1930s were: Yisroyel Biber, Mendl Blumental, Miriyam Brumberg-Gavenda, Motl Gilinski, Reyzl Graievski, Hershl Grinboym, Beti Gumener-Nutkevitsh, Zisl Gutman, Liuba Kantorovitsh-Gilinski, Yoysef Kats, Fela Lindeman-Vinik, Yitzkhok Man, Zundl Mandelbroyt, Khane Pishtshatsher-Man, Sonie Pludermakher-Vaysbrot, Menukhe Rabinovitsh, Yente Ruvin-Fishman, Rifke Savitsh, Gitl Segalovitsh-Kats, Leah Tempel, Yankl Trupianski, and Khane Zakheym. Biographical details on many of the sanatorium teachers may be gleaned from *Lerer-yizkhor-bukh*. This work does not include information on the small number of teachers who survived the Second World War.

22. Motl Gilinski, Graievski, Kats, Yitzkhok Man, Mandelbroyt, Pishtshatsher-Man, Pludermakher-Vaysbrot, Segalovitsh-Kats, and Trupianski were all graduates of the seminary. Biber was a teacher in and a director of the seminary beginning around 1924 *(Lerer-yizkhor-bukh,* 43, 92, 112–13, 180, 236–37, 283, 316, 372; *Medem-sanatorie bukh,* 234). After Vladimir Medem's death, the seminary was renamed in his honor (Kh[ayim] Sh[loyme] Kazdan, "Vl. medem un di yidish-veltlekhe shul," in *Vladimir medem tsum tsvantsikstn yortsayt* [New York: Amerikaner reprezentants fun algemeynem yidishn arbeter-bund ("bund") in poyln, 1943], 167). The year of the seminary's founding is noted in Kh. Pupko, "Vilna—dos vigele fun der yidish-veltlikher shul," in *Vilna,* ed. Ephim N. Jeshurin (New York: Vilner brentsh 367 arbeyter ring, 1935), 303. See A. Golomb, "Di lerer seminarn fun der tsysho," in *Lerer-yizkhor-bukh,* 506–13. Though named after a Bundist, the Yiddish Teachers Seminary was not a Bundist institution. In addition to the Bundists in attendance, there were individual students with Labor Zionist and Communist sympathies, as well as students not affiliated with any political party. Yekhiel Shtern, a Labor Zionist, served for three years as the student-selected representative to the seminary's Pedagogical Council. Both Bundists and non-Bundists taught at the seminary (Arthur Lermer, "Zikhroynes vegn dem vilner lerer-seminar," in *Un dokh—dem morgnroyt antkegn. Eseyen* [Tel Aviv: I. L. Peretz, 1999], 193–97).

23. Brumberg-Gavenda, Motl Gilinski, Graievski, Grinboym, Gutman, Kats, Mandelbroyt, Pishtshatsher-Man, and Trupianski all fall into this category.

24. Sh[loyme] Gilinski, "Dr. anna broydo-heler," in *Lerer-yizkhor-bukh,* 64–66. Other doctors closely associated with the sanatorium at one point or another, and who were not necessarily affiliated with the Bund in any way, included Anna Gotslav, Shaul Grosboym, Helena Kelson, Benyomin Kovarski, Tole Mints, Tsilina Rozengartn, and Natalia Shpilfogel-Likhtenboym (*Lerer-yizkhor bukh,* 10, 558; Kazdan, "Di medem-sanatorie in miedzeszyn," 51).

25. Kazdan, "Di medem-sanatorie in miedzeszyn," 56.

26. Gilinski, "Medem-sanatorie. Fun oyfbli—bizn heylikn umkum," 32.

27. Kazdan, "Di medem-sanatorie in miedzeszyn," 56.

28. Perl Vaysnberg, "Di medem-sanatorie," in *Medem-sanatorie-bukh,* 344.

29. Goldstein, *Tsvantsik yor in varshever "bund" 1919–1939,* 124.

30. Ibid., 159–60.

31. The dispute involving the Medem Sanatorium and a Communist-dominated trade union representing certain members of its staff was regularly reported on (from a Bundist perspective) in the party's Warsaw-based newspaper. See, for example, "Onfal fun komunistn oyf der medem-sanatorie," *Naye folkstsaytung* (Dec. 5, 1930): 2; "Vos azoyns kumt for in medem-sanatorie?" ibid. (Dec. 7, 1930): 4; "Vos hert zikh in der medem-sanatorie?" ibid. (Dec. 8, 1930): 5; "Derklerung fun der medem-sanatorie," ibid. (Dec. 9, 1930): 5; "Makht a sof tsu di komunistishe shand-tatn!" ibid. (Dec. 15, 1930): 4; "Derklerung fun pedagogish-meditsinishn personel in medem-sanatorie," ibid. (Dec. 15, 1930): 5.

32. For a contemporary account of events written from a perspective sympathetic to the sanatorium, see the flyer titled "Tsu di yidishe arbetndike masn," signed by the "Yidishe

shul-organizatsie hoyptfarvaltung," Algemeyner Yidisher Arbeyter Bund in Lite, Poylen, un Rusland 'Bund' Collection, folder 326, International Institute of Social History, Amsterdam. A non-Bundist newspaper, *Haynt*, reported that shots were fired both by the strikers and by those defending the sanatorium, and that it had not been determined who had fired first ("A nayer onfal oyf di medem-sanatorie," *Haynt*, Feb. 13, 1931). This account was not confirmed by the report in *Der moment* ("Blutiger onfal oyf'n yud. kinder-sanatorium in miedzeszyn," *Der moment*, Feb. 13, 1931, 12). The latter was not a Bundist organ. See "Pogrom-onfal fun di 'royte' oyf der medem-sanatorie," *Naye folkstsaytung* (Feb. 13, 1931): 2.

33. Goldstein, *Tsvantsik yor in varshever "bund" 1919–1939*, 161–65; *Medem-sanatorie-bukh*, 166–72.

34. [Shloyme Gilinski], *Vi azoy lebt dos kind in medem-sanatorie* (Warsaw: Farvaltung fun medem-sanatorie, 1932), 3.

35. "2278 kinder in sanatorie," *Kleyne folkstsaytung*, Sept. 5, 1930. Seventy two of the 2,278 children had come to the institution from Lodz, twenty-nine from Vilna, and twenty-six from Pinsk. The other children were from twenty-eight additional locations. See *Medem-sanatorie bukh*, 456.

36. Gezelshaft "kinder sanatorie," *Zun, likht un freyd far undzere kinder!* (Warsaw: [1938]), 3.

37. Brumberg, "Derinerungen fun a sanitarin," 152. Brumberg was given administrative responsibility for the questionnaire project and continued to fill that role until 1939.

38. A copy of the questionnaire is in the Bund Archives, M 12-35.

39. [Gilinski], *Vi azoy lebt dos kind in medem-sanatorie*, 4. There is detailed data available on the occupations of the parents of the 1,860 children who stayed at the sanatorium in the first three-and-a-half years of its existence. Just over 1,000 of these children had parents who were skilled workers (of whom the single largest numbers were in the garment, leather, and food industries). Two hundred fifty children had parents who were clerical employees. The parents of 150 of the children were professionals of one kind or another. Exactly 87 children had parents who were unskilled workers. More than 300 children came from families in which parents were employed as artisans, small shopkeepers, or in some other capacity. Liebmann Hersch, "The People's Preventorium for Children at Miedzeszyn [Poland]," *Annals of Public and Cooperative Economics* 5, no. 2 (May 1929): 195–97; "Medem-sanatorie (kurtser barikht)," ca. 1929, p. 2, Bund Archives, M 12-35.

40. Kinder sanatorie u. n. vl. medem in miedzeszyn, "Barikht tsu der 22-ter planir sesie fun der yidisher shul-organizatsie," p. 2, Mar. 26, 1938, Bund Archives, M 12-30, item 391.

41. Though the town of Miedzeszyn did not have electricity, drains, or water mains, the Medem Sanatorium itself had all three. Hersch, "The People's Preventorium," 197.

42. [Gilinski], Vi azoy lebt dos kind in medem-sanatorie; [Shloyme Gilinski], "Kristlekhe kinder in medem-sanatorie in miedzeszyn bay varshe," Bund Archives, p. 3, M 12-34.

43. Gilinski, "Kristlekhe kinder," 2.

44. [Yoysef Brumberg], "Tsu der redaktsie fun yidishn gezelsh. leksikon," p. 2, Bund Archives, M 12-30, item 460.

45. Gilinski, "Kristlekhe kinder," 1.

46. Contact between the children of Polish coal miners and those of the sanatorium is depicted in the film *Mir kumen on*.

47. Kinder sanatorie u. n. vl. medem in miedzeszyn, "Barikht tsu der 22-ter planir sesie fun der yidisher shul-organizatsie." There were approximately 500,000 Jewish school-aged children in Poland at most points in the interwar era. At least 80 percent of them attended schools run by the Polish government in which Polish was the language of instruction. A much smaller number attended bilingual (Polish/Hebrew or Polish/Yiddish) schools. In the late 1930s, the Horev Schools (Orthodox schools for boys) had a total of 49,000 students. Tarbut Schools (which were Zionist and Hebraist) had some 45,000 students. There were 35,500 girls in ultra-orthodox Beys Yankef schools. Yavneh (with which schools both Zionist and religiously observant affiliated) enrolled 16,000. The Shul-Kult (Right Labor Zionist–dominated) network had just over 2,000 students, and TSYSHO-related institutions contained approximately 16,486 students (Miriam Eisenstein, *Jewish Schools in Poland 1919–39. Their Philosophy and Development* [New York: King's Crown Press, 1950], 96). There is an extensive literature on Jewish schools in interwar Poland. See, for example, Nathan Eck, "The Educational Institutions of Polish Jewry (1921–1939)," *Jewish Social Studies* 9, no. 1 (Jan. 1947): 3–32; Aryeh Tartakower, "Di yidishe shul in poyln tsvishn tsvey milkhomes," in *Sefer ha-shanah/Yorbukh* (Tel Aviv: Velt federatsie fun poylishe yidn, 1967), 2:210–65; Shimon Frost, *Schooling as a Socio-Political Expression* (Jerusalem: Magnes Press, The Hebrew Univ., 1998), and the sources cited in these works.

48. Y[oysef] Rotenberg, "Der gayst fun an institutsie," in *Medem-sanatorie-bukh*, 214.

49. Liuba Kantorovitsh-Gilinski, "Shloyme gilinski un di medem-sanatorie," in *Medem-sanatorie-bukh*, 186.

50. Typical schedules are reproduced in *W słońcu i radoś ci: dziecko w Sanatorjum im Wł. Medema w Miedzeszynie* (Warsaw: Zarzą du Sanatorjum dla Dzieci im. Wł. Medema, 1933), 16–17.

51. Y[oysef] Giligitsh, "Zeks vokhn in kindershn gan-eden," in *Medem-sanatorie-bukh*, 129.

52. Yosl Mlotek, "Vi azoy iz geshafn gevorn 'der shpeykhler,'" in *Medem-sanatorie-bukh*, 135.

53. In the words of one of the sanatorium's teachers, "The focal point of the work lies in giving the children the possibility to jointly create and to carry together the responsibility for collective harmony through joyfulness and love of life." Sonie Pludermakher-Vaysbrot, "Umfargeslekhe epizodn," in *Medem-sanatorie-bukh*, 230.

54. M[otl] Gilinski, *Lialkes* (Warsaw: Kooperativer farlag "kultur-lige," 1937), [5]. During the Second World War, the play was also performed in both the Warsaw and the Vilna Ghetto (Kazdan, "Di medem-sanatorie in miedzeszyn," 63). Scenes from *Lialkes* appear in the film *Mir kumen on*.

55. Kazdan, "Di medem-sanatorie in miedzeszyn," 58.

56. Ibid., 64.

57. Yoysef Fishman, "Di idealn vos zey hobn farflantst in undz," in *Medem-sanatorie-bukh*, 351; Cf. Nekhe Vidrevitsh-Tukhmakher, "Mit libshaft un akhtung dermon ikh di medem-sanatorie," in *Medem-sanatorie-bukh*, 365–66.

58. Shoshke Fligel-Erlich, "Mayne zikhroynes fun der medem-sanatorie," in *Medem-sanatorie-bukh*, 376.

59. See Rozenbaum, "A mitglid fun der sanatorie-farvaltung dertseylt," 160.

60. Kinder sanatorie u. n. vl. medem in miedzeszyn, "Barikht tsu der 22-ter planir sesie fun der yidisher shul-organizatsie," 4; Gezelshaft "kinder sanatorie," 4.

61. Liuba [Kantorovitsh]-Gilinski, "Khane zakheym," in *Lerer-yizkhor-bukh*, 163.

62. Daniel Charney, *A litvak in poyln* (New York: Alveltlekher yidisher kultur-kongres, 1955), 74–92; Vaysnberg, "Di medem-sanatorie," 344; Fligel-Erlich, "Mayne zikhroynes fun der medem-sanatorie," 375.

63. Gezelshaft "kinder sanatorie," 2. In 1932, Yiddish cultural activist Pinkhes Vald, who had emigrated from the Russian Empire to Argentina in 1906 and who had been active in the Bund as a young man, visited Poland and was absolutely delighted to be taken by Shloyme Mendelson on a tour of the sanatorium, which Vald described in glowing terms as the Jewish secular "national park," "wonderful," "exemplary," and as a "free and democratic Jewish children's republic." P[inkhes] Wald [Vald], *Geshtaltn fun yidishn velt-folk (bundistn)* (Buenos Aires: Farlag "yidbukh" bay der "gezelshaft far yidish-veltlekhe shuln in argentine," 1964), 375.

64. Kazdan, "Di medem-sanatorie in miedzeszyn," 42. In 1927, Baruch Charney Vladeck informed one donor that the sanatorium was on the verge of closing. Baruch Charney Vladeck to Paul Baerwald, July 16, 1927, The Baruch Charney Vladeck Papers, Box 10, Tamiment.

65. See the report on the sanatorium to the editors of the *Zyd. Leksykon Społeczny*, ca. 1937, 9, Bund Archives, M 12-30, item 460.

66. Gilinski, "Kristlekhe kinder in medem-sanatorie in miedzeszyn bay varshe," 4.

67. Hersch, "The People's Preventorium for Children at Miedzeszyn (Poland)," 197–98; Cf. Shloyme Gilinski to Shatskin, May 16, 1928, Bund Archives, M 12-32, who reports that the municipality and the Sickness Insurance Fund were prepared to greatly increase the number of children that these agencies would support if the sanatorium would make substantial improvements to its facilities, such as the installation of central heating and of a disinfection facility. The sanatorium, however, did not have the financial ability to make such improvements.

68. Kantorovitsh-Gilinski, "Shloyme gilinski un di medem-sanatorie," in *Medem-sanatorie-bukh*, 191.

69. Gilinski, "Kristlekhe kinder in medem-sanatorie in miedzeszyn bay varshe," 4.

70. Kinder sanatorie u. n. vl. medem in miedzeszyn, "Barikht tsu der 22-ter planir sesie fun der yidisher shul-organizatsie," 3; Brumberg, "Tsu der redaktsie fun yidishn gezelsh. leksikon," 6.

71. Gez[elshaft], "medem-sanatorie," "Yedies vegn onnemen kinder fun der provints," May 1930, Bund Archives, M 12-30, item 393.

72. Three and one-half years after the sanatorium's creation, at which point in time it had one hundred spaces open in the summer months, only fifteen of those staying at the institution were supported by private means. Of the children in this group, eight seem to have come from TSYSHO schools, four from state-supported Polish- language schools, and three from

wealthy families that paid their own way. "Medem-sanatorie (kurtser barikht)," ca. 1929, Bund Archives, M 12-35.

73. "Es muz batsolt vern der khoyv tsum yidishn elentn kind, *Naye folkstsaytung* (Sept. 3, 1935): 4. See Shloyme Gilinski to Baruch Charney Vladeck, Jan. 25, 1936, Baruch Charney Vladeck Papers, Box 2, Tamiment.

74. "Di ekzistents fun medem-sanatorium bedroht!" *Der moment* (July 8, 1935), 5.

75. Brumberg, "Tsu der redaktsie fun yidishn gezelsh. leksikon," 10.

76. Medem komitet, "Medem-sanatorie, a heyl-dertsierisher anshtalt far yidishe kinder in poyln," p. 3, Feb. 1938, Bund Archives, M 12-30C, item 284.

77. Kinder sanatorie u. n. vl. medem in miedzeszyn, "Barikht tsu der 22-ter planir sesie fun der yidisher shul-organizatsie," 2.

78. Hilfs-komitet far dem medem-sanatorie in poyln, "Der kampeyn tsu shafn yerlekhe bayshtayerungen oystsuhaltn kinder in der medem-sanatorie geyt on mit derfolg," July 14, 1938, Bund Archives, M 12-32, item 372.

79. Shloyme Gilinski to the National Executive of the Workmen's Circle, Apr. 15, 1939, Bund Archives, M 12-35, item 106.

80. The American Jewish Joint Distribution Committee allocated funds to the Medem Sanatorium on a regular basis beginning with 1934, increasing its support in later years. The committee donated $1,053.35 in 1934, $6,306.34 in 1935, $1,828.03 in 1936, $8,167.76 in 1937, $10,456.90 in 1938 and $11,518.15 in 1939 ("Payments to Medem Sanatorium, Poland," Jan. 12, 1944, American Jewish Joint Distribution Committee Archives, Series 1933-1944, file 841). Support to the Medem Sanatorium extended well beyond the "usual suspects" affiliated with the Jewish socialist and labor movements. The Atlanta Jewish Welfare Fund, for one, allotted $150 to the sanatorium in 1937. Harold Hirsch to J. Baskin, Aug. 4, 1937, Bund Archives, M 12, item 617.

81. Medem komitet, "Medem-sanatorie, a heyl-dertsierisher anshtalt far yidishe kinder in poyln."

82. For additional material on this remarkable film see Kazdan, "Di medem-sanatorie in miedzeszyn," 43–45; Liuba Kantorovitsh-Gilinski, "Der film 'mir kumen on,'" in *Medem-sanatorie-bukh*, 174–78; Pickhan, *"Gegen den Strom,"* 249–53; and materials in the Bund Archives, M 12-18, M 12-30B, and M 12-30D. The funds to produce the film were raised with the help of Baruch Charney Vladeck. Gilinski, "Medem sanatorie," 24.

83. The unanticipated legal obstacles involved in screening *Mir kumen on* in Poland led to a deficit that was covered, in part, by Yitzkhok Giterman. Kantorovitsh-Gilinski, "Der film 'mir kumen on,'" 177–78.

84. Shloyme Gilinski to Baruch Charney Vladeck, Oct. 21, 1938, Bund Archives, M 12-38. A translation of an undated letter from the Medem Sanatorium to the Paris office of the American Jewish Joint Distribution Committee indicated that the cut in support by the municipality had forced the sanatorium to diminish the number of children it served: "The state of things has reached such a climax that, although we have room for 200 children, we only have 73 now. We cannot accept any sick children in the free wards, as we have no money." Medem

Sanatorium to American Joint Distribution Cttee. Paris, n.d., American Jewish Joint Distribution Committee Archives, Series 1933–44, file 841.

85. The Relief Campaign for the Jewish Masses in Poland disseminated the report in the United States. There is a copy in the Bund Archives, M 12-34. See Shloyme Mendelson and Shloyme Gilinski to the [Jewish] Labor Committee, Apr. 15, 1939, Bund Archives, M 12-4, item 107, which discusses the ways in which the sanatorium had increased the size of its gardens and the number of hens it was raising to help provide for the newly arrived refugee children.

86. M[endel] Racolin to Murray Thau, Apr. 22, 1939, YIVO Archives, RG 1471, file 107.

87. Frost, *Schooling as a Socio-Political Expression*, 39.

88. Mendelsohn, *The Jews of East Central Europe between the World Wars*, 65.

89. Gilinski, "Medem-sanatorie. Fun oyfbli—bizn heylikn umkum," 20–22.

90. Gilinski, *Vi azoy lebt dos kind in medem-sanatorie*, 3.

91. Gezelshaft "kinder sanatorie," 2–3. See Kinder sanatorie u. n. vl. medem in miedzeszyn, "Barikht tsu der 22-ter planir sesie fun der yidisher shul-organizatsie," 1.

92. Shloyme Mendelson and Shloyme Gilinski to the [Jewish] Labor Committee, Apr. 15, 1939, Bund Archives, M 12-4, item 107.

93. Charney, *A litvak in poyln*, 89.

94. Sh[loyme] Gilinski, D[avid] Dubinsky, and B. Levine to Federatsie fun poylishe yidn in amerika, Mar. 2, 1938, Bund Archives, MG 9-289.

95. Gilinski, *Vi azoy lebt dos kind in medem-sanatorie*, 4. Did the Bund's leaders use their power to obtain places in the sanatorium for their own children or for the children of the party's activists ahead of individuals on the waiting list? While this question cannot be answered definitively, it is known that children of such figures as Henryk Erlich, Victor Alter, Shmuel Zygielbaum, and Borukh Shefner stayed at the sanatorium (Kantorovitsh-Gilinski, "Shloyme gilinski un di medem-sanatorie," 188)—and it is hard to imagine that they were in greater need of such a stay than other children from the desperately poor neighborhoods of Warsaw or Lodz.

96. Brumberg, "Tsu der redaktsie fun yidishn gezelsh. leksikon," 7.

97. Kinder sanatorie u. n. vl. medem in miedzeszyn, "Barikht tsu der 22-ter planir sesie fun der yidisher shul-organizatsie," 2.

98. One source proclaims that the total number of children who attended the sanatorium in 1937 was as high as 755 (Gezelshaft "kinder sanatoria," 3). Another source noted that the number of children served in 1937 was only 695, a total still larger than those in any given year from 1934 through 1936 (Kinder sanatorie u. n. vl. medem in miedzeszyn, "Barikht tsu der 22-ter planir sesie fun der yidisher shul-organizatsie," 1).

99. Gezelshaft "kinder sanatorie," 5.

100. Rozenbaum, "A mitglid fun der sanatorie-farvaltung dertseylt," 158.

101. Sh[loyme] Gilinski, "Yozef der forzitser fun unzer kinder-sanatorie," *Unzer tsayt* 10 (Nov. 1941): 45.

102. Gezelshaft "kinder sanatorie," 3. Post–World War II sources have stated that there were more than 10,000 children served by the sanatorium. However, I have been unable to find contemporary documents corroborating that claim.

103. I. M. Alef, "In gan-eden far kinder (mit a prese-oysflug in der medem-sanatorie)," *Der moment* (Dec. 20, 1937), 4.

104. I. Sh. Goldshteyn, "Vos a yid. zhurnalist trakht bezukhendig dos medem-sanatorie," *Haynt* (Dec. 16, 1937).

105. Shloyme Mendelson, "Dos yidishe shul-vezn in poyln," in *Shloyme mendelson*, 233.

106. Kazdan, "Di medem-sanatorie in miedzeszyn," 63.

107. The success of the Medem Sanatorium in the interwar period did not protect the institution in any way once the Second World War began. On September 5, 1939, several days after the beginning of the Nazi invasion of Poland, a bomb struck a Jewish orphanage located nearby. In the wake of this bombing, the sanatorium's leadership decided to close the institution and send the children back to their families (Gilinski, "Medem-sanatorie. Fun oyfbli—bizn heylikn umkum," 19). The children and staff seem to have gone to Warsaw—which was itself subjected to bombardment at that point in time—shortly thereafter.

On September 6, 1939, the Central Committee of the Bund concluded that the party's leadership should leave Warsaw (Blatman, *For Our Freedom and Yours*, 4). Within hours of this decision, an announcement was made, via radio, that the Polish government was urging all men able to bear arms to leave the city and head east. Many people did leave Warsaw during this period, including Yekutiel Portnoy, Shloyme Mendelson, Shloyme Giliniski, and Yoysef Brumberg (as well as other members of the sanatorium's board and staff). However, on October 3, 1939, after Warsaw had already been occupied by the German army, two of the sanatorium's former staff members, Liuba Gilinski (Shloyme Gilinski's wife) and Khane Zakheym, approached Shloyme Abramson, who had worked closely with Shloyme Gilinski in the institution's founding period, and asked him whether he would be willing to try to reopen it (Sh[loyme] Abramson, "Di medem-sanatorie in shotn fun der natsisher okupatsie [Sept. 1939–April 1940]," in *Medem-sanatorie-bukh*, 77). The institution was in fact reopened with a reconstituted board and a different group of teachers than it had had in the prewar era. Administration members included Dr. Ana Broyde-Heler, Dr. Helena Kelson, Zdisław Muszkat, Sonie Nowogrodzki and Mania Zygielbaum (Kazdan, "Di medem-sanatorie in miedzeszyn," in *Medem-sanatorie-bukh*, 68). Teachers in the post–October 1939 period included Leah Rotnberg, Leybl Fridman, Roze Veksler, Bela Frukht, Roza Aykhner, and Gute Morgntaler-Pav. The sanatorium continued to function, under exceptionally difficult circumstances, until August 20, 1942, at which time the children in residence as well as much of its personnel were deported to Treblinka. Perl Ellenbogen-Cahan, "Di medem-sanatorie in milkhome-tsayt," in *Medem-sanatorie-bukh*, 100–111; Khayim Ellenbogen, "Unter der natsisher okupatsie, in ibid., 111–15.

5. The Bundist Women's Organization

1. A. Litvak [Khaim-Yankev Helfand], "Di yidishe arbeyter-froy," *Di naye velt*, Oct. 15, 1915, 11. Approximately 70 percent of those employed in the Pale of Settlement in cigarette factories owned by Jews were either women or children (Mendelsohn, *Class Struggle in the Pale*, 25).

2. Ibid., 40; Litvak, *Vos geven*, 58.

3. The term *half-intellectuals* was used to describe both men and women. The daughters of the head of Vilna's yeshiva, who were "half-intellectuals," were among the very first workers to be drawn into socialist circles in that city (Litvak, *Vos geven*, 59). Young Jewish women who became activists, it has been alleged, found it necessary to struggle against patriarchal traditions and despotic fathers. Fathers objected to their daughters coming home late and to their resistance to arranged marriages. Some are known to have attempted to physically restrain their daughters from participating in the movement. As a result, many young women who became involved in the Jewish socialist movement ultimately felt obliged to leave their parents' home. Leon Bernstein [Bernshteyn], *Ershte shprotsungen (zikhroynes)* (Buenos Aires: Farlag "yidbukh" bay der "gezelshaft far yidish-veltlekhe shuln in argentine," 1956), 26.

4. Litvak, "Di yidishe arbeyter-froy."

5. *Arkadi. Zamlbukh tsum ondenk fun grinder fun "bund" arkadi kremer* (New York: Farlag unzer tsayt, 1942), 361. Greenblat is known to have argued at this meeting that the Bund ought to publish and disseminate philosophical works by writers such as Friedrich Engels and Ludwig Feuerbach rather than propagandistic materials. However, her proposal was not formally accepted (Tobias, *The Jewish Bund in Russia*, 68). Greenblat later emigrated to Switzerland and became a Zionist (N. A. Buchbinder (Bukhbinder), *Di geshikhte fun der yidisher arbeter-bavegung in rusland* (Vilna: Farlag "tomor," 1931), 79).

6. For biographical information on Hurvitch see J[acob] S. Hertz, editor, *Doyres bundistn*, 1:228–31.

7. John Mill, [Yoysef Shloyme Mil], *Pionern un boyer* (New York: Farlag der veker, 1946), 1:16; Tobias, *The Jewish Bund in Russia*, 87.

8. The roles of women in Bundist printing shops are described in Sholom Levine [Sholem Levin], *Untererdishe kemfer* (New York: Sholom levin bukh-komitet, 1946), 238, 284–85.

9. Hertz, *Doyres bundistn*, 1:456.

10. Franz Kursky [Frants Kurski], *Gezamlte shriftn* (New York: Farlag der veker, 1952), 194. For a similar case see Paula E. Hyman, *Gender and Assimilation in Modern Jewish History. The Roles and Representation of Women* (Seattle: Univ. of Washington Press, 1995), 79.

11. Dubnow-Erlich, *Bread and Matzoth*, 107ff.

12. Dina Blond, "Di bundishe froyen-organizatsie un ir ershte sekretarin," 3, unpublished radio talk, n.d., Bund Archives, ME 17-65.

13. Frankel, *Prophecy and Politics*, 240.

14. Hertz, compiler, *Der bund in bilder 1897–1957* (New York: Farlag unzer tsayt, 1958), 57.

15. L[eybetshke] Berman, *In loyf fun yorn. Zikhroynes fun a yidishn arbeter* (New York: Farlag "unzer tsayt," 1945), 364.

16. Hertz, *Doyres bundistn*, 1:366–67.

17. Ibid., 1:364.

18. Ibid., 1:359, and B[eynish] Michalewicz [Mikhalevitsh] [Josef Isbitzki], *Geshtaltn un perzenlekhkaytn. Gezamlte artiklen vegn denker un tuer fun der arbeter-bavegung* (Warsaw: [Tsentral komitet fun bund in poyln], 1938), 157–63.

19. Henri Minczeles, *Histoire générale du Bund. Un mouvement révolutionnaire juif* (Paris: Austral, 1995), 212; Sophia Dubnow-Erlich, "In di yorn fun reaktsie," *Di geshikhte fun bund*, 2:576, 585; Gitelman, *Jewish Nationality and Soviet Politics*, 517.

20. Dubnow-Erlich, *Bread and Matzoth*, 118, 121–22; Vladimir Medem, *The Life and Soul of a Legendary Jewish Socialist*, ed. and trans. Samuel A. Portnoy (New York: KTAV Publishing House, Inc., 1979), 386.

21. Eichner's death is noted in Marek Edelman, *The Ghetto Fights* (London: 1990), 65.

22. Hertz, *Doyres bundistn*, 2:163.

23. Dubnow-Erlich, "In di yorn fun reaktsie," 585.

24. Gina Medem, *A lebensveg. Oytobiografishe notitsn* (New York: Gina medem bukh-komitet, 1950), 144ff.

25. Medem, *The Life and Soul of a Legendary Jewish Socialist*, 499.

26. Hillel Kats Blum, *Zikhroynes fun a bundist. Bilder fun untererdishn lebn in tsarishn rusland* (New York: Bildungs-komitet fun arbeter ring, 1940), 67–68.

27. Levine, *Untererdishe kemfer*, 241.

28. Dubnow-Erlich, *Bread and Matzoth*, 164.

29. Bernstein, *Ershte shprotsungen (zikhroynes)*, 26.

30. Hertz, *Doyres bundistn*, 1:154–56.

31. Frumkin herself, it ought to be noted, went on to play a prominent role in the Evsektsiia [the Jewish Section of the Communist Party of the Soviet Union], and was later appointed director of Moscow's Foreign Languages Institute, but eventually fell victim to Stalin's purges. Gitelman, *Jewish Nationality and Soviet Politics*, 516–17.

32. Harriet Davis-Kram, "The Story of the Sisters of the Bund," *Contemporary Jewry* 5, no. 2 (fall-winter 1980): 40. Davis-Kram does not explain the basis for her estimate. However, she is known to have interviewed veteran Bundists at the time that she was conducting her research.

33. McNeal has concluded that approximately 20 percent of the members of the Russian radical movement were female (Robert H. McNeal, "Women in the Russian Radical Movement," *Journal of Social History* 5, no. 2 (1971–72): 144]. Blatman has asserted that "the percentage of women in the Bund, both in Poland and Russia, was lower than the percentage of women in the Russian revolutionary movements" (Daniel Blatman, "Women in the Jewish Labor Bund in Interwar Poland," in *Women in the Holocaust*, ed. Dalia Ofer and Lenore J. Weitzman (New Haven and London: Yale Univ. Press, 1998), 71]. However, Blatman does not make use of the data provided by Davis-Kram, and derives his conclusion from analysis of the three-volume set *Doyres bundistn*. Though *Doyres bundistn* is a valuable source, it may not fully reflect the actual gender distribution of the Bundist movement. There are four caveats that must be taken into account when making use of *Doyres bundistn* for purposes of statistical analysis of the Bund:

Those individuals who were at one time prominent in the Bund, but who eventually affiliated with other movements—i.e., Roza Greenblat, who became a Zionist, and Esther

Frumkin, who became a Communist—do not appear in *Doyres bundistn*. There were many such individuals.

Those Bundists who were still alive when *Doyres bundistn* appeared in print—including Sophia Dubnow-Erlich and Dina Blond—also do not appear. There is some reason to believe that the life spans of Jewish women who were born in Eastern Europe at the end of the ninteenth century or in the first part of the twentieth century (and who survived the Holocaust) were longer than those of Eastern European Jewish men who were part of the same generational cohorts.

The editor of *Doyres bundistn* notes that the volumes do not include entries for those Bundists who had already published autobiographical works—but he neglects to mention that he chose not to solicit an entry for at least one prominent woman [Ruta Berman] whose spouse had published an autobiography, and whose life is discussed in her spouse's book.

The archives of the Polish Bund were destroyed during the course of World War II. Thus, the editor of *Doyres bundistn* was forced to rely, in part, on the memories of those who happened to survive the Holocaust. These memories may or may have been accurate.

For all these reasons, in sum, *Doyres bundistn* may not fully reflect the actual rate of participation by women in the Bundist movement, and Blatman's conclusion is open to question.

34. H[ershl] K[upfershtayn], "Dina blond-mikhalevitsh," *Unzer tsayt* 5 [520] (May 1985): 21–24.

35. Interview with Dina Blond, n.d., conducted by "Charlotte," 8 [Bund Archives, ME 17-64]. The interview dates from the period 1972–1981 [as evidenced by the fact that Blond alludes in it to there being 4 volumes in the history of the Bund].

36. Litvak, "Di yidishe arbeyter-froy."

37. Interview with Dina Blond, 12.

38. The period of the Polish–Soviet War of 1920–21, during which the Bund took an antiwar stance, is the most important exception to this generalization. In the midst of the Polish–Soviet War, Bundist activists in Poland were imprisoned, a Bundist was condemned to death by a military tribunal and promptly executed, and Bundist-oriented periodicals, such as *Lebens-fragen* and *Di sotsialistishe yugnt-shtime*, were forced to close (Hertz, "Der bund in umophengikn poyln, 1918–1925," 89–93). The Bund did in fact operate in a quasi-underground manner in Poland for some of the period and published illegal materials. Female members of the Tsukunft were among those who helped to disseminate an illegal antiwar proclamation issued by the Central Committee of the Bundist youth movement. Hertz, *Di geshikhte fun a yugnt*, 189–90.

39. Hertz, *Doyres bundistn*, 3:78.

40. Ibid., 3:26, 30.

41. Moshe Zalcman, [Moyshe Zaltsman] *Bela shapiro. Di populere froyen-geshtalt* (Paris: n.p., 1983); Pickhan—in a study which is, in general, scrupulously accurate—mistakenly identifies Szapiro as the person in charge of the Bund's organization in Vilna. Pickhan, *"Gegen den Strom,"* 114.

42. Hertz, *Doyres bundistn*, 1:190.

43. Hertz, *Di geshikhte fun bund in lodz*, 429, 439. There were other women on the Lodz City Committee of the Bund elected in 1938: Golda Jakubowicz Zilberberg and Blimele Kleyner-Rozenblum (417). The first of these two was a leading figure in the trade union of the textile workers (Hertz, *Doyres bundistn*, 2:168). Kleyner-Rozenblum was also a trade union activist.

44. Hertz, *Doyres bundistn*, 2:496–97.

45. Kh[ayim] Sh[loyme] Kazdan, "Froy un man in unzer bavegung," *Naye folkstsaytung*, Feb. 10, 1939, 6. Blatman cites Kazdan as asserting that 10 percent of Bund members were women (Blatman, "Women in the Jewish Labor Bund in Interwar Poland," 79]. However, Kazdan specifically underscored that he did not know the percentage of women in the Bund. Kazdan, "Froy un man," 6; see Pickhan, *"Gegen den Strom,"* 114.

46. B[enyomin] Nadel, "Tsu der geografie fun 'bund' in poyln," *Undzer tsayt* 11–12 [708–9] (Nov.–Dec. 2001): 27.

47. Pickhan, *"Gegen den Strom,"* 131.

48. Blond, "Di bundishe froyen-organizatsie un ir ershte sekretarin," 1.

49. Dina [Blond], "In organizatsie iz unzer kraft," *Naye folkstsaytung*, Mar. 19, 1926, 5.

50. Hertz, *Doyres bundistn*, 3:352. Blatman is mistaken in his claim that YAF was established in the early 1920s (Blatman,"Women in the Jewish Labor Bund in Interwar Poland," 73).

51. Blond, "Di bundishe froyen-organizatsie un ir ershte sekretarin."

52. K[hayim] L[eyb] Fuks, "Sheyne-feygl blond," in *Leksikon fun der nayer yidisher literatur*, vol. 1 (New York: Alveltlekher yidisher kultur-kongres, 1956), col. 315; K[upfershtayn], "Dina blond-mikhalevitsh," 23.

53. Blond came to the United States during the Second World War, worked at the YIVO Institute at one time, and died in New York.

54. "Khaverte tsipe edelman," *Naye folkstsaytung*, Nov. 20, 1937, 1.

55. Death notice for Tsipe Edelman placed by YAF, *Naye folkstsaytung*, Nov. 21, 1937.

56. Edelman was married to an individual who had been a Bundist in the czarist era and who died in the 1920s. A. B. "Tsipe edelman," in *Doyres bundistn*, 3:353.

57. Hertz, *Di geshikhte fun bund in lodz*, 439; E[frayim] L[uzer] Zelmanovitsh, "Roza eichner," in *Doyres bundistn*, 2:163–64. Eichner, who moved to Warsaw after the beginning of the Second World War, worked at the Medem Sanatorium and was deported from that institution, together with the children who were staying in it, in 1942.

58. Berman, *In loyf fun yorn*, 363–70; Kazdan, *Lerer-yizkhor-bukh*, 56–57. Ruta Batkhan was married to Leybetshke Berman, a prominent Bundist.

59. Bela Szapiro and Anna Rozental, both of whom had made names for themselves in the Bund long before the establishment of the YAF, were reportedly among YAF's founders, but do not appear to have made it their primary fields of endeavor.

60. Hertz, *Di geshikhte fun a yugnt*, 354–55. Rena Hister Hertz was elected to the Central Committee of the Tsukunft at that organization's fourth and fifth Poland-wide conventions.

Her role notwithstanding, women did not play a greater role in the leadership of the Bundist youth movement than they did in the leadership of the Polish Bund, and did not play more visible roles at the end of the interwar era than they had earlier. The sixth countrywide convention of the Tsukunft, the last such convention in prewar Poland, elected a central committee of fifteen members, all of whom were male. Hertz, *Di geshikhte fun a yugnt*, 420.

61. Hertz, *Doyres bundistn*, 3:368.

62. The list of YAF founders and activists is derived from Luba Blum, "Di yidishe arbeter-froy amol un haynt," *Folkstsaytung*, Nov. 15, 1947, 27. An article appearing in the *Naye folkstsaytung* in 1928 and describing an event in Warsaw refers to women named Rotman Sveber, Oroniak-Tenenboym, and to a Dr. Golde as YAF leaders. Cipe Edelman is mentioned in the same context.

63. "Vos vil di gezelshaft yidishe arb.-froy (y.a.f.)?," Reprinted from *Lodzer Weker [Lodzer veker]*, Dec. 30, 1926, Algemeyner Yidisher Arbeter Bund in Lite, Poylen un Rusland "Bund" Collection, item 324, International Institute of Social History, Amsterdam (hereafter known as Bund Collection, IISH).

64. Gezelshaft yidishe arbetndike froy "yaf" in vilna, "Tsu di yidishe arbetndike froyen!," [1927], Bund Collection, IISH.

65. Mordekhay V. Bernshteyn, "Der 'bund' in poyln," *Yorbukh*, vol. 1, edited by Shimen Federbush (New York: Velt federatsie fun poylishe yidn, Amerikaner ekzekutiva, 1964), 206.

66. "Lubliner 'yaf' efnt a dernerungs-punkt far kinder," *Naye folkstsaytung*, July 13, 1926, 5.

67. "Unzer bagrisung," *Naye folkstsaytung*, Dec. 12, 1937, 6.

68. Report of the Arbeter komitet far di aroysgeshikte fun daytshland, distributed in the United States by the Hilfs kampeyn far di yidishe masn in poyln, July 1939, Bund Archives, M 12-34, 3.

69. P. Shats, "Mit arbeter-kinder (a prese-bazukh oyf di halb-kolonies fun 'yaf')," *Naye folkstsytung*, July 30, 1928, 5.

70. "Groyse farzamlung fun arbeter-muters vegn halb-kolonies far arbeter-kinder," *Naye folkstsaytung*, July 3, 1929, 6.

71. "Varshever yaf," *Naye folkstsaytung*, Apr. 1, 1932, 7.

72. Dina Blond, "Vegn di fayerungen fun internatsionaln froyen-tog in 'bund,'" ca. 1960, Bund Archives, ME 17-65.

73. Dina [Blond], *Shvester mayne! A vort tsu der yidisher arbeter-froy* (Warsaw: n.p., 1928). See "Yidishe arbeterin, froy, un muter!" *Naye folkstsaytung*, Jan. 31, 1928; "Di tetikayt fun gezelshaft yidishe arbeter-froy (yaf)," ibid., Mar. 30, 1928, 6.

74. Mela Sufit and Yustina Blank, "Bagrisungen farn lodzer 'yaf,'" *Naye folkstsaytung*, Sept. 9, 1938, 10; "Di froyen-kolonie fun lodzer 'yaf' in teodori nemt oyf kh'tes oykh fun andere shtet," ibid., May 26, 1939, 9. YAF first formed a branch in Lodz in 1926. Hertz, *Di geshikhte fun bund in lodz*, 345.

75. "Vegn der arbet fun bialystoker 'yaf'-organizatsie," *Naye folkstsaytung*, Sept. 9, 1938, 10.

76. Pickhan, *"Gegen den Strom,"* 90. Locations in which there are known to have been YAF organizations include Warsaw, Lodz, Vilna, Lublin, Piotrków, Tarnów, Kutno and

Bialystok. Blum, "Di yidishe arbeter-froy amol un haynt"; "Vegn der arbet fun bialystoker 'yaf'-organizatsie."

77. "Di tetikayt fun gezelshaft yidishe arbeter-froy (yaf)," *Naye folkstsaytung,* Mar. 30, 1928, 6

78. [Bundisher klub in nu york], "Vegn di atakes ofn 'bund' in tsuzamenhang mit dem kempeyn fun yidishn arbeter komitet," [Apr. 1937], 4, Jewish Labor Committee Records, Wagner 025, box 9, file 23, 3, Tamiment.

79. Hertz, "Der bund in umophengikn poyln, 1926–1932," 41.

80. "Varshever 'yaf,'" *Naye folkstsaytung,* Apr. 1, 1932, 7.

81. Malke, "Vilner ya"f," ibid., Apr. 5, 1935, 7.

82. Algemeyner yidisher arbeter-bund "bund" in poyln. Varshever komitet, "Materialn tsu der shtotisher konferents fun der varshever organizatsie fun 'bund,'" Feb. 1939, Bund Archives, MG 2-293. Daniel Blatman, citing this document, has claimed that the total number of YAF members in Warsaw in 1939 was sixty-two (Blatman, "Women in the Jewish Labor Bund," 79). However, he has confused this with the number of Warsaw YAF members also in the YAF branch of the Bund. The fact that the document cited by Blatman does not refer to the total membership of the YAF in Warsaw is best demonstrated by comparing the figures provided in this document under the heading "YAF" with the figures provided under the heading "Morgnshtern." The Warsaw branch of Morgnshtern is known to have had 1,059 members early in 1936, 956 of whom were active in the branch (Arbeter-gezelshaft far fizisher dertsiung "morgnshtern" in poyln [yidishe sektsie fun arbeter-sport-internatsional]. Varshever optaylung, *Barikht tsu der alg. farzamlung dem 14tn fevruar 1936 far der tsayt fun—1. II. 1935—1 II. 1936,* RG 29, file 86, YIVO Archives). The document that forms the basis for Blatman's assertion, however, under the heading "Morgnshtern," and in a column referring to October 1, 1936, lists the number of members as sixty-three. These numbers do not refer to the total number of members in the constituent organizations but only to those who were members of the corresponding divisions of the Warsaw Bund.

83. R[oza] E[ichner], "Lodzer 'yaf' bay der arbet," *Naye folkstsaytung,* Feb. 13, 1938, 5. The Warsaw YAF was also involved in a recruitment effort at that time. A "well attended" meeting of the Warsaw YAF held on January 1, 1938, resolved unanimously to double the number of members by having YAF members visit homes in Jewish working-class neighborhoods and encouraging individual Jewish women to become activists. "Varshever 'yaf' tsugetretn tsu der verbir-aktsie," *Naye folkstsaytung,* Jan. 5, 1938, 6.

84. The Central Committee of the Bund in Poland declared the organizing of a countrywide YAF secretariat to be among a number of organizational tasks for the party in 1937 (see circular 49 of the Central Committee of the Bund in Poland, Warsaw, Oct. 15, 1937, Bund Archvies, MG 2-470). The Poland-wide gathering of female members of the Bund sponsored by YAF took place in Warsaw on November 14, 1937, in conjunction with the celebration of the fortieth anniversary of the founding of the Bund. It was officially announced as a conference of all female delegates (*Naye folkstsaytung,* Nov. 11, 1937, 6). Organizers underscored that the number of women in YAF was very small (Polie, "A por bamerkungen tsu der frage fun unzer

land-konferents," *Naye folkstsaytung*, Dec. 12, 1937, 6). YAF disseminated organizational news and the views of its leaders and members through *Naye folkstsaytung*, the Warsaw-based daily of the Bund, in which there was a column entitled "Froyen-vinkl" (Women's Corner), edited by Dina Blond (H[ershl] K[upfershtayn], "Dina blond-mikhalevitsh," *Unzer tsayt* (May 1985): 21–24.

85. Khane Rafalowicz, "A brif fun a hoyz-agitatorin," *Naye folkstsaytung* (Feb. 13, 1938): 5. A YAF activist in Vilna commented at one point, "It is difficult to organize because the element] is not female workers, but poor market women or women who work in their homes. Both elements live in very difficult conditions and are so backward that it is not easy to plow through their heads." Malke, "Vilner yaf," *Naye folkstsaytung* (Apr. 5, 1935): 7.

86. This debate has been discussed both by Daniel Blatman, "Women in the Jewish Labor Bund," pp. 79–80, and by Gertrud Pickhan. "'Where are the Women?' On the Discussion about Feminity, Masculinity and Jewishness within the General Jewish Workers Union ["Bund"] in Poland," unpublished paper delivered at the conference "Between Wars: Nations, Nationalisms, and Gender Relations in Central and Eastern Europe 1918–1939," Obory, Poland, May 12, 2000. Cf. Gertrud Pickhan, "'Wo sind die Frauen?' Zur Diskussion um Weiblichkeit, Männlichkeit und Jüdischkeit im Allgemeinen Jüdischen Arbeiterbund ("Bund") in Polen," in *Zwischen den Kriegen: Nationen, Nationalismen und Geschlechterverhältnisse in Mittel- und Osteuropa 1918–1939*, ed. Johanna Gehmacher, Elisabeth Harvey, und Sophia Kemlein. Einzelveröffentlichungen des Deutschen Historischen Instituts Warschau, 7 (Osnabrück: 2004), 187–99.

87. Kh[ayim] Sh[loyme] Kazdan, "Froy un man in unzer bavegung," *Naye folkstsaytung*, Feb. 10, 1939, 6.

88. Dina [Blond], "Vu zenen di froyen?" *Naye folkstsaytung*, Feb. 17, 1939, 9.

89. Ruta [Berman], "Vu lign di sibes?" *Naye folkstsaytung*, Mar. 3, 1939, 9.

90. *Naye folkstsaytung* seems to have received a number of letters from readers who wanted to state an opinion in the debate sparked by Kazdan's piece. In some cases, persistent readers wrote a second time in order to inquire as to why their letters had gone unpublished. "Tsu unzere lezer un lezerins," *Naye folkstsaytung*, June 2, 1939, 9.

91. Y-ke, "Tsi zenen take di froyen shuldik? (an entfer dem kh' kazdan)," *Naye folkstsaytung*, Mar. 10, 1939, 10.

92. A dantsiker froy, "A briv fun a lezerin," *Naye folkstsaytung*, June 9, 1939, 10.

93. In the wake of Warsaw's occupation by the German military in 1939, the Bund regrouped and began to operate underground. A new central committee was organized, on which Sheyne Gitl [Sonie] Czemelinski Nowogrudski (ca. 1893–1942) was the only woman (Hertz, *Doyres bundistn*, 2:108–11; Bernard Goldstein [Goldshteyn], *Finf yor in varshever geto* [New York: Farlag unzer tsayt, 1947], 120). Additional information on Nowogrudski may be found in Kazdan, *Lerer-yizkhor-bukh*, 256–62. Ruta Berman along with Gitl Skutelski, a long-term YAF activist in her own right and the widow of a Bundist pioneer, initially represented YAF in the body that reported to this central committee (Hertz, *Doyres bundistn*,

1:467). Neither Berman nor Skutelski survived the Holocaust. Miriam-Royze [Maria] Salomon Klepfisz served during the war on the central council of trade unions as a representative of the teachers (Hertz, *Doyres bundistn*, 2:360; see Kazdan, *Lerer-yizkhor bukh*, 380, for information on Klepfisz's earlier activities). Bela Szapiro was a member of the party council that represented Bundists outside of Warsaw. Szapiro was arrested in Lublin in 1941 and died in captivity. Three Bundist women—Ester Zdunski-Vaynberg, Blimele Kleyner-Rozenblum, and Golde Zilberberg—served on the underground committee of the Bund in the Lodz Ghetto (Hertz, *Di geshikhte fun bund in lodz*, 442).

Members of the YAF Committee of the Warsaw Bund during the period of the occupation included, in addition to Berman and Skutelski, Liuba Belitski and Waks *(In di yorn fun yidishn khurbn. Di shtim fun untererdishn bund* [New York: Farlag unzer tsayt, 1948], 331). YAF is also said to have operated in Lodz even after the Germans took control [Hertz, *Di geshikhte fun bund in lodz*, 442].

As in the czarist era, Bundist women once again became active in distributing literature and as couriers when the movement was forced to go underground. They also took up arms against the Nazis. Tsipore Aynshtayn (ca. 1915–43), Asie Big (d. 1943), Gute Blones (d. 1943), Tobcie Dawidowicz (1924–43), Miriam Szyfman Fainer (ca. 1915–43), Hannah Krystal Fryshdorf (1920–89), Bluma Klog (d. 1944), Feigel ["Wladka"] Peltel, Sore Rozenboym (1922–43), Leah Szyfman (ca. 1922–43), and Chaike Belchatowska Spiegel (d. 2002), some of whom had been active in SKIF or in Tsukunft before the Second World War rather than in the Bund itself, were among those who participated in the resistance movement. On Fryshdorf see Meir Rak, "Eyne fun di letste varshever geto-kemfer," *Forverts*, Feb. 3, 1989, 10, 25. On Spiegel see Paul Lewis, "Chaike Spiegel, 81, of Warsaw Revolt, Dies," *The New York Times*, Apr. 7, 2002, 35. Information on the other resistance fighters listed here is derived from Hertz, *Di geshikhte fun a yugnt*, 567, 574–78, 583–85, and idem, *Doyres bundistn*, 2:69, 384–86, 391–92, 404–5, 409–11, 444–45, 513–17.

The overwhelming bulk of YAF members were murdered or died during 1939–45. Immediately following the conclusion of World War II, Bundist women in Poland attempted to reorganize. There were YAF chapters in Legnica, Lodz, and Szczuczyn in 1947, and a childcare center named for Ruta Berman and run under the auspices of YAF in Szczuczyn (Blum, "Di yidishe arbeter-froy amol un haynt"). But the Bund in Poland was forced to liquidate itself as a result of pressure put on it by Communists, and YAF, as an affiliate of the Bund, folded as well. Female Bundist survivors participated in the activities of the Bundist groups that continued to operate in Argentina, Australia, Canada, France, Israel, the United States, and elsewhere in the decades directly following the Holocaust. These women, however, did not re-create a centrally run Bundist women's group following the dissolution of the Polish Bund.

94. Just how small was the organization of Bundist university students? In 1928, apparently the year in which Ringen was established, there was a group of unknown size in Warsaw, and the Bundist-oriented group had thirty members in Cracow (home of Jagiellonian

University, one of Poland's most important institutions of higher education). There were no more than ten Bundists active in a non-Bundist but still socialist grouping of Jewish university students in Vilna. There were, in addition, ten students affiliated with the movement in Lodz, and even smaller numbers of students sympathetic to the Bund in Piotrków, Lublin, and Tarnów (Report of the "Tsaytvayliker ekzekutiv fun akademishe bundishe grupn in poyln" to the Central Committee of the Bund in Poland, Feb. 22, 1928, Bund Archives, MG 9-270). The locations listed here seem to have been the only ones in Poland in which there were Bundist university students at that time. A report in the *Naye folkstsaytung* published in 1932 suggests that only the Warsaw group had had success. Activity in Cracow among students had become weaker, and the situation was at its worst in Lemberg (Pickhan, *"Gegen den Strom,"* 133). Victor Erlich has estimated that Ringen had forty to forty-five members in Warsaw in the late 1930s. Victor Erlich to Jack Jacobs, Jan. 3, 2007.

95. Simon Segal, *The New Poland and the Jews* (New York: Lee Furman, Inc., 1938), 197–201; Heller, *On the Edge of Destruction*, 119–22.

96. Arcadius Kahan, *Essays in Jewish Social and Economic History*, ed. Roger Weiss (Chicago and London: Univ. of Chicago Press, 1986), 166.

97. Marcus, *Social and Political History*, 160. Marcus points out other factors, such as economic conditions, in addition to the rise of anti-Semitism that help to explain the decrease in the proportion of Jewish university students.

98. Harry M. Rabinowicz, *The Legacy of Polish Jewry: A History of Polish Jews in the Inter-War Years 1919–1939* (New York and London: Thomas Yoseloff, 1965), 99.

99. Hertz, *Di geshikhte fun a yugnt*, 584.

100. Victor Erlich, *Child of a Turbulent Century* (Evanston, Ill.: Northwestern Univ. Press, 2006), 31, 33–34, 54; Erlich to Jacobs, Jan. 3, 2007.

101. There is little information available on other individual members of Ringen. Emanuel Scherer and L. Brandes headed the list of candidates in the elections intended to decide who would serve as delegates at the third countrywide gathering of Jewish academics in Poland ("Haynt—valn bay di akademiker," *Naye folkstsaytung*, May 25, 1930, 5). Gershon [Grisza] Yashunski [Gerszon Jaszuński], who spoke on behalf of Ringen at the Tsukunft's 1932 Poland-wide gathering (Hertz, *Di geshikhte fun a yugnt*, 307), was apparently at one point secretary-treasurer of Ringen in Warsaw (Erlich to Jacobs, Jan. 3, 2007). Yashunski later played a leading role in the Bund's efforts to reestablish itself in Poland beginning with 1944. *Leksikon fun der nayer yidisher literatur*, vol. 4, col. 227; David Engel, "The Bund after the Holocaust: Between Renewal and Self-Liquidation," in *Jewish Politics in Eastern Europe*, 216, 219; Daniel Blatman, *For Our Freedom and Yours*, 167, 169, 172, 173, 178, 181.

102. Sophia Dubnow-Erlich, "Biografie," in *Leon oler*, 22. Oler, the representative in question, had himself attended the University of Warsaw.

103. While incarcerated in a Soviet prison during WWII, Henryk Erlich wrote a history of the Polish Bund in which he noted that, as anti-Semitism in Poland became ever more militant, the Bundist student groups increased in significance. Gertrud Pickhan, "Das NKVD-Dossier

über Henryk Erlich und Wiktor Alter," *Berliner Jahrbuch für osteuropäische Geschichte* (1994), 185–86.

Conclusion

1. "Yugnt-bund 'tsukunft' in poyln"; "Der 4ter tsuzamenfor fun yugnt-bund 'tsukunft,'" *Yugnt-veker* 4, no. 8 (Nov. 20, 1925): 6; *Arbeter tashn kalendar 1930*, 34; "Der 6-ter kongres fun sots. yugnt-internatsional," *Yugnt-veker* 18, no. 16 (Aug. 15, 1939): 3.

2. *Tashn-kalendar mayn khaver 1930*, 32; "Referat vegn di problemen un tsushtand fun der skif-arbet"; *1-ter land-tsuzamenfor fun "skif" in poyln (varshe, 1–3 oktober 1936)*. Skif bibliotek 4 (Warsaw: Farlag skif-bilbiotek, 1937), 9.

3. Y[ankef] Patt, L[eyvik] Hodes, and K[almen] Vapner to the Jewish Labor Committee, Apr. 20, 1939, Bund Archives, MG 9-243.

4. Mor., "Der 'morgnshtern' geyt faroys," *Yugnt-veker* 6, no. 8 (Apr. 15, 1927): 10; Tsharnetski, "Unzere sportler marshirn faroys," 4; *Beckmanns Sport Lexikon A–Z*, col. 1370; Hertz, *Di geshikhte fun a yugnt*, 445; [Bundisher klub in nu york], "Vegn di atakes ofn 'bund' in tsuzamenhang mit dem kempeyn fun yidishn arbeter komitet," [Apr. 1937], 4, Jewish Labor Committee Records, Wagner 025, Box 9, file 23, Tamiment.

5. Gilinski, "Medem-sanatorie. Fun oyfbli—bizn heylikn umkum," 21; [Gilinski], *Vi azoy lebt dos kind in medem-sanatorie?* 3; Gezelshaft "kinder sanatorie," 3; Shloyme Mendelson and Shloyme Gilinski to the [Jewish] Labor Committee, Apr. 15, 1939), Bund Archives, M 12-4, item 107.

6. At an early point in SKIF's history, Hodes expressed concern that Skifistn did not know enough about the Tsukunft and were not eager to leave the Bund's children's movement for the party's youth movement (Hodes, *Materialn un onvayzungen far der sotsialistisher dertsiung-arbet*, 24). The situation changed after Hodes made these comments, however. Skif groups regularly transferred into the Tsukunft from 1929 onward. In 1938–39, for example, eight circles of the Warsaw SKIF, with a total of 120 members, were shifted from the Bund's children's movement to the Tsukunft. I. Ki-ki, "Ershte skif-grupe ibergefirt in 'tsukunft,'" *Yugnt-veker* 8, no. 5 (Mar. 1, 1929): 15; Sotsialistisher kinder-farband "skif" in poyln. Varshever organizatsie, "1 yor sotsialistishe dertsiungs-arbet fun varsh. skif 1938/39," Warsaw: 1939, Bund Archives, MG 9-245, 12.

7. Hertz, *Di geshikhte fun a yugnt*, 275.

8. "Unzere geveylte," *Yugnt-veker* 18, no. 1 (Jan. 1, 1939): 4.

9. Polonsky "The Bund in Polish Political Life," 572; Mendelsohn, "Jewish Politics in Interwar Poland," 10, 11–12.

10. Pickhan, *"Gegen den Strom,"* 205.

11. Zygielbaum's activities in the trade union movement are described in J[acob] S. Hertz, "Shmuel mordekhay zigelboym," in *Zigelboym-bukh* (New York: Farlag unzer tsayt, 1947), 18–20.

12. Sh[muel] M[ordechay] Zygielbaum, "Di profesionele bavegung fun di yidishe arbeter," in *Di geshikhte fun bund*, 4:211.

13. Zygielbaum, "Di profesionele bavegung fun di yidishe arbeter," 211. Another Bundist source notes that there were 35,479 workers in the unions that came to the founding convention of the *Land-rat* in 1921, and 47,500 workers in the unions in the *Land-rat* at the time of that organization's second convention in 1922. J[acob] S. Hertz, "Di profesionele fareynen fun di yidishe arbeter," in *Di geshikhte fun bund*, 4:227, 228.

14. Zygielbaum, "Di profesionele bavegung fun di yidishe arbeter," 211.

15. Sara [Szweber], "Der 'bund' un di profesionele bavegung in poyln," *Naye folkstsaytung*, Nov. 19, 1937, 22. Szweber's activities in the Polish Jewish trade union movement are described in Hertz, *Doyres bundistn*, 3:78.

16. Zygielbaum, "Di profesionele bavegung fun di yidishe arbeter," 212. Marcus reports significantly lower membership totals for the National Council of Jewish Class Trade Unions than does Zygielbaum. According to Marcus, this organization had 22,577 members in 1935, 27,465 members in 1936, 29,155 members in 1937, and 43,466 members in 1938 (Marcus, *Social and Political History*, 125). See the comments by Pickhan on Marcus's statistics (Pickhan, *"Gegen den Strom,"* 203).

17. A countrywide convention of trade unionists in the leather industry held in June 1935 was attended by fifty Jewish delegates. Thirty-eight were Bundists, eight were considered leftists (Communists), three were affiliated with the Left Poalei Zion, and two were unaffiliated. The unions in the clothing industry—the industry employing the single largest number of Jewish workers—held a similar Poland-wide convention in October 1935. The total number of Jewish delegates to this convention was seventy-seven. Sixty-one were Bundists, fifteen were leftists, and one was a member of the Left Poalei Zion. At a congress of the textile workers of Poland held in May 1936, all Jewish delegates were Bundists. A Poland-wide convention of the unions representing Jewish trade and office employees began in mid-February 1937, with fifty-five delegates in attendance. Forty-two were Bundists. Twelve were either leftists or unaffiliated. One delegate was a member of the Right Poalei Zion. The conference of the *Land-rat* held in Warsaw in February 1937 is perhaps the most telling example since it encompassed trade unions in a broad range of industries. Of the 253 official delegates in attendance, 191 were Bundists, 51 were leftists, 9 were members of the Left Poalei Zion, and 2 were unaffiliated. Tsentral-komitet fun "bund" in poyln, *Memorandum tsum yidishn arbeter-komitet in amerike*, 7–8.

18. Zygielbaum attributed the rise of the Jewish trade-union movement in Poland to a rise in anti-Semitism: "In the years 1935–1936, when, under the effect of Hitlerism, the reactionary parties in Poland enormously strengthened their activity, the activity of the workers also increased. The number of members in the general trade unions began to grow back little by little." Zygielbaum, "Di profesionele bavegung fun di yidishe arbeter," 211.

19. Johnpoll, *Politics of Futility*, 270; Polonsky, "The Bund in Polish Political Life," 572. I agree on this issue with Pickhan, *"Gegen den Strom,"* 252, 410–11, and Gechtman, "Yidisher Sotsializm," 26–27.

20. Hertz, *Di geshikhte fun a yugnt*, 467; Emanuel Scherer, "The Bund," in *Struggle for Tomorrow*, 149. Cf. Majer Bogdanski, *Jewish Chronicle* (Oct. 31, 1986), as cited by Polonsky, "The Bund in Polish Political Life," 571.

Glossary

aliya: immigration by Jews to the Land of Israel
batkhonim: wedding entertainers
davened: prayed
doikeyt: "hereness"; the idea, supported by the Polish Bund, that Jews ought to focus on improving their lot in Poland rather than on evacuation or the promotion of organized, mass emigration
Evsektsiia: the Jewish Section of the Communist Party of the Soviet Union
felker-has: hatred of other peoples
gmina: schools of the Jewish community
kehiles: organized Jewish religious communities
khalemoyed peysakh: the intermediate days of Passover
kheder, pl. **khedorim:** a traditional, privately funded Jewish primary-level religious school
kheyder-yinglekh: young male students in traditional Jewish religious schools
klezmorim: musicians
mishtayns gezogt: of whom some think so highly
naye mentshn: new people
sheliakh-tsibur: traditionally, a representative of the Jewish community acting as its emissary in its negotiations with God (used here to refer to a party speaking on behalf of the Jewish community to the non-Jewish society)
shtetlekh: towns or villages in Eastern Europe in which Jews lived
talmud toyre: an elementary school for Jewish boys providing religious instruction; typically funded by the Jewish community
tsveyer: the "twos"; as used here, an adherent of the left-wing faction of the Polish Bund
yasles: day-care centers

Selected Bibliography

Notes: Articles published in Bundist periodicals before the beginning of the Second World War are listed in the endnotes.

Unpublished Sources

Archival Material

American Jewish Joint Distribution Committee Archives, New York Series, 1933–44:
    Poland, general (file 795)
    Bund (file 818)
    Central Jewish School Organization, Warsaw (file 828)
    Medem Sanatorium (file 841)
Archiwum Akt Nowych, Warsaw
    Wajsbrot, Jakub. "'Jugunt-bund "Cukunft" in Pojłn'/ Młodzieżowa organizacja bundowska 'Przyszłość' w Polsce od zarania do 1939 r." (76/II-87)
International Institute of Social History, Amsterdam
    Algemeyner Yidisher Arbeyter Bund Collection
Tamiment Library/Robert F. Wagner Labor Archives, New York
    Baruch Charney Vladeck Papers (Tamiment 037)
    Jewish Labor Committee Records (Wagner 025)
YIVO Institute for Jewish Research, New York
    Autobiographies of Jewish Youth in Poland (RG 4)
    Bund Archives (RG 1400)
    Kligsberg, Moses Collection (RG 719)
    TSYSHO (RG 1471)
    Vilna Collection (RG 29)

YIVO (Vilna): Administration (RG 1.1)
Zajd, Yisroel Collection (RG 1467)

Masters' Essays, Dissertations, and Conference Papers

Davis-Kram, Harriet. "Jewish Women in Russian Revolutionary Movements 1869–1905." M.A. thesis, Hunter College, City Univ. of New York, 1979.

Gechtman, Roni. "Yidisher Sotsializm: The Origin and Contexts of the Jewish Labor Bund's National Program." Ph.D. diss., New York Univ., 2005.

Pickhan, Gertrud. "'Where are the Women?' On the Discussion about Femininity, Masculinity and Jewishness within the General Jewish Workers Union ('Bund') in Poland." Paper delivered at the conference "Between Wars: Nations, Nationalisms, and Gender Relations in Central and Eastern Europe, 1918–1939," Obory, Poland, May 12, 2000.

Published Sources

"A nayer onfal oyf di medem-sanatorie." *Haynt,* February 13, 1931.

Abramson, Sh. "Di medem-sanatorie in shotn fun der natsisher okupatsie (September 1939–April 1940)." In *Medem-sanatorie-bukh,* edited by Khayim Shloyme Kazdan, 76–99. Tel Aviv: Farlag "Hamenora," 1971.

Alef, I. M. "In gan-eden far kinder (mit a prese-oysflug in der medem-sanatorie)." *Der moment,* December 20, 1937, 4.

Arayn in der "tsukunft." Sotsialistishe yugnt-bibliotek, vol. 3. Warsaw: Farlag sotsialistishe yugnt-bibliotek, 1931.

Arbeter-gez[elshaft] far fizisher dertsiung "morgnshtern" in poyln. Varshever optaylung. *A yor arbet: Tetikayts-berikht far der tsayt fun II.1 1937 bizn II.1 1938.* Warsaw, 1938.

Arbeter-gezelshaft far fizisher dertsiung "morgnshtern' in poyln. Varshever optaylung. *1938: Yor barikht.* Warsaw, 1939.

Arkadi: Zamlbukh tsum ondenk fun grinder fun "bund" arkadi kremer. New York: Farlag unzer tsayt, 1942.

Aronson, G[regor], S[ophia] Dubnow-Erlich, J[acob] S. Hertz [I. Sh. Herts], E[manuel] Nowogrudski [Novogrudski], Kh[ayim] S[hloyme] Kazdan, and E[manuel] Scherer [Sherer], eds. *Di geshikhte fun bund,* vol. 2. New York: Farlag unzer tsayt, 1962.

Astour, Michael [Astur, Mikhl]. *Geshikhte fun der frayland-lige un funem teritorialistishn gedank.* Vol. 1. Introduction by L. M. Fruchtbaum [Frukhtboym]. Buenos Aires and New York: Frayland lige, 1967.

Bacon, Gershon C. "Agudat Israel in Interwar Poland." In *The Jews of Poland Between Two World Wars,* edited by Gutman, Yisrael, Ezra Mendelsohn, Jehuda Reinharz, and Chone Shmeruk, 20–35. Hanover, N.H.: Univ. Press of New England, 1989.

Balabanoff, Angelica. *My Life as a Rebel.* Bloomington, Ind.: Indiana Univ. Press, 1973.

Balberyszki, M. "Volkism and the Volksparty." In *Struggle for Tomorrow: Modern Political Ideologies of the Jewish People,* edited by Basil J. Vlavianos and Feliks Gross, 236–43. New York: Arts, Incorporated, 1954.

Barzilai, Zvi. *Tenuat ha-bund be-polin ben shete milhamot ha-olam.* Jerusalem: Carmel, 1994.

Beckmanns Sport Lexikon A–Z. Leipzig, Vienna: Verlagsanstalt Otto Beckmann, 1933.

Berman, Khariton. "Der umfargeslekher rovner 'morgnshtern.'" *Forverts,* October 4, 2002, 15.

Berman, L. [Leybetshke]. *In loyf fun yorn: Zikhroynes fun a yidishn arbeter.* New York: Farlag "unzer tsayt," 1945.

Bernshteyn, Mordekhay V. "Der 'bund' in poyln." *Yorbukh,* vol. 1, edited by Shimen Federbush, 159–223. New York: Velt federatsie fun poylishe yidn, Amerikaner ekzekutiva, 1964.

Bernstein, Leon [Bernshteyn]. *Ershte shprotsungen (zikhroynes).* Buenos Aires: Farlag "yidbukh" bay der "gezelshaft far yidish-veltlekhe shuln in argentine," 1956.

Blatman, Daniel. "The Bund in Poland, 1935–1939." *Polin* 9 (1996): 58–82.

———. *For Our Freedom and Yours: The Jewish Labour Bund in Poland 1939–1949.* Translated by Naftali Greenwood. Portland, Ore.: Vallentine Mitchell, 2003.

———. "National-Minority Policy, Bundist Social Organizations, and Jewish Women in Interwar Poland." In *The Emergence of Modern Jewish Politics: Bundism and Zionism in Eastern Europe,* edited by Zvi Gitelman, 54–70. Pitt Series in Russian and East European Studies. Pittsburgh, Pa.: Univ. of Pittsburgh Press, 2003.

———. "Women in the Jewish Labor Bund in Interwar Poland." In *Women in the Holocaust,* edited by Dalia Ofer and Lenore J. Weitzman, 68–84. New Haven: Yale Univ. Press, 1998.

Blecking, Diethelm. "Jüdischer Sport in Polen." *Sozial- und Zeitgeschichte des Sports* 13, no. 1 (Mar. 1999): 20–27.

———. "Marxism Versus Muscular Judaism—Jewish Sports in Poland." In *Sport and Physical Education in Jewish History: Selected Papers from an International Seminar Held on the Occasion of the 16th Maccabiah, Wingate Institute, Israel, July 12–15, 2001,* edited by George Eisen, Haim Kaufman, and Manfred Lämmer, 48–55. Israel: Wingate Institute, 2003.

———. "Marxismus versus Muskeljudentum: Die jüdische Sportbewegung in Polen von den Anfängen bis nach dem Zweiten Weltkrieg." *SportZeit* 1, no. 2 (2001): 31–52.

Blond, Dina [Sheyna-Feygl Szapiro Michalewicz]. "A froy—a symbol." *Unzer tsayt* 10–12 (Oct.–Dec. 1972): 77–78.

———. *Shvester mayne! A vort tsu der yidisher arbeter-froy.* Warsaw: n.p., 1928.

Blum, Hillel Kats. *Zikhroynes fun a bundist: Bilder fun untererdishn lebn in tsarishn rusland.* New York: Bildungs-komitet fun arbeter ring, 1940.

Blum, L[i]uba. "Di yidishe arbeter-froy amol un haynt." *Folkstsaytung,* November 15, 1947, 27.

———. "Dr. ana broyde-heler." *Kultur un lebn* (Mar.–Apr. 1969): 10–11.

"Blutiger onfal oyf'n yud. kinder-sanatorium in miedzeszyn." *Der moment,* February 13, 1931, 12.

Dos bono viner gedenkbukh. Montreal: n.p., 1997.

Bronsztejn, Szyja. "Polish-Jewish Relations as Reflected in Memoirs of the Interwar Period." *Polin* 8 (1994): 66–88.

Brumberg, Abraham. "The Bund: History of a Schism." In *Jewish Politics in Eastern Europe,* edited by Jacobs, 81–89.

———. "The Bund and the Polish Socialist Party in the Late 1930s." In *The Jews of Poland,* edited by Gutman et al., 75–94.

———. "Mayn foters 10 yor in der medem-sanatorium." In *Medem-sanatorie-bukh,* edited by Kazdan, 304–8.

Brumberg, Lola. "Derinerungen fun a sanitarin." In *Medem-sanatorie-bukh,* edited by Kazdan, 151–55.

Buchbinder, N. A. [Bukhbinder]. *Di geshikhte fun der yidisher arbeter-bavegung in rusland loyt nit-gedrukte arkhiv-materialn.* Translated by Dovid Roykhel. Vilna: Farlag "tomor," 1931.

Charney, Daniel. *A litvak in poyln.* New York: Alveltlekher yidisher kultur-kongres, 1955.

Cohen, Nathan. "The Bund's Contribution to Yiddish Culture in Poland between the Two World Wars." In *Jewish Politics in Eastern Europe,* edited by Jacobs, 112–30.

Davis-Kram, Harriet. "The Story of the Sisters of the Bund." *Contemporary Jewry* 5, no. 2 (fall–winter 1980): 27–43.

Dubnow-Erlich, Sophia. "Biografie." In *Leon oler: Zayn lebn,* by Oler, 9–63.

———. *Bread and Matzoth.* Translated by Alan Shaw. Tenafly, N.J.: Hermitage Publishers, 2005.

———. "In di yorn fun reaktsie." In *Di geshikhte fun bund,* 2:537–626.

———. "Dos lebn fun leyvik hodes." In Dubnow-Erlich, *Leyvik hodes. Biografie un shriftn*, 9–36.

———, ed. *Leyvik hodes. Biografie un shriftn*. New York: Farlag unzer tsayt, 1962.

Dubnow-Erlich, Sophia, J[acob] S. Hertz [I. Sh. Herts], Kh[ayim] Sh[loyme] Kazdan, and E[manuel] Scherer [Sherer], eds. *Di geshikhte fun bund*. Vol. 4. New York: Farlag unzer tsayt, 1972.

———. *Di geshikhte fun bund*. Vol. 5. New York: Farlag unzer tsayt, 1981.

Eck, Nathan. "The Educational Institutions of Polish Jewry (1921–1939)." *Jewish Social Studies* 9, no. 1 (Jan. 1947): 3–32.

Edelman, Marek. *The Ghetto Fights*. London: n.p., 1990.

Eisenstein, Miriam. *Jewish Schools in Poland, 1919–39: Their Philosophy and Development*. New York: King's Crown Press, 1950.

"Di ekzistents fun medem-sanatorium bedroht!" *Der moment*, July 8, 1935, 5.

Elenboygn, A. K. "Lublin in unzer tsayt." *A[rbeter r[ing] lubliner young men's br. 392. 25 yoriger yubileyum 1909–1934*, 23–25. [New York]: Tsentrale yidishe bibliotek un prese arkhiv, 1934.

Ellenbogen, Khayim. "Unter der natsisher okupatsie." In *Medem-sanatorie-bukh*, edited by Kazdan, 111–15.

Ellenbogen-Cahan, Perl. "Di medem-sanatorie in milkhome-tsayt." In *Medem-sanatorie-bukh*, edited by Kazdan, 100–111.

Engel, David. "The Bund after the Holocaust: Between Renewal and Self-Liquidation." In *Jewish Politics in Eastern Europe: The Bund at 100*, edited by Jacobs.

Erlich, H[enryk]. "Der 'forverts' un der 'bund.'" In *Der "forverts" un der "bund,"* 11–37. New York: Bundisher klub in nu york, 1935.

Erlich, Shoshke. "Dzielna 22." In *Leon oler: Zayn lebn*, by Oler, 83–88.

———. "Dzielna 22." In *Leon Oler: The Life*, by Oler, 67–71.

Erlich, Victor. *Child of a Turbulent Century*. Evanston, Ill.: Northwestern Univ. Press, 2006.

———. "Life with Grandfather." In Sophia Dubnow-Erlich [Sophie Dubnov-Erlich], *The Life and Work of S. M. Dubnov: Diaspora Nationalism and Jewish History*. Edited by Jeffrey Shandler. Translated by Judith Vowles, 249–56. Bloomington: Indiana Univ. Press, in association with the YIVO Institute for Jewish Research, 1991.

Die Falken Organisationen in Ost- und Mitteleuropas von 1923 bis Heute. Brussels: IFM-SEI.

Fishman, Yoysef. "Di idealn vos zey hobn farflantst in undz." In *Medem-sanatorie-bukh*, edited by Kazdan, 373–79.

Fligel-Erlich, Shoshke. "Mayne zikhroynes fun der medem-sanatorie." In *Medem-sanatorie-bukh*, edited by Kazdan, 350–56.

Frankel, Jonathan. *Prophecy and Politics: Socialism, Nationalism and the Russian Jews, 1862–1917.* Cambridge: Cambridge Univ. Press, 1981.

Frost, Shimon. *Schooling as a Socio-Political Expression.* Jerusalem: Magnes Press, The Hebrew Univ., 1998.

[Frumkin], Ester. Foreword to Levin, *Fun yene yorn: "Kleyn bund,"* 3–9.

Fuftsen yor yugnt-bund "tsukunft" in vilne: Yoyvl-heft, 1922–1937. Vilna: n.p., 1937.

Garntsarska-Kadari, Bine. *Di linke poyle-tsien in poyln biz der tsveyter velt-milkhome.* Tel Aviv: Farlag i. l. peretz, 1995.

Gechtman, Roni. "Playing on the Left Wing." *Jewish Socialist* 47 (winter 2002–3): 24–26.

———. "The Rise of the Bund as reflected in the *Naye Folkstsaytung*, 1935–1936." *Gal-Ed* 17 (2000): 29–55.

———. "Socialist Mass Politics though Sport: The Bund's Morgnshtern in Poland, 1926–1939." *Journal of Sport History* 26, no. 2 (summer 1999): 326–52.

Gelbard, Arye. *Der jüdische Arbeiter-Bund Russlands im Revolutionsjahr 1917.* Ludwig Boltzmann Institut für Geschichte der Arbeiterbewegung, Materialen zur Arbeiterbewegung. Vol. 26. Vienna: Europaverlag, 1982.

Gezelshaft "kinder sanatorie." *Medem-sanatorie.* Warsaw: n.p., 1938.

Gezelshaft "kinder-sanatorie." *Zun, likht un freyd far undzere kinder!* Warsaw: n.p., 1938.

Giligitsh, Y[oysef]. "Zeks vokhn in kindershn gan-eden." In *Medem-sanatorie-bukh,* edited by Kazdan, 127–33.

Gilinski, M[otl]. *Lialkes.* Warsaw: Kooperativer farlag "kultur-lige," 1937.

Gilinski, Sh[loyme]. "Medem-sanatorie. Fun oyfbli bizn heylikn umkum." In *Medem-sanatorie-bukh,* edited by Kazdan, 19–34.

———. *Vi azoy lebt dos kind in medem-sanatorie.* Warsaw: Farvaltung fun medem-sanatorie, 1932.

———. "Yozef der forzitser fun unzer kinder-sanatorie." *Unzer tsayt* 10 (Nov. 1941): 44–45.

Gitelman, Zvi. "A Century of Jewish Politics in Eastern Europe: The Legacy of the Bund and the Zionist Movement." In *The Emergence of Modern Jewish Politics,* 3–19.

———, ed. *The Emergence of Modern Jewish Politics: Bundism and Zionism in Eastern Europe.* Pitt Series in Russian and East European Studies. Pittsburgh, Pa.: Univ. of Pittsburgh Press, 2003.

———. *Jewish Nationality and Soviet Politics: The Jewish Sections of the CPSU, 1917–1930*. Princeton: Princeton Univ. Press, 1972.

Glikson, Tsipore. "Medem sanatorie, ver ken dikh fargesn?" In *Medem-sanatorie-bukh*, edited by Kazdan, 309–23.

Goldfinger, Hershl. "Fun shmoln gesl oyfn breytn trakt." In *Unter der fon fun k.p.p. zamlbukh*, edited by H[ershl] Goldfinger, M[ikhael] Mirksi, and Sz[imon] Zachariasz, 91–114. Warsaw: Książka i Wiedza, 1959.

Goldsamer, Mordekhay, "A bletl geshikhte fun der yidisher arbeter-yugnt," *Mir zaynen do* 3 (Apr. 1953): 11.

Goldshteyn, I. Sh. "Vos a yid. zhurnalist trakht bezukhendig dos medem-sanatorie." *Haynt,* December 16, 1937.

Goldstein, Bernard [Goldshteyn]. *Finf yor in varshever geto*. New York: Farlag unzer tsayt, 1947.

———. *Tsvantsik yor in varshever "bund" 1919–1939*. New York: Farlag unzer tsayt, 1960.

Gorny, Yosef. *Converging Alternatives: The Bund and the Zionist Labor Movement, 1897–1985*. Albany, N.Y.: State Univ. of New York Press, 2006.

Greenbaum, Henry. "To the memory of a Teacher and Friend." In *Leon Oler: The Life*, by Oler, 150–53.

——— [Henri Grinboym]. "Tsum ondenk fun a lerer un fraynt." In *Leon oler: Zayn lebn*, by Oler, 177–80.

Gruber, Helmut. *Red Vienna: Experiment in Working-Class Culture, 1919–1934*. New York and Oxford: Oxford Univ. Press, 1991.

Gutman, Yisrael, Ezra Mendelsohn, Jehuda Reinharz, and Chone Shmeruk, eds. *The Jews of Poland Between Two World Wars*. Hanover, N.H.: Univ. Press of New England, 1989.

Heller, Celia S. *On the Edge of Destruction: Jews of Poland between the Two World Wars*. New York: Columbia Univ. Press, 1977.

Hersch, Liebmann. "The People's Preventorium for Children at Miedzeszyn (Poland)." *Annals of Public and Cooperative Economics* 5, no. 2 (May 1929): 191–200.

Hertz, J[acob] S. [I. Sh. Herts], ed. *Der bund in bilder 1897–1957.* New York: Farlag unzer tsayt, 1958.

———. "Der bund in umophengikn poyln, 1981–1925." In *Di geshikhte fun bund*, 4:9–178.

———. "Der bund in umophengikn poyln, 1926–1932." In *Di geshikhte fun bund*, 5:9–144.

———, ed. *Doyres bundistn*. 3 vols. New York: Farlag unzer tsayt, 1956–68.

———. "Di ershte ruslender revolutsye." In *Di geshikhte fun bund*, 2:7–482.

———. *Di geshikhte fun a yugnt. Der klayner bund—yugnt-bund tsukunft in poyln.* New York: Farlag unzer tsayt, 1946.

———. *Di geshikhte fun bund in lodz.* New York: Farlag unzer tsayt, 1958.

———. "Ideyishe erlikhkayt." In *Yid, mentsh, sotsialist. I. artuski ondenk-bukh.* Tel Aviv: Farlag "lebns-fragn," 1976.

———. "Di profesionele fareynen fun di yidishe arbeter." In *Di geshikhte fun bund*, 4:219–85.

———. "Shmuel mordekhay zigelboym." In *Zigelboym-bukh*, 11–40. New York: Farlag unzer tsayt, 1947.

Hodes, Leyvik. "Di ideologie fun sotsialistishn scouting." *Ershter land tsuzamenfor fun "skif" in poyln (varshe, 1–3 oktober 1936)*, 40–47. Skif-bibliotek. Vol. 4. Warsaw: Farlag skif-bibliotek, 1937.

———. *Materialn un onvayzungen far der sotsialistisher dertsiung-arbet.* Skif-bibliotek, 1. [Warsaw]: n.p., 1928.

Hunt, Richard N. *German Social Democracy 1918–1933.* Chicago: Quadrangle Books, 1970.

Hyman, Paula E. *Gender and Assimilation in Modern Jewish History: The Roles and Representation of Women.* Seattle: Univ. of Washington Press, 1995.

In di yorn fun yidishn khurbn: Di shtim fun untererdishn bund. New York: Farlag unzer tsayt, 1948.

Jacobs, Jack. "Creating a Bundist Counter-Culture: Morgnshtern and the Significance of Cultural Hegemony." In *Jewish Politics in Eastern Europe*, edited by Jacobs, 59–68.

———. "I movimenti Bundisti per bambini: verso una prospettiva comparata." *Annali dell'Istituto Gramsci Emilia-Romagna*, no. 4–5 (2000–2001): 239–48.

———. ed. *Jewish Politics in Eastern Europe: The Bund at 100.* New York: New York Univ. Press, in association with the Jewish Historical Institute, Warsaw, 2001.

———. "Jewish Worker's Sports Movements in Interwar Poland: Shtern and Morgnshtern in Comparative Perspective." In *Jews, Sports, and the Rites of Citizenship*, edited by Jack Kugelmass, 114–28. Urbana: Univ. of Illinois Press, 2007.

———. "Der 'Kleine Bund.' Sozialistische Jugend im Zarenreich." *Israel Stimme. Zeitschrift des Israel-AK der SJD Die Falken*, no. 6 (Jan. 2001): 24–29.

———. "The Politics of Jewish Sports Movements in Interwar Poland." In *Emancipation Through Muscles: Jews and Sports in Europe*, edited by Michael Brenner and Gideon Reuveni, 93–105. Lincoln: Univ. of Nebraska Press, 2006.

———. "Sport." In *The YIVO Encyclopedia of Jews in Eastern Europe*, edited by Gershon David Hundert, 2:1794–98. New Haven: Yale Univ. Press, 2008.

———. "Women in the Bund." In *Jewish Women: A Comprehensive Historical Encyclopedia*, edited by Paula E. Hyman. Jerusalem: Shalvi Publishing, 2006 (CD-ROM).

Johnpoll, Bernard K. *The Politics of Futility: The General Jewish Workers Bund of Poland, 1917–1943*. Ithaca: Cornell Univ. Press, 1967.

Kahan, Arcadius. *Essays in Jewish Social and Economic History*, edited by Roger Weiss. Chicago and London: Univ. of Chicago Press, 1986.

Kantorovitsh-Gilinski, Liuba. "Der film 'mir kumen on.'" In *Medem-sanatorie-bukh*, edited by Kazdan, 174–78.

———. "Shloyme gilinski un di medem-sanatorie." In *Medem-sanatorie-bukh*, edited by Kazdan, 183–94.

Kantorowicz, N. [Kantorovitsh]. "Die tsienistishe arbeter-bavegung in poyln," *Yor-bukh*, vol. 1, edited by Shimen Federbush, 183–94. New York: Velt federatsie fun poylishe yidn, Amerikaner ekzekutiva, 1964.

Kasel, Dovid. *Meierke fun "kleynem bund."* Sotsialistishe yugnt-bibliotek, no. 4. Lodz: Tsentral-komitet fun yugnt-bund "tsukunft," 1947.

Kassow, Samuel. "The Left Poalei Tsiyon in Inter-War Poland." In *Yiddish and the Left*, edited by Gennady Estraikh and Mikhail Krutikov, 109–28. European Humanities Research Center. Studies in Yiddish, Vol. 3. Oxford: Legenda, 2001.

Katan, Ish. "Kinder-shpilen fun 'kleynem bund.'" *Der arbeyter*, May 2, 1908, 4.

Katz, Moise [Moyshe Kats]. *A dor, vos hot farloyrn di moyre. Bleter zikhroynes fun arum 1905*. New York: Moyshe kats yubiley-komitet, 1956.

Kazdan, Kh[ayim] Sh[loyme]. *Fun kheder un "shkoles" biz tsysho: Dos ruslendishe yidntum in gerangl far shul, shprakh, kultur*. Mexico City: Shloyme mendelson fond bay der gezelshaft far "kultur un hilf," 1956.

———. *Di geshikhte fun yidishn shulvezn in umophengikn poyln*. Mexico City: Gezelshaft "kultur un hilf," 1947.

———. "Di medem-sanatorie in miedzeszyn." In *Medem-sanatorie-bukh*, edited by Kazdan, 38–70.

———. *Mentshn fun gayst un mut (bundishe geshtaltn)*. Buenos Aires: Farlag "yid-bukh" bay der "gezelshaft far yidish-veltlekhe shuln in argentine," 1962.

———. "Shloyme feyvish gilinski." In *Doyres bundistn*, vol. 3, edited by J. S. Hertz [I. Sh. Herts], 109–15. New York: Farlag unzer tsayt, 1968.

———. "Di shul- un kultur-tetikayt." In *Di geshikhte fun bund*, 4:287–388.

———. "Der shul- un kultur-tuer." In *Shloyme mendelson: Zayn lebn un shafn*, 52–71. New York: Farlag unzer tsayt, 1949.

———, ed. *Lerer-yizkhor-bukh: Di umgekumene lerer fun tsysho shuln in poyln*. New York: Komitet tsu fareybikn dem ondenk fun di umgekumene lerer fun di tsysho shuln in poyln, [1954?].

———, ed. *Medem-sanatorie-bukh*. Tel Aviv: Farlag "Hamenora," 1971.

———. "Vl. medem un di yidish-veltlekhe shul." In *Vladimir medem tsum tsvantsikstn yortsayt*, 160–69.

———. "Yoysef brumberg." In *Medem-sanatorie-bukh*, edited by Kazdan, 299–301.

Kdusman, A. "Skif arbet in kleynem shtetl." *Ershter land tsuzamenfor fun "skif" in poyln (varshe, 1–3 oktober 1936)*, 60–64. Skif-bibliotek. Vol. 4. Warsaw: Farlag skif-bibliotek, 1937.

Kellman, Ellen. "*Dos yidishe bukh alarmirt!* Towards the History of Yiddish Reading in Inter-War Poland." *Polin* 16 (2003): 213–41.

Kener, Yankef. *Kvershnit (1897–1947): Fragmentn fun zikhroynes, epizodn, geshikhtlekhe momentn, gedenkverter vegn umgekumene kedushim, martirer un kemfer*. New York: Tsentral komitet fun linke poyle-tsien in di fareynikte shtatn un kanade, 1947.

Kessler, Mario. "The Bund and the Labour and Socialist International." In *Jewish Politics in Eastern Europe*, edited by Jacobs, 183–94.

Khmurner-bukh. New York: Farlag unzer tsayt, 1958.

Kiel, Mark W. "The Ideology of the Folks-Partey." *Soviet Jewish Affairs* 5, no. 2 (1975): 75–89.

Klepfisz, Irena. "Di mames, dos loshn/The mothers, the language: Feminism, Yidishkayt, and the Politics of Memory." *Bridges* 4, no. 1 (1994): 12–47.

Kligsberg, Moshe. "Di yidishe yugnt-bavegung in poyln tsvishn beyde velt milkhomes (a sotsiologishe shtudie)." In *Shtudies vegn yidn in poyln 1919–1939: Di tsvishnshpil fun sotsiale, ekonomishe un politishe faktorn inem kamf fun a minoritet far ir kiem*, edited by Joshua [Shikl] Fishman, 137–228. New York: Yidisher visnshaftlekher institut—YIVO, 1974.

Korzec, Pawel. *Juifs en Pologne: La question juive pendant l'entre-deux-guerres*. Paris: Presses de la foundation nationale des sciences politiques, 1980.

K[upfershtayn], H[ershl]. "Dina blond-michalewicz." *Unzer tsayt*, no. 5 [520] (May 1985): 21–24.

Kursky, Franz [Frants Kurski]. *Gezamelte shriftn*. New York: Farlag der veker, 1952.

Lermer, Arthur [Artur]. "Zikhroynes vegn dem vilner lerer-seminar." In *Un dokh—dem morgnroyt antkegn: Eseyen*, 187–97. Tel Aviv: Farlag i. l. peretz, 1999.

Lestschinsky, Jacob. *Di yidishe arbeter-yugnt in poyln*. N.p., 1929.

Levin, Yankl. *Fun yene yorn: "Kleyn bund."* Minsk: Beltrespetshat, 1924.

Levine, Sholom [Levin]. *Untererdishe kemfer*. New York: Sholom levin bukh-komitet, 1946.

Lewin, Isaac. *The Jewish Community in Poland: Historical Essays*. New York: Philosophical Library, 1985.

Lewis, Paul. "Chaike Spiegel, 81, of Warsaw Revolt, Dies." *The New York Times,* April 7, 2002, 35.
Libeskind, Nachman. "Far velkhe parteyen hobn yidn in lodz geshtimt bes di valn tsum shtotrat un seym in 1919–1938?" *Undzer tsayt* 7–8 (July–Aug. 2000): 27–28.
Litvak, A. [Khaim-Yankev Helfand]. *Vos geven: Etiudn un zikhroynes.* Vilna: Farlag fun b. kletskin, 1925.
———. "Di yidishe arbeyter-froy." *Di naye velt,* October 15, 1915, 11.
Maderthaner, Wolfgang. "Sport für das Volk." In *Die ersten 100 Jahre. Österreichische Sozialdemokratie 1888–1988,* edited by Helene Maimann, 174–78. Vienna: Verlag Christian Brandstätter, 1988.
Marcus, Joseph. *Social and Political History of the Jews in Poland, 1919–1939.* Studies in the Social Sciences. Berlin, New York: Mouton Publishers, 1983.
McNeal, Robert H. "Women in the Russian Radical Movement." *Journal of Social History* 5, no. 2 (1971–72): 143–63.
Medem, Gina. *A lebensveg: Oytobiografishe notitsn.* New York: Gina medem bukhkomitet, 1950.
Medem, Vladimir. *Fun mayn lebn.* Vol. 2. New York: Vladimir medem komite, 1923.
———. "Kinder vos zaynen farmishpet tsum toyt." *Forverts,* April 19, 1922, 4.
———. *The Life and Soul of a Legendary Jewish Socialist,* edited and translated by Samuel A. Portnoy. New York: KTAV Publishing House, Inc., 1979.
Melman, F. "Di arbet fun skif in unzere shuln un tsvishn di shiler fun unzere shuln." *Ershter land tsuzamenfor fun "skif" in poyln (varshe, 1–3 oktober 1936),* 17–21. Skif-bibliotek. Vol. 4. Warsaw: Farlag skif-bibliotek, 1937.
Melzer, Emanuel. *No Way Out: The Politics of Polish Jewry, 1935–1939.* Cincinnati: Hebrew Union College Press, 1997.
Mendel, Hersh. *Memoirs of a Jewish Revolutionary.* Preface by Isaac Deutscher. London: Pluto Press, 1989.
Mendelsohn, Ezra. *Class Struggle in the Pale: The Formative Years of the Jewish Workers' Movement in Tsarist Russia.* Cambridge: Cambridge Univ. Press, 1970.
———. "The Dilemma of Jewish Politics in Poland: Four Responses." In *Jews and Non-Jews in Eastern Europe,* edited by Bela Vago and George L. Mosse, 203–19. New York, Toronto: John Wiley and Sons; Jerusalem: Israel Universities Press, 1974.
———. "Jewish Politics in Interwar Poland: An Overview." In *The Jews of Poland,* edited by Gutman et al., 9–19.
———. *The Jews of East Central Europe between the World Wars.* Bloomington: Indiana Univ. Press, 1983.
———. *On Modern Jewish Politics.* New York, Oxford: Oxford Univ. Press, 1993.

———. *Zionism in Poland: The Formative Years, 1915–1926*. New Haven and London: Yale Univ. Press, 1981.

Mendelson, L[evi]. "Nokh vegn der arkadi-grupe in varshe." *Lebns-fragn* 38, nos. 445–46 (May–June 1989): 11–12.

Mendelson, Shloyme. "Dos yidishe shulvezn in poyln." In *Shloyme mendelson. Zayn lebn un shafn*, 229–43.

———. *Shloyme mendelson. Zayn lebn un shafn*. New York: Farlag unzer tsayt, 1949.

Michalewicz, B[einish] [Mikhalevitsh] [Josef Isbitzki]. *Geshtaltn un perzenlekhkeytn: Gezamlte artiklen vegn denker un tuer fun der arbeter–bavegung*. Warsaw: [Tsentral komitet fun bund in poyln], 1938.

Mill, John [Yoysef Shloyme Mil]. *Pionern un boyer*. 2 vols. New York: Farlag der veker, 1946–49.

Minc, P[inkus] (Alexander). *Di geshikhte fun a falsher iluzie (zikhroynes)*. Dos poylishe yidntum. Vol. 103. Buenos Aires: Tsentral-farband fun poylishe yidn in argentine, 1954.

———. *The History of a False Illusion: Memoirs on the Communist Movements in Poland (1918–1938)*. Translated from the Yiddish by Robert Michaels. Lewiston, Queenston, Lampeter: Edwin Mellen Press, 2002.

Minczeles, Henri. *Histoire générale du Bund: un mouvement révolutionnaire juif*. Paris: Denol, 1999.

Mishkinsky, Moshe. *Reshit tenuat ha-poalim ha-yehudit be-rusyah: megamot yesod*. Tel Aviv: Ha-kibutz Ha-meuchad, 1981.

Mlotek, Yosl. "Vi azoy iz geshafn gevorn 'der shpeykhler.'" In *Medem-sanatorie-bukh*, edited by Kazdan, 134–41.

Nadel, B[enyomin]. "Tsu der geografie fun 'bund' in poyln." *Undzer tsayt*, nos. 11–12 [708–9] (Nov.–Dec. 2001): 26–27.

Niewerth, Toni and Peiffer, Lorenz. "'Jüdischer Sport in Deutschland' eine kommentierte Bibliogrfie," *SportZeit* 1, no. 2 (2001): 81–106.

Niger, Shmuel, Shatzky, Jacob [Yankef Shatski], et al., eds. *Leksikon fun der nayer yidisher literatur*. 8 vols. New York: Alveltlekher yidisher kultur-kongres, 1956–81.

Nowogrodzki, Emanuel. *The Jewish Labor Bund in Poland: From its Emergence as an Independent Political Party Until the Beginning of World War II 1915–1939*. Rockville, Md.: Shengold Books, 2001.

Oler, Leon. "Di linke rikhtung in bund fun poyln." In *Khmurner-bukh*, 9–20. New York: Farlag unzer tsayt, 1958.

———. *Leon Oler: The Life of a Jewish Socialist*. Edited by Sophia Dubnow-Erlich. Translated by Hinda Oler Gutoff. Brookline, Mass.: n.p., 2006.

———. *Leon oler: Zayn lebn un tetikayt.* Edited by Sophia Dubnow-Erlich. New York: Farlag unzer tsayt, 1973.

Ollman, Bertell. *Social and Sexual Revolution: Essays on Marx and Reich.* Boston: South End Press, 1979.

Oppenheim, Israel. *The Struggle of Jewish Youth for Productivization: The Zionist Youth Movement in Poland.* East European Monographs, Vol. 273. New York: Columbia Univ. Press, 1989.

Patt, Emanuel [Pat]. "Gilinski mayn lerer, mayn khaver, mayn patsient." In *Medem-sanatorie-bukh,* edited by Kazdan, 281–91.

———. *In gerangl: Yankef pat un zayn dor.* New York: Yankef pat familie fond, 1971.

———. "Mir zaynen yung un dos iz sheyn. Leyvik hodes un der sotsialistisher kinder-farband 'skif.'" In Dubnow-Erlich, *Leyvik hodes. Biografie un shriftn,* 342–56.

———. *Di skif-grupn: Loyt dem proyekt, vos iz gevorn ongenumen oyf dem plenum fun der skif-tsentrale dem 15-tn november 1937. Hant-bikhl far skif-helfer.* Skif bibliotek. Vol. 5. Warsaw: Farlag skif-bibliotek, 1938.

Peled, Yoav. *Class and Ethnicity in the Pale: The Political Economy of Jewish Workers' Nationalism in Late Imperial Russia.* New York: St. Martin's Press, 1989.

Pickhan, Gertrud. *"Gegen den Strom": Der Allgemeine Jüdische Arbeiterbund "Bund" in Polen, 1918–1939.* Schriften des Simon-Dubnow Instituts Leipzig, vol. 1. Stuttgart, Munich: Deutsche Verlags-Anstalt, 2001.

———. "Kossovsky, Portnoy and Others: The Role of Members of the Bund's Founding Generation in the Interwar Polish Bund." In *Jewish Politics in Eastern Europe,* edited by Jacobs, 69–80.

———. "Das NKVD-Dossier über Henryk Erlich und Wiktor Alter." *Berliner Jahrbuch für osteuropäische Geschichte* (1994): 155–86.

———. "'Wo sind die Frauen?' Zur Diskussion um Weiblichkeit, Männlichkeit und Jüdischkeit im Allgemeinen Jüdischen Arbeiterbund ("Bund") in Polen." In *Zwischen den Kriegen: Nationen, Nationalismen und Geschlechterverhältnisse in Mittel- und Osteuropa 1918–1939,* edited by Johanna Gehmacher, Elisabeth Harvey, und Sophia Kemlein, 187–99. Einzelveröffentlichungen des Deutschen Historischen Instituts Warschau, 7. Osnabrück: 2004.

Pludermakher-Vaysbrot, Sonie. "Umfargeslekhe epizodn." In *Medem-sanatorie-bukh,* edited by Kazdan, 230–34.

Polonsky, Antony. "The Bund in Polish Political Life, 1935–1939," In *Jewish History: Essays in Honour of Chimen Abramsky,* edited by Ada Rapoport-Albert and Steven J. Zipperstein, 547–77. London: Peter Halban, 1988.

———. "The New Jewish Politics and its Discontents." In *The Emergence of Modern Jewish Politics,* edited by Gitelman, 35–53.

Pupko, Kh. "Vilna—dos vigele fun der yidish-veltlikher shul." In *Vilna*, edited by Ephim N. Jeshurin, 296–312. New York: Vilner brentsh 367 arbeyter ring, 1935.

Rabinowicz, Harry M. *The Legacy of Polish Jewry: A History of Polish Jews in the Inter-War Years, 1919–1939.* New York: Thomas Yoseloff, 1965.

Rak, Meir. "Eyne fun di letste varshever geto-kemfer." *Forverts*, February 3, 1989, 10, 25.

Reyzen, Zalman. *Leksikon fun der yidisher literatur.* 4 vols. Vilna: Farlag fun b. kletskin, 1926–29.

Rogoff, Dovid. "Sport in vilne." *Forverts*, September 8, 2000, 20.

Rosenfarb, Chava. "An Oak Has Fallen." In *Bono Wiener Remembered* [Dos bono viner gedenkbukh], 1–39. Montreal: Privately published, 1997.

Rotenberg, Y[oysef] [Rotnberg]. "Der gayst fun an institutsie." In *Medem-sanatorie-bukh,* edited by Kazdan, 211–16.

Rowe, Leonard. "Jewish Self-Defense: A Response to Violence." In *Shtudies vegn yidn in poyln 1919–1939,* edited by Fishman, 105–49. New York: Yidisher visnshaftlekher institut—YIVO, 1974.

Rozen, Neytn. "Iberlebungen fun a 'kleyenem bundist' (derinerungen fun vilne, vitebsk un polotsk)." *Unzer tsayt* 12 (Dec. 1943): 29–32.

Rozenbaum, Menukhem. "A mitglid fun der sanatorie-farvaltung dertseylt." In *Medem-sanatorie-bukh,* edited by Kazdan, 157–60.

Samuś, Pawel. "The Bund Organization in Lodz, 1898–1939." In *Jewish Politics in Eastern Europe,* edited by Jacobs, 90–111.

Scherer, Emanuel. "The Bund." In *Struggle for Tomorrow,* edited by Vlavianos and Gross, 135–96. New York: Arts, Incorporated, 1954.

Schweizer, Shlomo [Shloyme Svaytser], ed. *Shures poyle-tsien. Portretn.* Tel-Aviv: I. l. peretz farlag, 1981.

Segal, Simon. *The New Poland and the Jews.* New York: Lee Furman, Inc., 1938.

Shapiro, Aharon. *Mentsh un goyrl.* Tel Aviv: I. l. peretz farlag, 2002.

———. "Zikhroynes fun der arkadi-grupe." *Lebns-fragn* 37, nos. 433–34 (May–June 1988): 8.

Shapiro, Robert Moses. "The Polish *Kehillah* Elections of 1936: A Revolution Reexamined." *Polin* 8 (1994): 206–26.

Sharaf, Myron. *Fury on Earth: A Biography of Wilhelm Reich.* New York: Da Capo Press, 1994.

Shmeruk, Chone. "Hebrew-Yiddish-Polish: A Trilingual Jewish Culture." In *The Jews of Poland,* edited by Gutman et al., 285–311.

Shpizman, Leyb, ed. *Khalutsim in poyln,* vol. 1. New York: Forsh-institut fun der tsionistisher arbeter-bavegung, 1959.

Steenson, Gary P. *"Not One Man! Not One Penny!" German Social Democracy, 1863–1914.* Pittsburgh: Univ. of Pittsburgh Press, 1981.

Steingart, Tsirl [Shtayngart]. "Di froyen in 'bund.'" *Unzer tsayt,* nos. 3–4 [398–99] (Mar.–Apr. 1975): 19–22.

Steinlauf, Michael C. "Jewish Politics and Youth Culture in Interwar Poland: Preliminary Evidence from the YIVO Autobiographies." In *The Emergence of Modern Jewish Politics,* edited by Gitelman, 95–104.

Shvarts, P[inkus]. "Folkstsaytung." In *Fun noentn over,* 2:303–439. New York: Alveltlekher yidisher kultur-kongres, 1956.

Szulman, W[iktor] [Viktor Shulman]. *Bletlekh geshikhte fun der yidisher arbeter-bavegung.* Warsaw: Farlag "di velt," 1929.

Tartakower, Aryeh. "Di yidishe shul in poyln tsvishn tsvey milkhomes." *Sefer hashanah/Yorbukh,* 2:210–65. Tel Aviv: Velt federatsie fun poylishe yidn, 1967.

Tashn-kalendar mayn khaver 1930. Skif bibliotek. Vol. 2. Warsaw: n.p., 1930.

Tennenbaum Becker, Nina. "Leon Oler, Teacher and Spiritual Leader." In *Leon Oler: The Life,* by Oler, 57–62.

———. "Der lerer un der gaystiker firer." In *Leon oler: Zayn lebn,* by Oler, 72–77.

Tobias, Henry J. *The Jewish Bund in Russia: From Its Origins to 1905.* Stanford, Calif.: Stanford Univ. Press, 1972.

Tobias, Henry J., and Charles E. Woodhouse. "Political Reaction and Revolutionary Careers: The Jewish Bundists in Defeat, 1907–1910." *Comparative Studies in Society and History* 19 (1977): 367–96.

———. "Revolutionary Optimism and the Practice of Revolution: The Jewish Bund in 1905." *Jewish Social Studies* 47 (1985): 135–50.

"Tsentral-komitet fun 'bund' in poyln." *Memorandum tsum yidishn arbeter-komitet in amerike.* New York: Bundisher klub in nu york, 1937.

Vaysnberg, Perl. "Di medem-sanatorie." In *Medem-sanatorie-bukh,* edited by Kazdan, 337–45.

Vidrevitsh-Tukhmakher, Nekhe. "Mit libshaft un akhtung dermon ikh di medem-sanatorie." In *Medem-sanatorie-bukh,* edited by Kazdan, 365–68.

Vladeck, B. Charney [Vladek]. "Tsvey yinglekh." In *B. vladek in leben und shafen,* edited by Ephim Jeshurin [Yefim Yeshurin], 156–57. New York: "Forverts" Association, 1936.

Vladimir medem tsum tsvantsikstn yortsayt. New York: Amerikaner reprezentants fun algemeynem yidishn arbeter bund ("bund") in poyln, 1943.

W słońcu i radości: dziecko w Sanatorjum im Wł. Medema w Miedzeszynie. Warsaw: Zarządu Sanatorjum dla Dzieci im. Wł. Medema, 1933.

Wachowska, Barbara. "Łódź Remained Red: Elections to the City Council of 27 September 1936." *Polin* 9 (1996): 83–106.

Wald, P[inkhes]. [Pinkhes Vald]. *Geshtaltn fun yidishn velt-folk (bundistn).* Buenos Aires: Farlag "yidbukh" bay der "gezelshaft far yidish-veltlekhe shuln in argentine," 1964.

Wapner-Lewin, Paie [Paie Vapner-levin]. *Mayn flikht tsu dertseyln: Derinerungen fun a lererin in vilner geto.* Buenos Aires: Memoria, 1999.

Weill, Claudie. *Les cosmopolites. Socialisme et judéité en Russie (1897–1917).* Paris: Éditions Syllepse, 2004.

Wróbel, Piotr. "From Conflict to Cooperation: The Bund and the Polish Socialist Party, 1897–1939." In *Jewish Politics in Eastern Europe*, edited by Jacobs, 155–71.

Der yidisher arbeter-klas in yor 1936. Lodz: n.p., 1937.

"Yidn in youston gibn op koved a yidisher kultur-tuerin tsu ir 100stn geboyrnyor." *Forverts*, May 4, 1990, 16.

Yismakh, Borukh. "Sports Clubs and Self-Defense." In *From a Ruined Garden: The Memorial Books of Polish Jewry*, edited by Jack Kugelmass and Jonathan Boyarin, 60–63. New York: Schocken Books, 1983.

Yonas, Elka. "Skif-arbet tsvishn arbeter-kinder un gasn-kinder." *Ershter land tsuzamenfor fun "skif" in poyln (varshe, 1–3 oktober 1936)*, 21–29. Skif-bibliotek. Vol. 4. Warsaw: Farlag skif-bibliotek, 1937.

Zalcman, Moshe. *Bela shapiro: Di populere froyen-geshtalt.* Paris: n.p., 1983.

Zelmanowich, F. L. [Efrayim Luzer Zelmanovitsh]. *Epizodn fun mayn lebn.* Mexico City: Shloyme mendelson fond bay der gezelshaft far kultur un hilf, 1956.

Zimmerman, Joshua D. *Poles, Jews, and the Politics of Nationality: The Bund and the Polish Socialist Party in Late Tsarist Russia, 1892–1914.* Madison, Wis.: Univ. of Wisconsin Press, 2004.

Zygielbaum, Sh[muel] M[ordekhay]. "Di profesionele bavegung fun di yidishe arbeter." In *Di geshikhte fun bund*, 4:179–217.

Index

Italic page number denotes illustration.

abortion, 22, 23, 117n. 67
Abramowicz, Yulia, 83
Abramson, Sh., 133n. 6
Agranov, Yankl Moyshe, 32
Agudes Yisroel: city council elections (1936), 3; *kehiles* elections (1936), 3, 107n. 11; parliamentary elections (1919) and, 106n. 4; sanatorium and, 80; sports clubs and, 49
Aizenshtat, Isai, 86
aliya, 5, 59, 153
Alter, Victor, 75, 88, 140n. 95
American Jewish Joint Distribution Committee, 63, 77, 139–40n. 84
Amsterdam, Avrom Meyer, 86
Amsterdam, Liza Grinblat, 86
anarchist children's movements, 34
anticlericalism, 42
anti-Semitism: electoral victories and, 100; Henryk Erlich on, 150n. 103; Medem Sanatorium and, 77; Sotsialistisher kinder farband and, 46; sports movements and, 58, 130n. 59; trade unions and, 152n. 18; Tsukunft Storm and, 19–20; university students and, 96, 150n. 97, 150n. 103
Antman, Rifke, 88
apprentices, 30, 31, 32

Arbeiterbund für Sport und Körperkultur in Oesterriech, 127–28n. 27
Arbeter-gezelshaft far fi zisher dertsiung "morgnshtern" in poyln. *See* Morgnshtern
Arbeter-gezelshaft far fi zisher dertsiung "shtern." *See* Shtern
Arbeter-tsaytung (Left Poalei Zion), 54–55, 58, 130n. 53
Arkadi Group, 15, 114n. 31, 114n. 32
asceticism, revolutionary, 86
Asch, Sholem, 75
assimilation, 94, 95, 148n. 90
Austria, 41, 127–28n. 27
autobiographies, youth, 26–27
Aykhner, Roza, 141n. 107
Aynshtayn, Tsipore, 149n. 93
Ayzenshtat, B., 133n. 6

Baranowicze (Poland), 40
Bar Kochba, 51–52, 55
basketball, 55
Batkhan, Ruta. *See* Berman, Ruta Batkhan
Belgium youth organizations, 18
Belitski, Liuba, 149n. 93
Berkovitsh Circle, 15

Berman, Leybetshke, 145n. 58
Berman, Ruta Batkhan (Mina): activities of, 84, 90; *Doyres bundistn* on, 144n. 33; marriage of, 145n. 58; on women, 94; World War II era and, 148–49n. 93
Bernshtayn, Matvey, 15
Beys Yankef schools, 80, 137n. 47
Bialystok (Poland): children's movements in, 34; city council elections (1938–39), 4; *kehiles* elections (1937), 3; parliamentary elections (1922), 2; Sanatorium Home, 75; women Bundists in, 84; women City Council members, 88; Yidisher arbeter froy branch, 92, 146–47n. 76; Youth Bund Tsukunft survey in, 11
Big, Asie, 149n. 93
bilingual schools, 137n. 47
birth control, 92
Blatman, Daniel: on electoral victories, 5–6; on founding YAF, 145n. 50; on Warsaw YAF members, 147n. 82; on women Bund members, 143–44n. 33, 145n. 45; on women leaders, 148n. 86
Blit, Lucjan, 19–20, 117n. 55, 129n. 46
Blond, Dina: *Doyres bundistn* listing, 144n. 33; on early women Bund members, 87; post–World War II life of, 145n. 53; "Where Are the Women?", 94; YAF and party activities, 89
Blones, Gute, 149n. 93
Bloody Sunday, 31
Blum, Luba, 146n. 62
Bobruisk (Russian Empire), 31
Bolshevik Revolution, 86, 105n. 1
Bolsheviks, 36
Borislav (Poland), 15–16
Borochov, Ber, 127n. 23
boxing, 51, 53–54, 56, 127n. 24, 128n. 31, 131n. 64
boycotts, 107n. 8
Boy-Zelenski, Tadeusz, 23, 117n. 67

Brandes, L., 150n. 101
Brisk, 58
Broniewski, Władysław, 70
Broyde-Heler, Ana, 66, 133n. 6, 133n. 10, 135n. 24, 141n. 107
Brumberg, Yoysef, 65–66, 133n. 10
Bub und Maedel (Hodann), 22
Bund, the: Central Committee (World War I), 86; Central Committee (World War II), 141n. 107, 148n. 93; Central Committee members (1898), 83; Central Committee women members, 86, 88; children's organization of (*see* Sotsialistisher kinder farband); on children's organizations, 38; Comintern and, 9; constellation of organizations, 1, 98; counterculture of, 6–7, 82, 97, 101, 109n. 30, 116–17n. 53; Eighth Conference (1910), 85; on the election boycott (1919), 2; electoral victories of, 5–7, 99–100, 101 (*see also* elections); Fifth Congress (1903), 84; founding of, 83, 142n. 5; growth of, 98–99; influence of, 1, 98–99; Kleyner bund and, 30–33; Labour and Socialist International and, 5, 10, 42, 111–12n. 9; legal status of, 87, 94; libraries of, 19, 116–17n. 53; Medem Sanatorium and, 67, 140n. 95; Shloyme Mendelson and, 64; Morgnshtern and, 50, 60–61, 125–26n. 13, 132n. 81; 1920 split of, 86; Ninth Conference (1912), 85; Otvosk summer colony and, 133n. 6; Polish Socialist Party and, 57; Polish-Soviet War (1920–21) and, 144n. 38; post–Revolution of 1905 decline of, 35, 119–20n. 25; Social Democratic Party of the Kingdom of Poland and Lithuania and, 8–9; Sotsialistisher kinder farband and, 38, 40–42, 47, 121n. 41; success of, 101; Tenth Conference (1917), 86; tuberculosis sanatorium of (*see* Medem Sanatorium); underground operation of, 148–49n. 93;

university students organization, 96–97, 115n. 45, 149–50n. 94, 150n. 101; women leaders and, 86, 93–94, 148n. 86; women members of (Polish Bund), 87–89, 145n. 45; women members of (Russian Empire), 82–87, 143–44n. 33, 143n. 32; women's division (1917), 87; women's organization of (*see* Yidisher arbeter froy); during World War II, 141n. 107, 148–49n. 93; YAF founding and, 89, 93, 147–48n. 84; Youth Bund Tsukunft members in, 18, 99, 115n. 45; youth organization of (*see* Youth Bund Tsukunft). *See also* Bundist candidates

Bund Archives, 31

Bundist candidates, 1–7, 99–100; from 1936–1939, 99–100; boycotts (1935 and 1938), 107n. 8; city council elections (1919), 108n. 17; city council elections (1936), 3, 107n. 10, 107n. 13; city council elections (1936–39), 99–100; city council elections (1937), 107n. 15; city council elections (1938–39), 3–4, 108n. 17; Heller on, 108n. 25; *kehiles* elections, 2–3, 99–100, 107n. 10, 107n. 11, 107n. 15; parliamentary elections, 1–2, 106n. 4, 106n. 6; Sotsialistisher kinder farband workers for, 47; sports movements and, 61; Youth Bund Tsukunft and, 19

camps, 43–44, 45, 46, 91, 123n. 65

Central Jewish School Organization. *See* TSYSHO

Charney, Daniel, 75

chess, 126n. 14

children: day-care centers for, 92, 93, 153; newspapers for, 40, 122n. 55; refugee, 78, 85n. 140, 91; street, 39–40

children's movements: anarchist, 34; communist, 44–45; czarist era, 29–37, 47; Medem Sanatorium and, 66–67; membership in, 34–35, 45–46; Pioneers, 44–45; Polish Socialist Party, 35, 42, 45; relationships with the Kleyner bund, 33–34; rivalry between, 34; scouting movement, 41–42; socialist, 34–35, 41–42, 44, 122n. 57; working class and, 37; Zionist, 33. *See also* Fraye skoytn; Kleyner bund; Sotsialistisher kinder farband; Yungbor

Chwoinik, Abraham, 97

city council: elections (1919), 108n. 17; elections (1936), 3, 107n. 10, 107n. 13; elections 1936–39, 99–100; elections (1937), 107n. 15; elections (1938–39), 3–4, 108n. 17; women members of, 88, 90, 145n. 93

coal miners, 70, 137n. 46

Comintern, 9

communal elections. *See kehiles*

communist party of Poland: children's movements for, 44–45; dissolution of (1938), 4, 100; Kombund and, 110n. 3; Medem Sanatorium and, 67–68, 135–36n. 32, 135n. 31; opposition to Sotsialistisher kinder farband, 46, 123n. 75; sports clubs, 49; Yidisher arbeter froy and, 149n. 93; youth organizations and, 9–10, 14, 37, 110–11n. 6

communist trade unions, 67–68, 135n. 31, 135–36n. 32

Communist Workers' Party of Poland, 110n. 3

Communist Youth International, 9–10, 13, 110–11n. 6, 111n. 7

contraception, 22

Council of Trade Unions, 3

counterculture, 6–7, 101; libraries and, 116–17n. 53; vs. subculture, 108–9n. 30; Yidisher arbeter froy and, 82, 97

Cracow (Poland), 4, 49, 125n. 10, 149–50n. 94

cycling, 50–51

czarist era, 8, 29–37, 47, 82–87. *See also* Russian Empire

Czech sports movement, 127–28n. 27

Dalton System, 71
Davis-Kram, Harriet, 143n. 32
Dawidowicz, Tobcie, 149n. 93
day-care centers, 91, 92, 153
Dinezon, Yankef, 133n. 5, 133n. 6
Dinezon Committee, 63, 133n. 5, 133n. 6
doikeyt, 5, 153
Doyres bundistn, 143–44n. 33
Dubnow, Simon, 21
Dubnow, Sophia. *See* Dubnow-Erlich, Sophia
Dubnow-Erlich, Sophia: *Doyres bundistn* listing, 144n. 33; early activities of, 85; literature distribution by, 83; marriage of, 86; Medem Sanatorium and, 133n. 6; on sexuality, 21–25, 27, 117n. 67, 118n. 74; sons of, 97
Dvinsk (Russian Empire), 32–33, 84

Eberil, I., 36
Edelman, Cipe, 83, 90, 145n. 56, 146n. 62
education: Frost's study on, 78; Medem Sanatorium and, 62, 71–74, 81, 137n. 53; religious, 74; sex, 22, 23, 28; socialist, 67; Sotsialistisher kinder farband and, 38; for street children, 40; Youth Bund Tsukunft and, 20, 113n. 24. *See also* schools
Eichner, Roza, 85, 88, 90, 145n. 57
elections, 1–7, 99–100, 101; boycotts (1935 and 1938), 107n. 8; city council, 3–4, 99–100, 107n. 10, 107n. 13, 107n. 15, 108n. 17; Heller on, 108n. 25; *kehiles*, 2–3, 99–100, 107n. 10, 107n. 11, 107n. 15; 1936–39, 99–100; parliamentary, 1–2, 106n. 4, 106n. 6, 107n. 8; Sotsialistisher kinder farband workers in, 47; Youth Bund Tsukunft and, 19
Engels, Friedrich, 142n. 5
Epstein, Liza, 83

Erlich, Alexander, 25, 97, 118n. 75
Erlich, Henryk: on anti-Semitism, 150n. 103; on Lestschinsky, 112n. 11; marriage of, 21, 86; Medem Sanatorium and, 75, 140n. 95; sons of, 97
Erlich, Victor, 97, 150n. 94
evening schools, 20, 67, 123n. 75
Evsektsiia (Jewish Section of the Communist Party), 37, 143n. 31, 153

Fainer, Miriam Szyfman, 149n. 93
Faraynikte, 112n. 11
Federation of Polish Jews in America, 77
Feiner, Leon, 126n. 13
Feldhendler, Yankef, 15
Ferrière, Adolphe, 75
Feuerbach, Ludwig, 142n. 5
Fiksenbaum, Judka, 114n. 27
Folkist party, 49, 106n. 4
Folkstsaytung. *See Naye folkstsaytung*
football. *See* soccer
Football Association of Warsaw, 54
Ford, Aleksander, 77
Forward Association, 77
France, 18
Fraye skoytn (children's movement), 45
Frayhayt (youth movement), 19, 116n. 52
Frayland Lige, 14, 17
free love, 21, 26–27, 28
Frejlich, S., 26–27
Freud, Sigmund, 23
Fridman, Leybl, 126n. 13, 141n. 107
Friedrich, Zalmen, 126n. 13
Frost, Shimon, 78
Frukht, Bela, 141n. 107
Frumkin, Esther, 36–37, 84–86, 143–44n. 33, 143n. 31
Fryshdorf, Hannah Krystal, 149n. 93
Fun yene yorn (Levin), 33–34

Galicia (Poland), 4
gangs, street, 34
Gants, Khane Sore, 32
Gechtman, Roni, 51
Gelborn, Morris, 126n. 13
General Jewish Workers' Bund. *See* Bund, the
General Zionists, 3, 5, 33, 106n. 4, 107n. 11
Germany: boxing in, 128n. 31; children's movements in, 41, 122n. 57; refugee children from, 78, 85n. 140, 91; Social Democratic Party, 108–9n. 30; sports movements in, 48; youth organizations in, 18
Gilinski, Motl, 72, 74
Gilinski, Shloyme: Brumberg and, 65, 66; career of, 65; educational programs and, 71; on Jewish holidays, 74; Medem Sanatorium board member, 133n. 6, 133n. 10; Medem Sanatorium funding and, 75, 77, 139–40n. 84; Warsaw City Council and, 75; during World War II, 141n. 107
Gitelman, Zvi, 109n. 30
Giterman, Yitzkhok, 133n. 10
gmina schools, 71, 121n. 47, 153
Golde, Dr., 146n. 62
Goldman, Emma, 24
Goldshmid, A., 21
Goldshtayn, Moyshe, 36
Gotlib, Yitskhok, 128–29n. 43
government. *See* Polish government
Grabolski, Fruma (Vera), 84
Great Britain, 5
Greenbaum, Henry, 118n. 75
Greenblat, Rosa, 83, 142n. 5, 143–44n. 33
Grinfeld, Nadia (Frume) Kenigshats, 84
Grodno (Poland), 3, 107n. 10
Gurvich, Evgeniia Adolovna. *See* Hurvitch, Zhenia
Gwiazda. *See* Shtern
gymnastics, 49, 50–51, 56, 57, 125n. 5, 125n. 11

half-intellectuals, 82, 142n. 3
handball, 56
Hapoel (sports movement), 49
Hashomer Hatsair, 18, 114n. 27, 116n. 49, 116n. 50, 126–27n. 19
Haynt (newspaper), 80, 136n. 32
health care, 63. *See also* Medem Sanatorium
Hebrew, 51–52, 62, 96
Hekhalutz Hatsair (youth movement), 116n. 52
Helfand, Khaim-Yankev, 82–83, 87
Heller, Anna. *See* Rozental, Anna Heller
Heller, Celia, 108n. 25
Hertz, Jacob S., 112n. 10
Hertz, Rena Hister, 90, 145–46n. 60
hiking, 50–51
Himelshtayn, Avremele, 32
Hocke, Willi, 122–23n. 62
Hodann, Max, 22
Hodes, Leyvik, 40–42, 120–21n. 37, 122n. 55, 151n. 6
holidays, Jewish, 74
Homel (Russian Empire), 29, 30, 32, 33–34, 35–36
Honigwil, Ludwik, 133n. 10
Horev schools, 80, 137n. 47
Hurvitch, Tsivia, 83
Hurvitch, Zhenia, 84

illiteracy, 13
imprisonment, 85
Independent Socialist Party, 2
intelligentsia, 70, 83
International Information Bureau of Revolutionary Socialist Parties (Paris Bureau), 9, 10, 110n. 4, 111n. 7
International Socialist Sports Congress, 58
International Workers Olympics, 58, 129n. 51, 130n. 53

Iwińska, Esther Alter, 88
Izbitski, Yoysef. *See* Michalewicz, Beynish

Jewish Academic Union, 55
Jewish Communist Workers' Bund of Poland. *See* Kombund (of Poland)
Jewish immigration to the Land of Israel. *See* aliya
Jewish political cycles, 108n. 29
Jewish population (Poland), 1, 116n. 48
Jewish religious communities. *See* kehiles
Jewish trade unions. *See* trade unions
Jewish women. *See* women; women's organizations; working-class women
Jewish working youth. *See* working youth
Johnpoll, Bernard K., 4, 101
Jutrzenka (Bundist sports club), 125n. 10. *See also* Morgnshtern

Kahan, Arcadius, 96
Kahan, Virgily, 96
Kalisz (Poland), 107n. 10
Kantorowicz, N., 116n. 52
Kasel, Dovid, 36
Katalianski, Pesl. *See* Szweber, Sara
Kats, Yoysef, 72
Katz, Dovid, 85
Katz, Moyshe, 34
Kazdan, Khayim Shloyme: on assimilation of women, 94–95, 148n. 90; *Kleyne folkstsaytung* editor, 122n. 55; on Medem Sanatorium, 74, 81; on women Bund members, 145n. 45
Kegn shtrom (Bundist periodical), 41
kehiles: definition of, 153; elections (1936), 2–3, 107n. 10, 107n. 11; elections (1936–39), 99–100; elections (1937), 3, 107n. 15
Kellman, Ellen, 116–17n. 53

Kelson, Helena, 141n. 107
Khavershaft (SKIF periodical), 43
Kindersanatorie u. n. vladimir medem. *See* Medem Sanatorium
Klepfisz, Miriam-Royze (Maria) Salomon, 149n. 93
Kleyne folkstsaytung, 40, 122n. 55
Kleyner bund, 29–37, 47; the Bund and, 30–33; decline of, 35–36; flyer from, 31; later lives of members, 36; leadership of, 32, 33; legacy of, 37; literary works on, 36–37; membership in, 30, 34, 119n. 24; political activities of, 30–33; relationships with other children's movements, 33–34; compared with Sotsialistisher kinder farband, 47; strikes and, 31, 32; study circles by, 34
Kleyner SS, 33, 34
Kleyner-Rozenblum, Blimele, 145n. 43, 149n. 93
Kligsberg, Moshe (Moses), 20, 126n. 13
Klog, Bluma, 149n. 93
Kombund (of Poland), 9, 110n. 3
Kombund (of Russia), 86
Komtsukunft (youth movement), 10, 110–11n. 6
Kremer, Arkadi (Alexsandr), 15, 85
Kruk, A., 133n. 6, 133n. 8
Kruk, Shmuel. *See* Shvarts, Pinkhes
Kulkes, Eljasz, 50
Kultur-lige, 90
Kutno (Poland), 146–47n. 76

Labor Zionists: on boxing, 53–54; children's movements and, 33; kehiles elections (1937), 3; sports clubs, 51, 52, 124–25n. 5, 127n. 23; on table tennis, 127n. 19. *See also* Left Poalei Zion; Right Poalei Zion
Labour and Socialist International (LSI), 5, 10, 42, 58, 111–12n. 9

Land-rat fun di profesionele klasn-fareynen, 100–101, 152n. 13, 152n. 16
language: Hebrew, 51–52, 62, 96; Polish, 39, 71, 121n. 47, 137n. 47; sports movements and, 51–52, 59, 127n. 21. See also Yiddish
leadership: of Kleyner bund, 32, 33; of Morgnshtern, 51, 125–26n. 13; of Sotsialistisher kinder farband, 40–42; by women, 86, 93–94, 95, 148n. 86, 149n. 93; of Yidisher arbeter froy, 89–90, 145n. 59, 146n. 62; of Youth Bund Tsukunft, 145–46n. 60
Lebens-fragen (Bundist newspaper), 2
Left Poalei Zion: *Arbeter-tsaytung*, 54–55, 58, 130n. 53; on boxing, 53–54; city council elections and, 3, 4; on the International Workers Olympics, 130n. 53; parliamentary elections (1919) and, 106n. 4; Shtern sports movement and, 49, 51, 52–53, 125n. 5, 127n. 24; on soccer, 52–53, 127n. 24; Yungbor children's movement, 45, 67; Yungt youth organization, 19, 116n. 51, 124–25n. 5
Legnica (Poland), 149n. 93
Lemberg (Poland), 4, 150n. 94
Lestschinsky, Jacob, 10, 112n. 11, 113n. 17
Letste pasirungen, Di (Bundist periodical), 31
Levin, Yankel, 33–34, 36
Levinson, Liuba, 83, 86
Levit, Rosa (Fride), 85
Lialkes (Gilinski and Trupianski), 72, 74, 137n. 54
libraries, 19, 116–17n. 53
Lifshits, Malke. See Frumkin, Esther
Lipshits, Anna (Gaponsha), 84
Lipshits, Esther (Eza), 84
Lipshits, Gita, 83
literature distribution, 83–84, 144n. 38, 149n. 93
Little Bund. See Kleyner bund
Litvak, A., 31
Lodz (Poland): children attending Medem Sanatorium, 136n. 35; city council elections, 3–4, 107n. 13, 108n. 17; Ghetto underground operation, 149n. 93; Kleyner bund in, 29, 32; Morgnshtern branch, 52, 131–32n. 76; parliamentary elections (1922), 2; post–Revolution of 1905 decline of the Bund in, 119–20n. 25; post–World War II era YAF, 149n. 93; Ringen branch, 150n. 94; Sanatorium Home, 75; Shtern branch, 125n. 5; women Bundists in, 84, 85; women City Council members, 88, 90, 145n. 43; Yidisher arbeter froy branch, 90, 92, 93, 146–47n. 76, 149n. 93; Youth Bund Tsukunft branch, 11, 115n. 42
love, 85–86
LSI. See Labour and Socialist International
Lublin (Poland): Arkadi Group members from, 15, 114n. 31, 114n. 32; city council elections (1938–39), 4; day-care centers, 91; *kehiles* elections (1936), 3, 107n. 10; Kleyner bund in, 32; Ringen branch, 150n. 94; Sanatorium Home, 75; women Bundist leaders in, 88; Yidisher arbeter froy branch, 146–47n. 76
Lukover Rebbe, 15
Luxemburg, Rosa, 124–25n. 5
Lwów (Poland). See Lemberg (Poland)

Maccabi groups, 49, 52, 55, 59
Marcus, Joseph, 4, 150n. 97, 152n. 16
Mariampol (Russian Empire), 34
marriage, 24, 85–86
Marx, Karl, 127n. 23
Marxism, 32, 87
May Day, 67
McNeal, Robert H., 143–44n. 33
Medem, Gina (Genie) Birentsvayg, 85
Medem, Vladimir, 63–64, 85, 135n. 22
Medem Sanatorium, 62–81, 73; administration of, 64–66, 133–34n. 10, 134n. 12, 141n. 107; alumni of, 74; anti-Semitism and, 77; attack

Medem Sanatorium (*cont.*)
   on, 68, 135–36n. 32; board members, 133n. 6; the Bund and, 67, 140n. 95; children attending, 68–71, 78–79, 98–99, 136n. 35, 138–39n. 72, 140n. 95, 140n. 98, 140n. 100; children's educational background, 71; children's home environment, 69; children's movements and, 66–67; Communist Party and, 67–68, 135–36n. 32, 135n. 31; cost per child, 77; educational program of, 62, 71–74, 81, 137n. 53; facilities available at, 136n. 41; first temporary location, 133n. 8; founding of, 63–64, 133n. 8, 135n. 22; funding for, 75–78, 138–39n. 72, 138n. 64, 138n. 67, 139–40n. 84, 139n. 80; *Lialkes* (play) by, 72, 74, 137n. 54; medical staff of, 66, 135n. 24; *Mir kumen on* (film) on, 77, 137n. 46, 139n. 83; newspapers on, 80; non-Jewish children attending, 70–71; parents occupation and, 69–70, 136n. 39; post-October 1939 staff of, 141n. 107; questionnaire from, 69–70; refugee children and, 78, 85n. 140; religious education by, 74; strikes at, 67–68, 135–36n. 32, 135n. 31; success of, 78–79, 80, 141n. 107; teaching staff of, 66, 134n. 21, 135n. 22, 141n. 107; TSYSHO and, 62, 63–64, 71–72, 81, 138–39n. 72; tuition for, 77, 138–39n. 72; visitors and commentary on, 75–76, 138n. 63; Warsaw and, 68–69, 75–76; working-class children attending, 69, 136n. 39; during World War II, 141n. 107, 145n. 57

Meirke fun "kleynem bund" (Kasel), 36
Mendel, Hersch, 110n. 2
Mendelsohn, Ezra: on the cycle of Jewish politics, 108n. 29; on electoral victories, 5, 99; on schools, 62, 78, 81
Mendelson, Levi, 15, 114n. 31
Mendelson, Shloyme, 64, 133n. 10, 138n. 63, 141n. 107
Meyer, Dovid, 133n. 6

Michalewicz, Beynish, 32, 33, 67, 89
Michalewicz, Prof., 70
Michalewicz, Sheyne-Feygl Szapiro. *See* Blond, Dina
Miedzeszyn Sanatorium. *See* Medem Sanatorium
"Mikhalevitsh's eyniklekh," 123n. 77
Ministry for Social Defense, 76–77
Minsk (Russian Empire), 34
Mir kumen on (film), 77, 137n. 46, 139n. 83
Moment (newspaper), 80
Morgnshtern, 48, 49–61; activities of, 50–51, 58–59, 126n. 14, 131n. 64; boxing and, 51, 53–54, 56; the Bund and, 50, 60–61, 125–26n. 13, 132n. 81; Bundist candidates and, 61; conference (April 1929), 50; delegation to the SWSI 1929 conference, 57–58; differences and similarities with Shtern, 51–57, 126–27n. 19; emblem of, 51, 126n. 18; founding of, 48, 49–50; growth of, 59–60, 98, 100; International Workers Olympics delegation, 58; language and, 51–52, 59, 127n. 21; leadership of, 51, 125–26n. 13; local branches of, 58–59, 60, 131–32n. 76; membership booklet, *50*; membership changes in (1927–39), 59–60, 98, 131–32n. 76, 132n. 81; membership demographics of, 59, 130–31n. 62, 131n. 63, 131n. 64; Polish Workers' Sport Federation and, 56–57, 129n. 46; political repression of, 58, 60, 130n. 57; soccer and, 51, 53, 54–55, 56, 127–28n. 27, 131n. 64; Warsaw branch, 50, 54, *55, 57,* 126–27n. 19, 131–32n. 76, 147n. 82; working-class members, 59, 130–31n. 62, 131n. 63, 131n. 64; Youth Bund Tsukunft and, 50, 125–26n. 13
Morgnshtern, Tseshke, 15
Morgntaler-Pav, Gute, 141n. 107
Mosaic fatih, 18, 116n. 47
Muszkat, Zdisław, 141n. 107

Nadir, Moyshe, 75
Nasz Przeglad, 54–55
National Bloc, 3
National Council of Professional Class Unions, 100–101, 152n. 13, 152n. 16
Naye folkstsaytung (Bundist newspaper), 23, 41, 43, 54–55, 66, 89, 94–95, 148n. 90
Naye kultur (journal of Youth Bund Tsukunft), 114–15n. 37
naye mentshn, 20, 153
Neustadt, Leova, 133n. 10
newspapers: for children, 40, 122n. 55; on Medem Sanatorium, 80, 135–36n. 32; on Shtern and soccer, 58. *See also specific publications*
Nomberg, H. D., 75
Notkovski, Shloyme, 126n. 13
Nowe Pismo (journal), 23
Nowogrodzki, Emanuel, 15
Nowogrudski, Sheyne Gitl (Sonie) Czemelinski, 141n. 107; 148–49n. 93
Noyakh. *See* Portnoy, Yekutiel
numerus clausus, 96

Odessa Committee, 84
Ogniwo. *See* Ringen
Oler, Leon, 25–26, 118n. 75, 150n. 102
Opnhaym, Ber, 128–29n. 43
Orioniak-Tenenboym, 146n. 62
orthodox Jews, 15, 48, 80–81, 137n. 47. *See also* Agudes Yisroel
Otto, Berthold, 71
Otvosk (Poland), 63, 133n. 5, 133n. 6

Pale of Settlement, 82, 141n. 1
Palestine, 5
Paris Bureau. *See* International Information Bureau of Revolutionary Socialist Parties

parliamentary elections, 1–2, 106n. 4, 106n. 6, 107n. 8
patriarchy, 142n. 3
patriotism, 41–42
Patt, Emanuel, 38, 123n. 77
Patt, Yankef, 40
Peltel, Feigel (Wladka), 149n. 93
People's Relief, 63
Perenson, Ruta Rutman, 90
Peysakhzon, Sonie Glikman, 84
physical education. *See* sports movements; Youth Bund Tsukunft
Pickhan, Gertrud: on electoral victories, 100, 101; on socioeconomic factors, 6, 20, 100; on Szapiro, 144n. 41; on women, 148n. 86
Pilsudksi, Jósef, 37
Pinsk (Poland), 34, 136n. 35
Pioneer (children's movement), 44–45
Piotrków (Poland): *kehiles* elections (1936), 3, 107n. 10; Kleyner bund in, 29, 31–32; Ringen branch, 150n. 94; Yidisher arbeter froy branch, 146–47n. 76
Pizshits, Khayim, 125–26n. 13
Poalei Zion. *See* Labor Zionists; Left Poalei Zion; Right Poalei Zion
Poland: Jewish population in, 1, 116n. 48; Jewish schools in, 137n. 47
Polish government, 46, 129n. 44
Polish language, 39, 71, 121n. 47, 137n. 47
Polish Socialist Party (PPS): the Bund and, 57; children's movement of, 35, 42, 45; Medem Sanatorium and, 76; Polish Workers' Sport Federation and, 56–57, 128–29n. 43
Polish-Soviet War (1920–21), 9, 144n. 38
Polish Workers' Sport Federation (ZRSS), 56–57, 58, 128–29n. 43, 129n. 44, 129n. 46, 130n. 54
political cycles, Jewish, 108n. 29
Polonsky, Antony, 6, 99, 101

Polotsk (Russian Empire), 34, 119n. 24
Portnoy, Yekutiel, 64, 80, 133n. 10, 134n. 12, 141n. 107
Potemkin uprising, 84
PPS. *See* Polish Socialist Party
prayer, 11–12, 112n. 13, 112n. 14
Pribulski, Dr., 51–52
Pritkin, Dina, 30
proletarian sports, 127n. 24
Prometheus group, 115n. 45
"Propaganda for Conscious Motherhood" section (YAF), 92
prostitution, 24
Pruszków (Poland), 58
public schools, 39, 121n. 47. *See also* schools

Red Falcons (of German Social Democratic Movement), 122n. 57
refugee children, 77–78, 85n. 140, 91
Reich, Wilhelm, 22, 117n. 66
Relief Campaign for the Jewish Masses, 85n. 140
religiosity, 41–42, 95
religious education, 74
religious observance, 11–12, 112n. 13, 112n. 14
resistance movement (World War II), 124n. 78
Revisionist-Zionists, 49
revolutionary asceticism, 86
Revolution of 1905, 34–35, 84–85
Right Poalei Zion: children's movement of, 45; city council elections (1937), 107n. 15; parliamentary elections (1919) and, 106n. 4; parliamentary elections (1928), 2; sports club of, 49; youth organization of, 19
rights, women's, 24–25
Ringen, 96–97, 115n. 45, 149–50n. 94, 150n. 101
Riskind, Esther (Hinda, a.k.a. Tamara), 84
Rosenfarb, Chava, 44, 123n. 65
Rotholts, Shepsl, 53, 128n. 31
Rotnberg, Leah, 141n. 107

rowing, 130–31n. 62
"Royte falkn," 123n. 77
Rozenbaum, Menakhem, 133n. 10
Rozenboym, Sore, 149n. 93
Rozental, Anna Heller, 45, 84, 85, 88, 145n. 59
Rozental, Pavel, 85
Russian Empire: Bolshevik Revolution, 86; children's movements in, 29–37, 47; radical movement in, 143–44n. 33; Revolution of 1905, 34–35, 84–85; women bundists in, 82–87, 143n. 32; youth organizations in, 8. *See also specific locations*

sabotage, 32
Sanacja regime, 76
Sanatorium Home (Warsaw), 74–75, 78
sanatoriums, 80–81. *See also* Medem Sanatorium
schools: bilingual, 137n. 47; evening, 20, 67, 123n. 75; *kheydorim*, 31, 153; for orthodox Jews, 137n. 47; Polish language, 39, 71, 121n. 47, 137n. 47; public, 39, 121n. 47; strikes in, 31; talmud toyre, 113n. 24, 153; tuition for, 39; for working class, 39; Yiddish, 39, 71, 137n. 47; Zionist, 80. *See also* Beys Yankef schools; education; *gmina* schools; Horev schools; Shul-Kult; Tarbut Schools; TSYSHO
Schutzbund (Austria), 117n. 55
scouting movement, 41–42
SDKPiL. *See* Social Democratic Party of the Kingdom of Poland and Lithuania
secularism, 11
Segal, Shaine Raizel, 83
SEI. *See* Sozialistische Erziehungs International
Sejm. *See* parliamentary elections
self-defense groups, 19–20, 84, 117n. 55
sex education, 22, 23, 28

sexuality, 20–28, 118n. 74, 118n. 75
Shafran, Nakhman, 109–10n. 2
Shapiro, Robert Moses, 107n. 10, 114n. 32
Shefner, Borukh, 140n. 95
Sherer, Emanuel, 150n. 101
Shpilfogel-Likhtenbaum, Natalia, 133–34n. 10
Shtern: boxing and, 53–54, 127n. 24, 128n. 31; differences and similarities with Morgnshtern, 51–57, 126–27n. 19; emblem of, 51, 126n. 18; founding of, 49, 124–25n. 5; goals of, 127n. 23; Labour and Socialist International and, 58; language and, 51–52, 127n. 21; membership in, 60; Polish Workers' Sport Federation and, 56, 57, 58, 128–29n. 43; political repression of, 58, 130n. 57; soccer and, 52–53, 54–55, 58, 125n. 5, 127n. 24; Third Workers Sports Olympics and, 130n. 54; women's section of, 56, 128n. 41; working class and, 52, 127n. 23
Shtern, Yekhiel, 135n. 22
Shtern Workers' Sport Club, 125n. 5
Shtral, 14
Shul-Kult (school network), 137n. 47
Shvarts, Pinkhes, 12, 125–26n. 13
Sickness Insurance Fund, 76, 138n. 67
Simkhovitsh, Dr., 79
Skała (sports club), 49
SKIB. *See* Sotsialistisher kinder-bund
SKIF. *See* Sotsialistisher kinder farband
Skutelski, Gitle, 90, 148–49n. 93
soccer, 51; anti-Semitism and, 58; Morgnshtern and, 51, 53, 54–55, 56, 127–28n. 27, 131n. 64; Shtern and, 52–53, 54–55, 58, 125n. 5, 127n. 24; Vilna Morgnshtern branch and, 131n. 64
Social Democratic Party (Germany), 108–9n. 30
Social Democratic Party of the Kingdom of Poland and Lithuania (SDKPiL), 8–9, 35, 86
Social Democratic Workers' Party of Austria, 117n. 55

Social Democratic Youth Organization Tsukunft, 9
socialism: children's movements and, 34–35, 41–42, 44, 122n. 57; education and, 67; half-intellectual women and, 142n. 3; Medem Sanatorium and, 62, 70; Pilsudksi and, 37; women and, 82–83; Youth Bund Tsukunft and, 20–21, 27; youth organizations and, 18
Socialist Children's Union. *See* Sotsialistisher kinder farband
Socialist Society of Sexual Advice and Sexual Research, 22
Socialist Workers' Sports International (SWSI), 53, 57–58; Congress of, 51
Socialist Workers' Youth (of German Social Democratic movement), 122n. 57
Socialist Youth International (SYI), 10, 111–12n. 9
Society for the Protection of Health (TOZ), 49, 125n. 11
Sotsialistisher kinder-bund (SKIB), 120n. 35
Sotsialistisher kinder farband (SKIF), 27, 37–47; activities of, 42–44; age for membership in, 38, 112n. 14, 120–21n. 37, 123n. 77; the Bund and, 47; camps by, 43–44, 45, 46, 123n. 65; communists and, 46, 123n. 75; conference (October 1936), 43; creation of, 37–38, 121n. 41; current events discussions, 42; education and, 38; growth of, 98, 100; Hodes and, 40–42; internal divisions in, 123n. 77; *Khavershaft*, 43; vs. Kleyner bund, 47; later lives of members, 124n. 78; leadership of, 40–42; Medem Sanatorium and, 66–67; membership in, 39–40, 45–46, 98, 121n. 47; opposition to, 46, 123n. 75; principles of, 41–44, 122n. 60; scouting movement and, 42; as a socialist movement, 42, 44; Sozialistische Erziehungs International and, 42, 122–23n. 62; street

182 | Index

Sotsialistisher kinder farband (SKIF) (*cont.*) children and, 39–40; teachers opposition to, 38–39; TSYSHO and, 38–39; working youth and, 39–40; Youth Bund Tsukunft members from, 14, 99, 151n. 6; Zionism and, 43
Soviet Union, 9, 24–25, 37, 144n. 38
Sozialistische Erziehungs International (SEI), 42, 46, 122–23n. 62
Spartakus, 124–25n. 5
Spiegel, Chaike Belchatowska, 149n. 93
sports, proletarian, 127n. 24
sports clubs, 49, 124–25n. 5. *See also* Jutrzenka; Skała; Typhoon
sports movements: anti-Semitism and, 58, 130n. 59; Austria, 127–28n. 27; Czech, 127–28n. 27; difference and similarities between, 51–57, 126–27n. 19; emergence of, 48–49, 124–25n. 5, 124n. 3, 125n. 10; language and, 51–52, 59, 127n. 21; Maccabi groups, 49, 52, 55, 59; Polish government and, 129n. 44; political repression of, 58, 130n. 57; soccer and, 127–28n. 27, 127n. 24. *See also* Hapoel; Morgnshtern; Shtern
Srednitsky, Matle (Pati), 83, 85
Stefan Batory University, 96
street children, 39–40
street gangs, 34
strikes: apprentices, 31; Kleyner bund and, 31, 32; at Medem Sanatorium, 67–68, 135–36n. 32, 135n. 31; working women in, 82
students. *See* university students
study circles, 34
subculture, 108–9n. 30
summer camps. *See* camps
summer colonies, 63, 133n. 5, 133n. 6
Sveber, Rotman, 146n. 62
swimming, 50–51
SWSI. *See* Socialist Workers' Sports International
SYI. *See* Socialist Youth International

Szapiro, Esther Beyla (Bela), 88, 144n. 41, 145n. 59, 149n. 93
Szczuczyn (Poland), 149n. 93
Szweber, Sara, 88, 100
Szyfman, Leah, 149n. 93

table tennis, 125n. 5, 126–27n. 19, 126n. 14
Tarbut Schools, 137n. 47
Tarnów (Poland), 146–47n. 76, 150n. 94
teachers, 38, 66, 134n. 21, 135n. 22. *See also* education; schools
Temporary Jewish National Council, 106n. 4
Tobias, Henry J., 35
Todres, Henakh, 17
Tomaszów Mazowiecki, 107n. 10
TOZ. *See* Society for the Protection of Health
trade unions: anti-Semitism and, 152n. 18; communist, 67–68, 135–36n. 32, 135n. 31; conventions of, 152n. 17; electoral victories and, 6; growth of, 100–101, 152n. 13, 152n. 16, 152n. 18; half-intellectual women and, 82–83; Medem Sanatorium funding and, 77; street children and, 40; youth sections of, 19
Trupianski, Yankl, 72, 74
Tsukunft. *See* Youth Bund Tsukunft
"Tsukunftistka," 114n. 27
Tsukunft-shturem, 19–20, 117n. 55
tsveyer, 41, 42, 65, 153
"Tsvey yinglekh" (Charney), 36
TSYSHO: decline of, 78; Gilinski and, 65; Medem Sanatorium and, 62, 63–64, 71–72, 81, 138–39n. 72; number of children attending, 137n. 47; Pioneer movement and, 45; Shloyme Mendelson and, 64; Sotsialistisher kinder farband and, 38–39; sports movements and, 51
tuberculosis, 62, 63, 68, 70, 133n. 5, 133n. 6. *See also* Medem Sanatorium
Typhoon (sports club), 125n. 5

underground operations, 148–49n. 93
Undzer veg (periodical of United Jewish Socialist Workers' Party), 65
unions. *See* trade unions
United Jewish Electoral Bloc, 3
United Jewish Socialist Workers' Party, 65, 112n. 11
United Zionist Bloc, 3
university students: anti-Semitism and, 150n. 97, 150n. 103; Ringen and, 96–97, 115n. 45, 149–50n. 94, 150n. 101
Unzer tsayt (Bundist periodical), 41

Vald, Pinkhes, 138n. 63
Vapner, Kalmen, 43
Vayner, Frida, 30, 36
Vaysvol, Ester, 84
Veksler, Roze, 141n. 107
Vilna (Poland): children attending Medem Sanatorium, 136n. 35; city council elections (1936), 107n. 10; city council elections (1938–39), 4; day-care centers, 91, 92; Kleyner bund in, 32; Maccabi group in, 59; Morgnshtern branch in, 59, 60, 130–31n. 62, 131n. 63, 131n. 64; Ringen branch in, 150n. 94; socialist women in, 83; Sotsialistisher kinder farband branch in, 46; Szapiro in, 144n. 41; women Bundist leaders in, 88; working women in, 82; Yiddish Teachers Seminary, 135n. 22; Yidisher arbeter froy branch in, 93, 146–47n. 76
Vladeck, Baruch Charney, 36, 138n. 64
Volkovishki (Russian Empire), 34

wages, 12, 113n. 17
Warsaw (Poland): Arkadi Group, 15; city council elections (1938–39), 3; *kehiles* elections (1936), 2–3; Kleyner SS in, 33; Komtsukunft committee of, 110–11n. 6; Medem Sanatorium and, 68–69, 70, 75–76; Morgnshtern branch in, 50, 54, 55, 57, 126–27n. 19, 131–32n. 76, 147n. 82; parliamentary elections, 1–2; post-Revolution of 1905 decline of the Bund in, 119–20n. 25; Ringen branch in, 149–50n. 94; Sanatorium Home, 74–75, 78; SDKPiL and, 8–9; Shtern branch in, 53, 55, 60, 128n. 41; Sotsialistisher kinder farband branch in, 38, 151n. 6; sports movement in, 49; Tsukunft-shturem in, 19–20; women City Council members, 88; Workers Sports Association, 126–27n. 19; YAF camps in, 91; Yidisher arbeter froy branch in, 93, 146–47n. 76, 147n. 82, 147n. 83, 149n. 93; Youth Bund Tsukunft branch, 9, 17–18, 19–20, 27, 115n. 42, 115n. 45; Youth Bund Tsukunft survey in, 11
Wasilewska, Wanda, 70
Weimer Republic, 122n. 57
Wolna Młodzież (periodical of Youth Bund Tsukunft), 16–17
women, 82–97; assimilation of, 94, 95, 148n. 90; as City Council members, 88, 90, 145n. 93; Communist Party and, 143n. 31; as early members of the Bund, 83–84; half-intellectuals, 82, 142n. 3; as leaders, 86, 93–94, 95, 148n. 86, 149n. 93; literature distribution by, 83–84, 144n. 38, 149n. 93; love, marriage, and, 85–86; Polish Bund members, 87–89; Revolution of 1905 and, 84–85; rights of, 24–25; Russian Empire Bundists, 82–87, 143n. 32; in the Russian radical movement, 143–44n. 33; Shtern section for, 56, 128n. 41; socialism and, 82–83; Warsaw City Council members, 88; during World War II, 148–49n. 93; Youth Bund Tsukunft members, 144n. 38.

women (*cont.*)

    See also women's organizations; working-class women

women's division (the Bund, 1917), 87

women's organizations, 82, 89–97. *See also* Yidisher arbeter froy

Woodhouse, Charles C., 35

Worker Sports Olympics, 58, 129n. 51, 130n. 54

Workers' Society for Physical Education "Morgnshtern." *See* Morgnshtern

Workers Sports Association (of Warsaw), 126–27n. 19

Workers Sports International. *See* Socialist Workers' Sports International

working class: children attending Medem Sanatorium, 69, 136n. 39; children's movements for, 37; Morgnshtern members, 59, 130–31n. 62, 131n. 63, 131n. 64; schools for, 39; sports movements for, 50–51, 52, 127n. 23

working-class women: in the Russian Empire, 82–83, 87, 141n. 1; socioeconomic factors and, 95; Yidisher arbeter froy and, 89, 91, 97, 101, 148n. 85

working youth: evening schools for, 20, 67, 123n. 75; illiteracy of, 13; Sotsialistisher kinder farband membership for, 39–40; survey of, 10–13, 112n. 13, 112n. 14; wages for, 12, 113n. 17

Workmen's Circle, 77

World War I, 86

World War II: the Bund during, 96, 141n. 107, 148–49n. 93; Medem Sanatorium during, 141n. 107, 145n. 57; resistance movement, 124n. 78; women during, 148–49n. 93; Yidisher arbeter froy during, 148–49n. 93

YAF. *See* Yidisher arbeter froy

Yashunski, Gershon (Grisza), 150n. 101

Yavneh, 137n. 47

Yiddish: schools, 39, 71, 137n. 47; sports movements and, 52, 59, 127n. 21; university students and, 96; youth organizations and, 16

Yiddish Teachers Seminary, 135n. 22

Yidisher arbeter froy (YAF), 82, 89–97; activities and services of, 91–92; conference (November 1937), 147–48n. 84; day-care centers, 91, 92; debate on women leaders, 93–94, 148n. 86; failure of, 101; founding of, 89, 145n. 50, 145n. 59, 146n. 62; goals of, 90–91; leadership of, 89–90, 145n. 59, 146n. 62; local branches of, 92–93, 146–47n. 76, 147n. 82, 147n. 83; membership in, 92–93, 97, 147n. 82, 147n. 83; post–World War II era, 149n. 93; "Propaganda for Conscious Motherhood" section, 92; target population of, 93–94, 148n. 85; working-class women and, 89, 91, 93–94, 97, 101, 148n. 85; during World War II, 148–49n. 93

YIVO Branch for the Jewish Sports Movement, 124n. 3

YIVO youth autobiographies, 26–27

Young Falcons (of German Social Democratic movement), 122n. 57

Young Socialists (of German Social Democratic movement), 122n. 57

youth, Jewish working. *See* working youth

youth autobiographies, 26–27

Youth Bund Tsukunft, 8–28; activities and services of, 19, 116–17n. 53; Berkovitsh Circle, 15; Communist Youth International and, 9–10, 13, 110–11n. 6, 111n. 7; cultural department of, 116–17n. 53; current events discussions, 27; education and, 20, 113n. 24; as a feeder group for the Bund, 18, 99, 115n. 45; feeder groups for, 13–14, 99, 151n. 6; female members of, 144n. 38; formation of, 8–9, 109–10n. 2; Fourth Conference (1925), 10, 111n. 7; growth of, 98, 100; Hashomer Hatsair and, 18, 116n. 50; leadership of, 145–46n. 60; local affiliates, 10, 17, 112n. 10; Lodz branch, 115n. 42; membership in, 13–19, 27, 28, 98, 110n. 2, 113n. 24, 114n. 26, 114n. 27, 115n. 42, 116n. 48, 116n. 50; Morgnshtern and, 50, 125–26n. 13; Mosaic fatih and, 18, 116n. 47; *Naye kultur,* 114–15n. 37; organization of a children's movement by, 37; paramilitary group of, 19–20, 117n. 55; Paris Bureau and, 10, 111n. 7; Polish-language periodical, 16–17; poster by, *16*; Prometheus group, 115n. 45; religious observance and, 11–12, 112n. 13, 112n. 14; Ringen group, 115n. 45; sexuality and, 20–28, 118n. 74, 118n. 75; sixth conference of, 111–12n. 9; socialism and, 20–21; Socialist Youth International and, 10, 111–12n. 9; survey of Jewish working youth, 10–13, 112n. 13, 112n. 14; Warsaw branch, 9, 17–18, 19–20, 27, 115n. 42, 115n. 45; *Wolna Młodzież,* 16–17; on Yugnt, 116n. 51. *See also Yugnt-veker*

youth organizations: communist, 9–10, 14, 37, 110–11n. 6; czarist era, 8–9; ideological similarity of, 20; membership in, 18–19, 110n. 2; movement among, 17; sexuality and, 27–28; socialist, 18; Youth Bund Tsukunft members from, 13–14. *See also* Frayhayt; Hashomer Hatsair; Hekhalutz Hatsair; Komtsukunft; Shtral; Youth Bund Tsukunft; Yugnt

youth workers. *See* working youth

Yugnt (youth organization), 19, 116n. 51, 124–25n. 5

Yugnt-Bund Tsukunft. *See* Youth Bund Tsukunft

Yugnt-veker (periodical of Youth Bund Tsukunft), *14*; on Borislav members, 15–16; on communists, 13; on Hashomer Hatsair, 116n. 50; on sexuality, 21, 22, 23–24, 25, 27, 118n. 74; on soccer, 53; on young workers, 12; on Yugnt, 116n. 51

Yungbor (children's movement), 45, 67

"Yung-falkn," 123n. 77

Zakhaym, Gitl, 84

Zakheym, Khane, 75

Zeire Zion, 19

Zhaludsky, Marya, 83, 85

Zilberberg, Golda Jakubowicz, 145n. 43, 149n. 93

Zionists: children's movement and, 33; city council elections (1938–39), 4; counterculture and, 109n. 30; electoral victories and, 100; Hashomer Hatsair and, 18; *kehiles* elections (1936), 3; Mendelson on, 5; parliamentary elections (1922), 106n. 6; schools, 80; Sotsialistisher kinder farband and, 43. *See also* General Zionists; Labor Zionists; Left Poalei Zion; Right Poalei Zion; United Zionist Bloc

Zionist Socialist Workers' Party, 33

ZRSS. *See* Polish Workers' Sport Federation

Zygielbaum, Mania, 141n. 107

Zygielbaum, Shmuel, 100, 140n. 95, 152n. 13, 152n. 16, 152n. 18

Zylberberg, Perec, 123n. 75

www.ingramcontent.com/pod-product-compliance
Lightning Source LLC
Chambersburg PA
CBHW032253150426
43195CB00008BA/441